Giulia, 1750, 2000 1962-78 Autobook

By Kenneth Ball

Associate Member, Guild of Motoring Writers
and the Autobooks Team of Technical Writers

Alfa Romeo Giulia 1300 TI, GT Junior 1967-72
Alfa Romeo Giulia 1600 TI, Super 1962-72
Alfa Romeo Giulia 1600 Sprint GT, GTV 1963-68
Alfa Romeo Giulia 1600 Spider, Duetto 1962-68
Alfa Romeo Giulia 1.6 Super 1972-75
Alfa Romeo GT Junior 1.6 1972-75
Alfa Romeo GT Junior 1600 1975-76
Alfa Romeo 1750, GT Veloce 1968-72
Alfa Romeo 1750 Spider Veloce 1968-72
Alfa Romeo 2000, GT Veloce 1971-75
Alfa Romeo 2000 Spider Veloce 1971-78

Autobooks

Autobooks Ltd. Golden Lane Brighton BN1 2QJ England

The AUTOBOOK series of Workshop Manuals is the largest in the world and covers the majority of British and Continental motor cars, as well as the majority of Japanese and Australian models.

Whilst every care has been taken to ensure correctness of information it is obviously not possible to guarantee complete freedom from errors or omissions or to accept liability arising from such errors or omissions.

CONTENTS

ISBN 0 85147 997 9

First Edition   1971
Second Edition, fully revised   1972
Third Edition, fully revised   1972
Fourth Edition, fully revised   1973
Fifth Edition, fully revised   1974
Sixth Edition, fully revised   1975
Seventh Edition, fully revised   1976
Eighth Edition, fully revised   1978

©Autobooks Ltd 1978

724

Printed in Brighton England for Autobooks Ltd by G. Beard and Son Ltd
Bound in Hove England for Autobooks Ltd by Jilks Ltd

E

ACKNOWLEDGEMENT

My thanks are due to Alfa Romeo for their unstinted co-operation and also for supplying data and illustrations.

Considerable assistance has also been given by owners, who have discussed their cars in detail, and I would like to express my gratitude for this invaluable advice and help.

Kenneth Ball
Associate Member, Guild of Motoring Writers
Ditchling Sussex England.

INTRODUCTION

This do-it-yourself Workshop Manual has been specially written for the owner who wishes to maintain his vehicle in first class condition and to carry out the bulk of his own servicing and repairs. Considerable savings on garage charges can be made, and one can drive in safety and confidence knowing the work has been done properly.

Comprehensive step-by-step instructions and illustrations are given on most dismantling, overhauling and assembling operations. Certain assemblies require the use of expensive special tools, the purchase of which would be unjustified. In these cases information is included but the reader is recommended to hand the unit to the agent for attention.

Throughout the Manual hints and tips are included which will be found invaluable, and there is an easy to follow fault diagnosis at the end of each chapter.

Whilst every care has been taken to ensure correctness of information it is obviously not possible to guarantee complete freedom from errors or omissions or to accept liability arising from such errors or omissions.

Instructions may refer to the righthand or lefthand sides of the vehicle or the components. These are the same as the righthand or lefthand of an observer standing behind the vehicle and looking forward.

CHAPTER 1

THE ENGINE

1 : 1 Description

The various cars covered in this manual are all equipped with high performance, twin overhead camshaft, engines which, although of four different sizes, are sufficiently alike for one set of instructions to suffice for their maintenance and overhaul. For servicing purposes the four engines are similar, their differences being in dimensional specifications, details of which will be found in **Technical Data** at the end of the book.

The four engines and their principal dimensions are as follows:

Type	Capacity	Bore Stroke
1300	1290 cc	74 x 75 mm
1600	1570 cc	78 x 82 mm
1750	1779 cc	80 x 88.5 mm
2000	1962 cc	84 x 88.5 mm

A light alloy cylinder block is used, cast integrally with the crankcase and carrying cast iron wet liners for the cylinder bores. **FIG 1:1** shows a cutaway view of the engine and **FIGS 1:2** and **1:3** the engine internal components. The detachable cylinder head is of light alloy with machined hemispherical combustion chambers and the valve seat inserts and valve guides are of cast iron and shrunk fitted into the head.

The counterbalanced crankshaft, which is a treated alloy steel forging, is provided with five plain shell bearings all of which are pressure lubricated. Axial thrust is accommodated at the centre main bearing position. The forged steel connecting rods have plain shell big-end bearings and bronze gudgeon pin bushes. A single belt drives both the generator and the centrifugal type water pump from a pulley mounted at the front of the crankshaft.

The gear type oil pump, which is driven from a gear on the crankshaft, is located inside the light alloy sump and draws oil through a pipe and strainer assembly. Pressure oil is fully filtered before being fed to the engine. The external filter is of the fullflow type and incorporates a relief valve which operates to return excess oil to the sump in the event of oil pressure becoming higher than the desired maximum.

The light alloy pistons have cut-outs in their crowns to provide working clearance for the valves and are equipped with three rings, one oil control ring and two compression rings, the upper ring being chrome plated.

The exhaust manifold is mounted on the opposite side to the inlet manifold to provide a crossflow pattern for the inlet and exhaust gases.

1 : 2 Removing the engine

The normal operations of decarbonizing and servicing the cylinder head can be carried out without removing the engine, as described in **Sections 1:3** and **1:4**. The camshafts and upper timing chain can be removed and worked

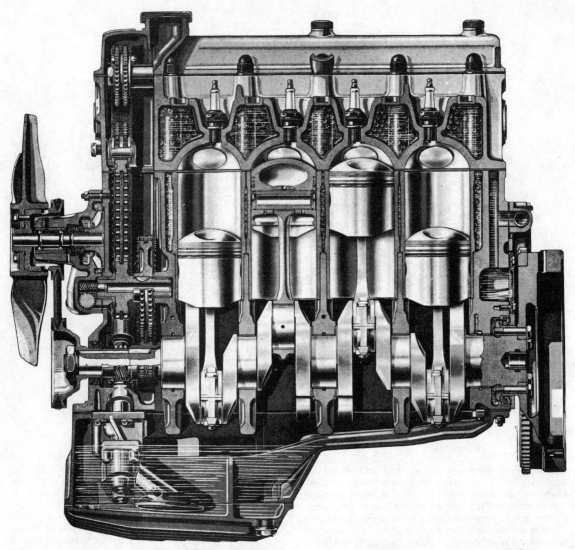

FIG 1:1   Longitudinal section of the engine

on in the same manner, as described in **Sections 1:4** and **1:6**. A major overhaul however can only be carried out with the engine removed from the car. If the operator is not a skilled automobile engineer it is suggested that he will find much useful information in **Hints on Maintenance and Overhaul** at the end of this manual, and that he should read it before starting work.

The engine and gearbox should be removed as a unit by lifting it from the car, using a suitable gantry and lifting tackle. Assistance will be essential to tilt and carefully guide the assembly upwards and forwards. **As the major castings in the engine assembly are of light alloy, care must be exercised to avoid stripping the threads in the castings when tightening fixings or connections.** Always adhere to the torque figures given in **Technical Data** and ensure that threads are clean and lightly lubricated before tightening.

1 Open the drain taps at the bottom of the radiator and the lefthand side of the engine. If the coolant contains antifreeze and is to be re-used, drain it into a clean container. Remove the bonnet at the hinge pins then remove the bonnet support strut. Disconnect the battery cables. Unscrew the sump drain plug and drain the engine oil.

2 Refer to **FIG 1:4** and detach the following from the underside of the car. The propeller shaft at the intermediate joint flange 1, after marking the front and rear parts for correct reassembly. The propeller shaft central bearing support 2 and the cross-plate 3. The speedometer cable 4 and the exhaust pipe bracket 5.

3 Refer to **FIG 1:5** and detach the clutch cover 6, the gear selector lever 7, the reversing light wires 8, the clutch operating lever 9, the manifold joint 10 and the

gear engagement lever 11. Remove the tachometer cable if fitted, from the front of the engine.

4 Remove the air cleaner. Refer to **FIGS 1 : 6** and **1 : 7** and remove the following from the engine compartment. The top hose 1, the bottom hose and the radiator 2 as described in **Chapter 4**. The hose 3 from the water pump to the manifold, also the heater hoses. The fuel pipe 4, temperature gauge connector 5, coil leads 6, choke control cable 7, accelerator hand control cable 8, generator leads 9, oil pressure gauge wire 10 and the engine earth strap 11. Remove the throttle control rod and the cables from the starter.

5 Attach the lifting equipment to the engine and give a light pull just to take the engine weight. Refer to **FIG 1 : 8** and remove the gearbox crossmember to car floor attaching bolts. Remove the bolt fixing the crossmember to the gearbox and remove the crossmember, as shown in **FIG 1 : 9**.

6 Lift the engine and gearbox assembly from the car, tilting it in order to clear the engine compartment. To separate the engine from the gearbox, remove the bolts attaching the clutch bellhousing to the engine and carefully withdraw the gearbox, taking great care to avoid the weight of the gearbox resting on the clutch driven plate.

7 Clamp the engine into a mounting stand and remove the ignition coil, generator complete with mounting bracket, cooling fan, water pump, starter, oil filter and bracket and the oil sump.

1 : 3 Removing and refitting the head

Before removing or dismantling the cylinder head the following warnings must be noted to avoid warping the head or damaging the valves against each other or against the pistons.

1 Make sure that the engine is cool before removing the cylinder head.

2 Do not rotate the engine or the camshafts after the camshaft drive has been disconnected.

3 When the cylinder head is removed, do not rotate either camshaft unless the other has been removed.

4 Before refitting the cylinder head, follow the instructions for positioning the camshafts in relation to each other and to the crankshaft.

Removal:

FIG 1 : 10 shows the components of the cylinder head.

1 Disconnect the battery. Drain the radiator and cylinder block, collecting the coolant in a clean container if it is to be re-used. Remove the radiator and heater hoses from the head and remove the vacuum line from the distributor.

2 Remove the air cleaner and the throttle operating linkage. Disconnect the choke cable and the hand throttle cable from the carburetter. Remove the fuel pipe from the fuel pump.

3 Remove the exhaust tube bracket from the gearbox mounting. Remove the exhaust manifold to cylinder head fixing nuts and pull the manifold off the studs. Remove the sparking plugs and the camshaft cover.

4 Rotate the crankshaft until the No. 1 piston is at TDC on the compression stroke, using the method described in **Section 1 : 7**. This should bring the timing

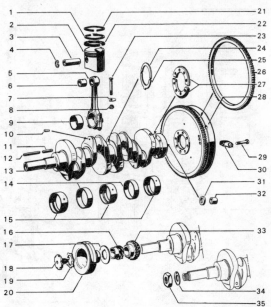

FIG 1 : 2 The crankshaft, pistons and flywheel assemblies

Key to Fig 1 : 2   1 Compression ring   2 Piston
3 Gudgeon pin   4 Circlip   5 Connecting rod
6 Small-end bush   7 Lockplate   8 Nut
9 Big-end bearing shells   10 Plugs   11/12 Keys
13 Crankshaft   14/15 Main bearing shells
16 Oil pump drive gear   17 Oil seal   18 Special bolt
19 Lockplate   20 Crankshaft pulley   21 Compression ring
22 Oil control ring   23 Big-end bolt   24/25 Thrust washers
26 Starter ring gear   27 Half-rings   28 Flywheel
29 Flywheel bolt   30 Lockplate   31 Felt washer
32 Guide bush   33 Crankshaft sprocket   34 Lockplate
35 Pulley nut

chain connecting link between the two camshaft sprockets. Slacken the chain tensioner securing screw as shown in **FIG 1 : 11** and push the tensioner away from the chain against its spring, retightening the securing screw to hold it in this position. If this is not done the tensioner will move out when the timing chain is removed and the clamp plate will drop into the sump.

5 Tie two pieces of wire to the chain ends at each side of the connecting link, then remove the link. The wires will prevent the chain from falling into the cylinder block if they are tied to part of the car frame when the head is removed. If the chain is to be renewed, tie a long enough piece of wire to one end, and remove the chain from the other end, pulling the wire into the chain position. Leave the wire installed so that it can be used to pull the chain into position when it is fitted. **Do not turn the crankshaft when the timing chain is disconnected.** The timing marks on the lower sprockets are not visible with the timing cover fitted, so if their positions are disturbed the engine will have to be further dismantled and the timing checked as described in **Section 1 : 7**.

6 Slacken the cylinder head bolts by a part of a turn at a time in the order shown in **FIG 1 : 12** until they are free. Remove the head nuts and the two screws fixing the front cover to the head, then lift off the head.

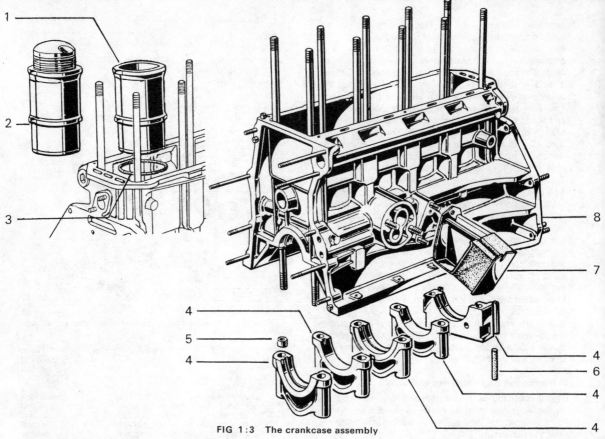

FIG 1:3   The crankcase assembly

Key to Fig 1:3 1 Cylinder liner 2 Liner with piston 3 Liner seal ring 4 Main bearing caps 5 Hollow dowel 6 Rubber plug
7 Engine mounting   8 Cylinder block

Refitting:

Refit the carburetter and inlet manifold assembly. Check that the timing marks on the camshafts and bearing caps are aligned as described in **Section 1:6**. Place a new head gasket onto the cylinder block and refit the head. Oil the head nuts and tighten them in the order shown in **FIG 1:12** to the torque specified in **Technical Data**. Refit the timing chain without disturbing the alignment of the camshaft timing marks. Refitting of all other parts is the reversal of the removal procedure.

Upon completion, drive the car to warm the engine to normal operating temperature and retighten the cylinder head nuts to the specified hot torque. Drive the car for about 300 miles, then allow the engine to cool right down. With the engine cold, slacken the head nuts $1\frac{1}{2}$ turns then tighten them finally to the specified cold torque. Always follow the order given in **FIG 1:12**. Adjust the timing chain tension as described in **Section 1:6**.

1:4 Servicing the head and valves

Take care to avoid damage to the light alloy cylinder head during servicing. The head should be supported on blocks of wood at each end, particularly while the cam-

shafts are installed and the valve gear liable to damage. When removing sealing compound, old gasket material or carbon deposits avoid the use of pointed tools and use worn emerycloth and paraffin only for cleaning purposes.

Dismantling:

Drain the oil from the camshaft housings and thoroughly clean the cylinder head. Remove the inlet manifold and carburetter as a unit. Mark the camshaft journal bearing caps for correct refitting and remove the caps and the camshafts.

Service tools A.2.0121 valve holder and A.3.0103/1, 2 and 3 spring compressor should be used to remove the valves. If these tools are not available a block of wood must be shaped to fit into the combustion chamber to hold the valves in the closed position while the springs are compressed. In either case, work on one pair of valves at a time, removing the tappets and adjusting shims with suitable pliers, then compressing the springs to remove the cotters. Release the compressor and remove the upper spring collars, springs, shims and lower spring collars into the order shown in **FIG 1:13**. Store all parts in the correct order for refitting in their original positions. Loosen the securing screw as shown in **FIG 1:11** and remove the timing chain tensioner from its housing, collecting the spring and clamp plate.

FIG 1:4 Items to be detached for engine removal. The numbers are referred to in the text

FIG 1:5 Items to be detached for engine removal. The numbers are referred to in the text

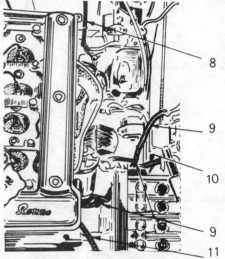

FIG 1:7 Items to be removed from the engine compartment. The numbers are referred to in the text

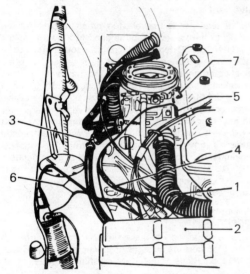

FIG 1:6 Items to be removed from the engine compartment. The numbers are referred to in the text

Valves:

When the valves have been cleaned of carbon deposits they must be inspected for serviceability. Valves with bent stems or badly burned heads must be renewed. Valves that are too pitted to clean up on grinding to their seats may be refaced by a garage, but the amount of metal that can be removed in this operation is limited and new valves will be required if refacing cannot be successfully carried out. The valve seat angle is 30 deg. in all cases. Check the valve stems for correct diameter against the dimension given in **Technical Data** for the various engines.

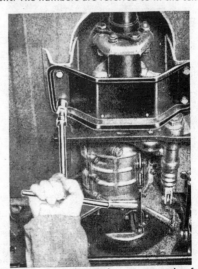

FIG 1:8 Detaching the gearbox crossmember from the car floor

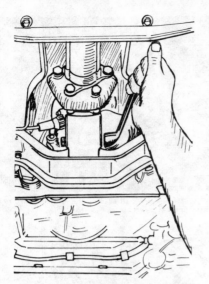

FIG 1:9 Removing the crossmember from the gearbox

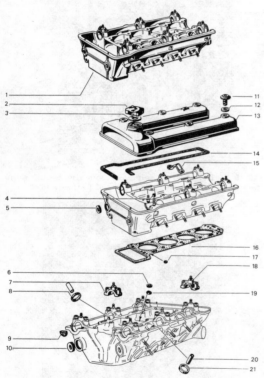

FIG 1:10 Components of the cylinder head

Key to Fig 1:10   1 Cylinder head   2 Oil filler cap
3 Gasket   4 Centralizing bush   5 Expansion plug
6 Screw plug   7 Camshaft bearing cap   8 Valve seat insert
9 Rubber seal   10 Expansion plug   11 Camshaft cover bolt
12 Gasket   13 Camshaft cover   14 Cover gasket
15 Lifting bracket   16 Cylinder head gasket   17 Seal ring
18 Camshaft bearing cap   19 Seal ring   20 Valve guide
21 Valve seat insert

Valve springs:

Test the valve springs either by reference to the specifications in **Technical Data** or against a new spring, discarding any that are shorter or weaker than standard.

To compare the performance of an old spring with a new one, insert the two springs end to end with a metal plate between them into the jaws of a vice or under a press. If the old spring has weakened it will close up first as the pressure is applied.

Valve guides:

Clean carbon deposits from the inside of the guides with a suitable brush. Using a service tool C.5.0115 or a similar gauge, check the inside diameter of the valve guides against the specification. Any guide bore outside the limit given or showing signs of damage must be removed and replaced. Tool A.3.0134 is available for guide removal and A.3.0133 for fitting the new guide.

The new guides must be driven in until they project from the cylinder head by the amounts stated and finally reamed to the correct bore.

Valve seat inserts:

Valve seat inserts that are too pitted to clean up on grinding to the valve may be refaced at a garage to the correct angle of 30 deg. If the inserts are too far gone to be refaced in this manner they must be renewed. As some special equipment is required, this job may be best left to a specialist. For removal, use service tool A.30053 fitted with tap U.4.004 and the appropriate spacer for inlet valve inserts, or tap U.4.0002 for exhaust valve inserts also with the appropriate spacer. Screw the tap into the insert then drive it out by tapping the tool with a soft-faced hammer as shown in **FIG 1:14**. When fitting new inserts, the cylinder head must be evenly heated to a temperature of 100° to 120°C. After installation the valve seat insert must be cut to the correct angle and the valve ground-in as described later.

Tappets:

Inspect the tappets to make sure that the top surface is flat and that there are no signs of scoring or seizing. Check that the top surface of the adjusting shim is not damaged.

FIG 1:11 The timing chain tensioner securing bolt

Refer to **FIG 1:15** and check that the outside diameter of the tappets (d) is between 1.3769 and 1.3775 inch (34.973 and 34.989 mm) standard, or if oversize tappets are fitted, between 1.3848 and 1.3854 inch (35.173 and 35.189 mm). Check that the tappet bore diameter in the cylinder head (D) is between 1.3780 and 1.3789 inch (35.000 and 35.025 mm) standard, or between 1.3859 and 1.3868 inch (35.200 and 35.225 mm) for oversize tappets. The clearance G should be between .0005 and .0020 inch (.011 and .052 mm).

Renew loose or damaged tappets, using oversize components if necessary.

Decarbonizing and valve grinding:

Avoid the use of sharp tools which could damage the light alloy surfaces. Remove all traces of carbon deposits from the combustion chambers, inlet and exhaust ports and joint faces. Check the joint face of the cylinder head for distortion by placing a long straightedge over the surface. The surface should be within .002 inch (.05 mm) of true. High spots can be removed by the careful use of a scraper.

Clean the carbon from the piston crowns, noting that the crankshaft must not be turned or the timing will be lost and further dismantling will be necessary to retime the engine at the lower sprockets.

Grind the valves to their seats, using a suction type valve grinding tool and, on completion, ensure that all traces of grinding paste are removed from the valves and the head.

1:5 Valve clearance adjustment

Refit all the valves with their springs, caps and cotters into the cylinder head and replace the adjusting shims and tappets all in their original position. Fit one of the camshafts and, referring to **FIG 1:16**, measure and record the clearance on each valve in turn using feeler gauges in the gap at G. Remove the camshaft and repeat the operation with the second camshaft so that the actual clearance on every valve is noted.

Adjustment shims are available in thicknesses from 1.3 to 3.5 mm in steps of .025 mm and from this range the correct shim must be selected for each valve position as

FIG 1:13   Valve springs, caps, shims and cotters

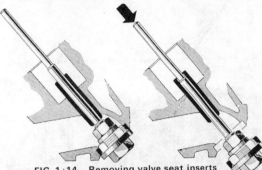

FIG 1:14   Removing valve seat inserts

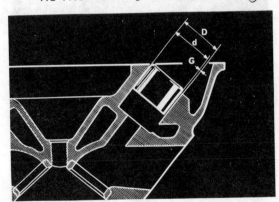

FIG 1:15   Measuring tappet clearance in the cylinder head

follows, noting that the correct clearances with a cold engine are:

Inlet   ..   .019 to .020 inch (.475 to .500 mm)
Exhaust ..   .021 to .022 inch (.525 to .550 mm)

	Specified	Measured	Correction required
Example 1 ..	.500 mm	.425 mm	+.075
Example 2 ..	.550 mm	.605 mm	—.055

In example 1, therefore, a shim .075 **thinner** than the one in use is required. In example 2 the new shim must be .055 mm **thicker** than the one in use.

Use a micrometer to measure each shim fitted to the engine and calculate the thickness of the new shim required in accordance with the method described.

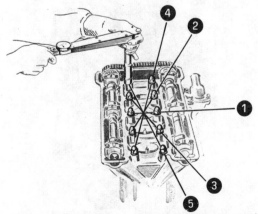

FIG 1:12   Slacken or tighten the cylinder head nuts in this order

ARG1600

15

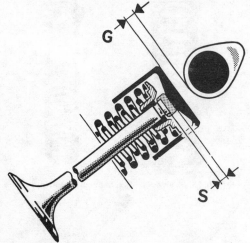

FIG 1:16 Checking valve clearance and adjusting shim thickness

FIG 1:17 Removing the engine front cover assembly

FIG 1:18 The lower sprocket and chain assembly, showing the valve timing marks on the sprockets

FIG 1:19 Aligning and refitting the front cover

Refitting:

With the appropriate adjusting shims in position, finally fit one camshaft so that the timing mark coincides with the mark on the front bearing cap. Fit the second camshaft in the same manner, noting that during this operation neither camshaft must be rotated until the timing procedure has been completed. Check that the timing marks are correctly aligned as described in **Section 1:7** and reconnect the timing chain around the sprocket, with the closed end of the clip on the connecting link facing the direction of chain travel.

1:6 Overhauling the camshaft drives

If work on the camshaft drives is to be carried out with the engine installed in the car the radiator must be removed as described in **Chapter 4**. If the engine is to be removed, refer to **Section 1:2**. In either case the servicing of the camshaft drives is as follows.

Removal:

1 Remove the water pump as described in **Chapter 4**. Remove the generator and its mounting flange. Remove the oil sump. Refer to **Chapter 2** and remove the fuel pump and bracket. Remove the cylinder head as described in **Section 1:3**. Undo the crankshaft pulley securing nut and remove the pulley.
2 Remove the front cover complete with the oil pump and distributor assemblies as shown in **FIG 1:17**. Slide out the sprockets, chain, oil pump drive pinion and idler sprocket as a unit.

Servicing:

Check the sprockets for wear and the chain for signs of wear or damage. Inspect the spacer between the idler sprocket and the crankcase abutment for wear. Renew any part found unserviceable. Measure the diameters and calculate the clearance between the idler shaft and the bushes in the crankcase and cover. Correct clearance is .0016 to .0029 inch (.040 to .074 mm) with a wear limit of .0040 inch (.100 mm).

If clearance is excessive, the bushes can be pulled out and new bushes installed. Ream after fitting to an inside diameter of .8141 to .8148 inch (20.677 to 20.698 mm).

Reassembly:

Install the chain, sprockets and spacer to the front of the engine as a unit, fitting the lower sprocket over the crankshaft key and aligning the sprocket timing marks as shown in **FIG 1 : 18**. Correct valve timing depends on the alignment of the sprockets, so take care to fit them as shown. Once the alignment is set, do not turn the crankshaft until the head is fitted and the upper timing chain correctly fitted or the timing will be wrong, leading to serious valve damage.

Fit two new gaskets between the crankcase and the front cover. Rotate the ignition distributor shaft so that the rotor arm is pointing toward the front of the engine as shown in **FIG 1 : 19** then fit the front cover. If necessary, pull the cover off again and turn the oil pump drive shaft so as to position the rotor arm correctly. Tighten the cover bolts. Drive the front oil seal into the cover and over the crankshaft, using service tool A.3.0146. Refit the crankshaft pulley.

Reassemble all other parts in the reverse order of dismantling, and check the valve timing as described in **Section 1 : 7** and the ignition timing as described in **Chapter 3**.

Timing chain tensioner:

The removal of the timing chain tensioner is described in **Section 1 : 4**. **FIG 1 : 20** shows the components of the timing chain tensioner. Check all parts and renew any that are worn or damaged. The spring specification is quoted in **Technical Data**.

Adjusting timing chain tension:

The tensioner is spring loaded to take up any slack in the chain, but is locked in a fixed position by the securing bolt once adjustment is complete.

Remove the camshaft cover. Loosen (but do not remove) the securing bolt as shown in **FIG 1 : 11** and check that the tensioner is free to move against its spring. **The engine must not be started from rest with the tensioner loose as chain backlash can cause valve and piston damage.** Retighten the securing bolt and refit the camshaft cover.

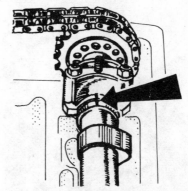

FIG 1 : 21   Timing marks on the camshaft and front bearing cap

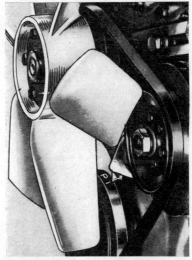

FIG 1 : 22   Crankshaft pulley timing mark and reference plate alignment

FIG 1 : 23   Loosening the camshaft securing nut

FIG 1 : 20   Timing chain tensioner components

FIG 1 : 24   Removing the camshaft locating bolt

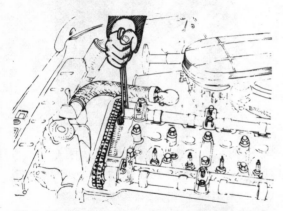

FIG 1 : 25   Aligning the camshaft timing marks with the special tool

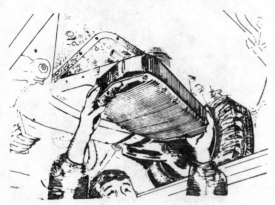

FIG 1 : 26   Removing the sump

Warm the engine up to normal operating temperature, then set it to run at 1000 to 1200 rev/min. During the following operation. the engine speed must remain constant. Slacken the tensioner securing bolt just enough to allow the tensioner to take up any slack in the chain, then retighten securely.

1 : 7   Valve timing

The setting of the timing marks on the lower camshaft drive sprockets is as described in **Section 1 : 6**. To check the final setting for the camshafts, the camshaft covers must be removed and the timing marks on the camshaft journals and front bearing cap brought into alignment as shown in **FIG 1 : 21**, and the timing mark P on the crankshaft pulley in line with the reference plate on the front cover as shown in **FIG 1 : 22**. If the camshaft marks are not in alignment when the crankshaft pulley mark is brought into alignment with the reference plate, the camshafts must be turned to the correct positions. Before adjusting the camshaft positions, adjust the timing chain tension as described in **Section 1 : 6** and check the valve clearances as instructed in **Section 1 : 5**. Then proceed as follows.

Set the piston of No. 1 cylinder at TDC on the compression stroke. This is when the timing marks shown in **FIG 1 : 22** coincide and the front cam lobes are facing outwards. Under these conditions, check that the timing marks on the camshafts and bearing caps line up as shown in **FIG 1 : 21**. If not, slacken the camshaft sprocket securing nut as shown in **FIG 1 : 23** and remove the splitpin and locating bolt shown in **FIG 1 : 24**. Using service tool A.5.0103, turn the camshafts without moving the chain or sprockets until the timing marks line up. Refit the locating bolt and secure it with a new splitpin in the castellated nut, then tighten the camshaft securing nut. **FIG 1 : 25** shows the method of camshaft alignment.

1 : 8   Sump

The light alloy sump is a two-part casting consisting of a main upper unit and a lower finned coverplate. Gaskets are fitted at the joint faces between the sump and coverplate and the sump and crankcase.

Removing the sump:

Drain and discard the sump oil. Loosen and remove the nuts securing the sump to the crankcase and, tilting it forwards, remove it from the car as shown in **FIG 1 : 26**.

Refitting:

Clean the inside of the sump and fit new gaskets between the sump and crankcase and between the lower coverplate and the sump. Refit in the reverse order of removal.

1 : 9   Oil pump

A gear-type oil pump is fitted in the lower part of the crankcase and access to the pump is by removing the sump as described in **Section 1 : 8**. A relief valve is fitted to the pump body which feeds surplus oil back to the sump when the correct oil pressure is exceeded. **FIG 1 : 27** shows the components of the oil pump.

Removal:

Turn the crankshaft until the piston in No. 1 cylinder is at TDC on the compression stroke, this being when the timing mark P is aligned with the reference mark as shown in **FIG 1 : 22** and the distributor rotor arm pointing towards the front of the engine. Remove the screws fixing the oil pump housing to the crankcase and withdraw the pump, strainer and drive shaft assembly out of the crankcase.

Servicing:

Refer to **FIG 1 : 27** and remove the nuts securing the gear housing to pump body. Withdraw the pump driven gear from its spindle and press off the pump drive gear from the drive shaft. Remove the retaining pin 6 and remove the pinion 5. Remove the splitpin and withdraw the relief valve spring, spring seat and plunger.

Refer to **FIG 1 : 28** and check the gear end play 'g' in the housing with a feeler gauge. Permissible play is .0078 to .0197 inch (.200 to .500 mm). Refer to **FIG 1 : 29** and check the radial clearance 'r' between gears and housing, which should be .0008 to .0024 inch (.020 to .062 mm).

Check the relief valve components shown in **FIG 1 : 27** as a faulty valve can be the cause of a drop in oil pressure. Examine the working surfaces of plunger 1 and smooth out any scratches with fine emerycloth. Check the spring 2 for a free length of 1.9 inch (48.25 mm). Check the distributor drive slot 3 for damage and distortion. Inspect the flange 4 to ensure that it is perfectly flat and smooth to prevent oil leakage.

Any parts found worn or damaged, or any which do not meet the specifications stated must be renewed.

Reassembly:

Reassemble the pump in the reverse order of dismantling, noting the following. When fitting the pump drive gear it must be heated to a temperature of 80 to 100°C in hot oil then placed in position over the shaft. On completeion, check that the gears 8 and 9 run freely. Tap lightly on the housing with a soft-faced hammer if it is necessary to free the gears. When refitting the pump assembly to the crankcase, ensure that the timing marks are aligned as shown in **FIG 1 : 30** before inserting the drive shaft. If the rotor to pump coupling does not engage take the pump out again and rotate the drive shaft slightly in either direction to engage the drive pinion in the next tooth. Repeat this operation until the coupling engages, then bolt the pump into position. Check the ignition timing as described in **Chapter 3**.

1:10 Flywheel

The flywheel is a steel forging, the starter ring gear being shrunk-fitted to its outer circumference. Flywheel removal will be necessary to fit a new starter ring gear, or when removing the crankshaft during a major overhaul.

Removal:

1 Remove the gearbox as described in **Chapter 6** and the clutch as described in **Chapter 5**. Mark the position of the flywheel on the crankshaft for refitting.
2 Refer to **FIG 1 : 31** and loosen and remove in alternate sequence one of each pair of flywheel attaching bolts.

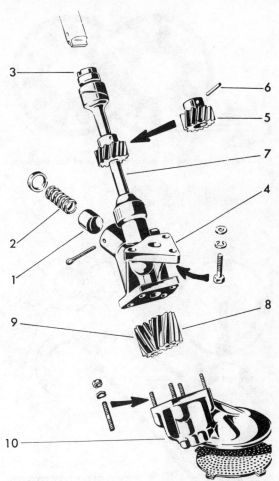

FIG 1 : 27   Components of the oil pump and drive

Key to Fig 1 : 27   1 Pressure relief valve plunger
2 Compression spring   3 Distributor drive slot
4 Pump mounting flange   5 Drive pinion   6 Retaining pin
7 Drive shaft   8/9 Pump gears   10 Pump casing and strainer assembly

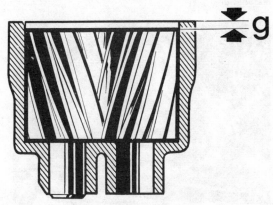

FIG 1 : 28   Checking the oil pump gear end play

FIG 1:29   Checking the radial clearance of the oil pump gears

FIG 1:30   Alignment of the timing marks for oil pump installation

FIG 1:31   The flywheel and attaching bolts

Screw four similar studs into the holes from which the bolts have been removed to prevent the half-rings from moving, then remove the remaining four attaching bolts and slide off the flywheel over the studs.

Servicing:

The starter ring gear can be removed from the flywheel with the aid of a press. The new ring gear must be shrunk into position by heating it to a temperature of 100°C in a hot oil bath before fitting it over the flywheel.

With the flywheel removed, check for any signs of leakage from the rear main bearing oil seal and renew it if necessary. Lever out the old seal and drive in a new seal with service tool A.3.0178 as shown in FIG 1:32. Also check the condition of the gaskets on the cover of the oil vent chamber and on the vent pipe connection, these being arrowed in FIG 1:32. Renew the gaskets if they are faulty.

Refitting:

Index the alignment marks made when dismantling and fit the flywheel over the studs. Use new lockplates. Screw in the first four bolts, then remove the studs and fit the remaining four bolts, noting that all bolts should be lightly lubricated. Tighten the bolts evenly to the correct torque.

1:11 Liners, pistons and rods

As there is insufficient working clearance beneath the engine when it is fitted to the car, the engine must be removed before the liners, pistons and connecting rods can be removed and serviced.

Removal:

1 Remove the engine and gearbox assembly and detach the gearbox and ancillary components all as described in Section 1:2. Fit the engine in a mounting stand. Remove the cylinder head as described in Section 1:3.
2 Fit service tools A.2.0117 to the cylinder head studs to retain the cylinder liners or make up similar holding tools using large washers and pieces of tubing, making sure that the bores are not obstructed. The holding tools fitted in position can be seen in FIG 1:34.

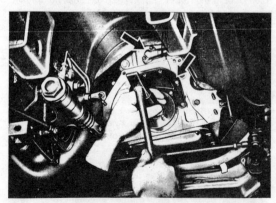

FIG 1:32   Installation of the rear main bearing oil seal. The arrows show the locations of the oil vent chamber cover and the vent pipe connection

3 Mark the connecting rod bearing caps so that they will be refitted in their original positions and, with the engine inverted in the mounting stand, remove the caps as shown in **FIG 1 : 33**. As each cap is removed, withdraw the connecting rod and piston from the cylinder block, taking care not to hit or scratch the liners with the connecting rod. Mark the pistons for reassembly in the original order. Remove the circlips and push out the gudgeon pins from the pistons.

4 Remove the holding tools and withdraw the cylinder liners from the crankcase, noting their positions for refitting to the same bores from which they were removed, and in the same position in the bore, marking both liner and bore.

Servicing :

FIGS 1 : 2 and **1 : 3** show exploded views of the crankshaft, liner, piston and connecting rod assemblies.

Pistons and rings:

Remove the rings and wash them in petrol. Clean off carbon deposits from the piston crowns and ring grooves. Inspect the piston and rings for score marks or any signs of seizure. Fit the piston rings one at a time into their liners as shown in **FIG 1 : 34** and measure their fitted gap, using feeler guages. Refer to **Technical Data** for the gap dimension for each model.

Inspect the pistons for deep score marks, chipped ring grooves and any signs of seizure. Refit the piston rings to the pistons and, using a feeler gauge as shown in **FIG 1 : 35**, check the clearance of the rings in their grooves. Refer to **Technical Data** for the clearance dimensions. If any piston is found to be unserviceable, a new piston complete with rings and cylinder liner must be fitted.

Connecting rods:

Check the big-end and small-end bearings for signs of scoring or seizure. The big-end bearing shells must be renewed if any signs of the pink metal layer can be seen under the whitemetal bearing surface. The bearings must never be hand-scraped, nor must the rod or cap be filed to take up wear. Small-end bushes may be renewed by pressing out the old bush, pressing in a new bush and reaming it to the dimensions given in **Technical Data**. Check that the difference in weight between connecting rods complete with caps, bearings and bolts does not exceed 2 grammes (.07 oz). Repeat the weighing pro-

FIG 1 : 34   Checking the piston ring fitted gaps

FIG 1 : 35   Measuring the ring clearance in the piston grooves

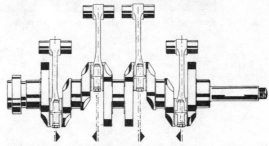

FIG 1 : 36   The correct assymmetric fitting of the connecting rods to the crankshaft

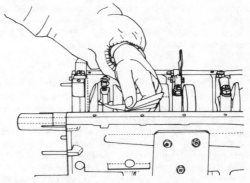

FIG 1 : 37   Checking the bearing cap clearance

FIG 1 : 33   Removing the big-end bearing caps

FIG 1:38 Removing the main bearing cap nuts

FIG 1:39 Peening the aluminium plugs in the crankshaft oilways

FIG 1:40 The crankshaft felt washer and guide bush details

cedure with the pistons, rings, gudgeon pins and rods assembled. The weight difference between assemblies should not exceed 5 grammes (.17 oz). If necessary, carefully grind away the flashing on the connecting rod seams to bring the weights within the limits stated.

Liners:

Inspect the bore in the liners. Minor scratches in the bores can be removed by polishing with fine glasspaper. But more serious damage such as scoring will necessitate renewing the liner. If suitable measuring equipment is available, measure the internal diameter of the liner bores and the external diameter of the pistons and compare them with the dimensions specified in **Technical Data**.

Liner bores should be measured between .40 inch (10 mm) from the upper end and 1.20 inch (30 mm) from the lower end, taking several measurements to check for

taper wear and ovality. Pistons should be measured at right angles to the gudgeon pin bore and .43 inch (11 mm) or .47 inch (12 mm) from the lower edge of the skirt for Mahle and Borgo pistons respectively. If the maximum wear limit of .0059 inch (.15 mm) for piston to liner clearance is exceeded, or if piston or liner show obvious signs of damage or localised wear, the piston and liner assemblies should be renewed. Markedly uneven piston and liner wear could indicate a distorted connecting rod.

Refitting:

Place one rubber seal ring over the shoulder on the cylinder liners and refit them to their original bores, indexing the marks made when dismantling. Check the projection of the liners from the cylinder block which should be .0004 to .0024 inch (.01 to .06 mm). Fit the liner holding tools in position. Arrange the rings on the pistons so that the ring gaps are staggered 120 degrees from each other and use a piston ring clamp when entering the pistons into the bores. Fit the asymmetric connecting rods as shown in **FIG 1:36**. Use new lockplates, oil the big-end cap bolts and tighten them to the specified torque. Having done so, loosen one bolt and check the bearing cap clearance as shown in **FIG 1:37** with a feeler gauge. The clearance should be .0030 to .0039 inch (.08 to .10 mm). If necessary, polish the bearing cap surfaces with very fine emerycloth to obtain the specified clearance. Tighten the bolts and tab the lockplates. Reassembly and refitting is a reversal of the removal procedure. Lubricate all moving parts with engine oil during reassembly.

1:12 Crankshaft and main bearings

Removal

1 Remove the engine and gearbox assembly and detach the gearbox and the ancillary components all as described in **Section 1:2**. Remove the pistons and rods as described in **Section 1:11** and the flywheel as instructed in **Section 1:10**. Remove the engine front cover and the lower timing chain and pinions as described in **Section 1:6**. The crankshaft and main bearing components can be seen in **FIGS 1:2** and **1:3**.

2 Remove the nuts securing the main bearing caps as shown in **FIG 1:38**, starting at the centre bearing and working outwards. Mark the bearing caps for refitting in their original positions. The rear bearing cap must be removed with the special puller A.3.0139/1 and A.3.0139/2, and the remaining bearing caps with puller A.3.0182.

3 Lift out the crankshaft and remove the thrust washers from the sides of the centre bearing. Remove the upper shell halves from the bearings and keep them with the corresponding lower shells and caps for correct refitting.

Servicing:

Inspect the main journals and the crankpins and remove possible minor scratches with a fine oilstone. If the bearing surfaces are deeply scored or show signs of seizure the journals and crankpins should be reground to one of two undersizes (and the appropriate oversize bearing shells fitted) in the case of a 1300, 1600 or 1750 engine. Journal dimensions and undersizes are listed in **Technical Data**.

In the case of 2000 engines, the nominal sizes of main journals and crankpins are listed, and these must be observed. The crankshaft on these engines cannot be reground.

Bearing clearances can be checked, if necessary, using the Plastigage method described in **Hints on Maintenance and Overhaul** in the **Appendix**.

Drill out the aluminium plugs which seal the crankshaft oil passages. Thoroughly clean the oil passages and fit new plugs, peening them in place with service tool A.2.0103 as shown in **FIG 1 : 39**. Place the crankshaft in a lathe or between V-blocks and check the runout at the main journals and crankpins. Runout should not exceed .0004 inch (.01 mm) for main journals or .0027 inch (.07 mm) for crankpins. It may be possible for an Alfa Romeo main dealer to carry out remedial work to a distorted crankshaft, but if not, it must be renewed.

Check that the felt washer and the guide bush shown in **FIG 1 : 40** are in good condition. If not, they must be removed and new components installed as follows: Soak the felt washer in engine oil heated to 45°C for an hour, then allow it to cool and fit it to its seat. Soak the guide bush in engine oil heated to 120°C for four hours, then allow it to cool and fit it to the crankshaft with the aid of a punch.

Check the gaskets at the rear of the crankcase as described in **Section 1 : 10**.

Refitting:

Fit new shell bearings into the housings in the crankcase and caps, using the correct oversize if the crankshaft has been reground, standard size if not. Lubricate the bearings and all moving parts with engine oil during reassembly. Fit the crankshaft to the crankcase together with the rear oil seal half-rings. Fit the upper thrust washers at each side of the centre main bearing with their oil grooves facing the crankshaft. Install the centre main bearing cap and shell and fit the remaining caps and shells in accordance with the location marks. Fit the lower thrust washer to the centre bearing with the oil groove towards the crankshaft and fit the rubber plugs between the rear main bearing cap and crankcase, using service tool A.3.0113 as shown in **FIG 1 : 41** or a similar punch. Oil the main bearing cap nuts and tighten them to the specified torque, starting with the centre bearing and working outwards. Check the bearing cap clearances by loosening one bolt and inserting a feeler gauge in the same manner as that shown for big-end bearings in **FIG 1 : 37**. The clearance should be .0030 to .0039 inch (.08 to .10 mm). Polish the bearing cap surfaces with very fine emerycloth if necessary, to obtain the specified clearance. Retighten the nuts.

Check for correct crankshaft end play, which should be .0028 to .0100 inch (.07 to .26 mm), using a dial gauge. If the end play is beyond the limit of .0190 inch (.50 mm), fit thicker thrust washers at the centre main bearing. Two thrust washer oversizes are available. Refit the rear main bearing oil seal as described in **Section 1 : 10**.

Reassembly and refitting is now a reversal of the removal procedure, referring to the appropriate sections in this Chapter for fitting details of the component parts.

FIG 1 : 41 Fitting the rubber plugs at the rear main bearing position

FIG 1 : 42 Removing the oil filter element

1 : 13 External oil filter

The external oil filter is of the fullflow type and pressure oil is fed to it direct from the oil pump, the oil then passing to the lubrication bores and galleries in the engine. The filter should normally be removed at intervals of 2500 to 5000 miles and the filter element renewed if it is of FRAM manufacture, or washed in petrol, dried and refitted if it is a FISPA unit.

The oil pressure during normal running should be 64 to 71 lb/sq in and between 7 and 14 lb/sq in at idling speed. If the oil pressure is below 50 lb/sq in, or if the oil pressure warning light comes on during normal running, the filter element should be checked and renewed or cleaned according to the previous instructions. If the fault remains, the pressure relief valve should be checked as described in **Section 1 : 9**. If the relief valve and filter element are in order, suspect worn main or big-end bearings. Always keep the engine oil topped-up to the level indicated on the dipstick.

Renewable element type:

Unscrew the threaded plug on the filter housing and remove the canister as shown in **FIG 1 : 42**. Drain the oil from the canister and lift out the element. Renew or service the element as previously described. When refitting, check that the gaskets between the canister and bracket, between the canister and filter and at the threaded plug are in good condition, renewing them if necessary. Fill the canister with engine oil, refit it to the housing and tighten the threaded plug. Do not overtighten to avoid distortion. Run the engine and check for oil leakage at the filter housing.

Disposable cartridge type:

Unscrew the cartridge complete and discard it. Clean the filter mounting face on the engine and lightly coat the new seal with engine oil. Make sure that the seal is correctly fitted, then screw the new cartridge into place until it just contacts its seating. From this point tighten a further three-quarters of a turn by hand only. Do not overtighten the filter or oil leaks may result. A strap wrench may be used to remove the old filter cartridge if it is too tight to be unscrewed by hand, but never use anything but hand pressure to tighten a new unit. On completion, check the engine oil level, start the engine and check for leaks around the filter unit. Top up the oil level to compensate for that used to fill the new filter.

1:14 Refitting the engine

Refitting the engine and gearbox unit to the car is the reverse of the removal procedure given in **Section 1:2** and reference should be made to that section and to the various chapter and section numbers quoted in it. New hoses must be obtained to replace any which show signs of deterioration and the required quantities of engine oil and gearbox oil obtained. Observe the torque tightening figures for the various components listed in **Technical Data**, noting where the torque applies to oiled threads.

When installation is complete and all systems made serviceable, the valve timing should be checked as described in **Section 1:7** and the ignition timing checked as described in **Chapter 3**. The instructions given in **Section 1:3** must be carried out when refitting the cylinder head to ensure that the head nuts are correctly tightened. If necessary, adjust the carburetter(s) or fuel injection as described in **Chapter 2**.

1:15 Fault diagnosis

(a) Engine will not start
1 Defective coil
2 Faulty distributor capacitor (condenser)
3 Dirty, pitted or incorrectly set contact breaker points
4 Ignition wires loose or insulation faulty
5 Water on spark plug leads
6 Battery discharged, corrosion of terminals
7 Faulty or jammed starter
8 Sparking plug leads wrongly connected
9 Vapour lock in fuel pipes
10 Defective fuel pump
11 Overchoking or underchoking
12 Blocked petrol filter or carburetter jet(s)
13 Leaking valves
14 Sticking valves
15 Valve timing incorrect
16 Ignition timing incorrect

(b) Engine stalls
1 Check 1, 2, 3, 4, 5, 10, 11, 12, 13 and 14 in (a)
2 Sparking plugs defective or gaps incorrect
3 Retarded ignition

4 Mixture too weak
5 Water in fuel system
6 Petrol tank vent blocked
7 Incorrect valve clearances

(c) Engine idles badly
1 Check 2 and 7 in (b)
2 Air leak at manifold joints
3 Carburetter adjustment wrong
4 Air leak in carburetter
5 Over-rich mixture
6 Worn piston rings
7 Worn valve stems or guides
8 Weak exhaust valve springs

(d) Engine misfires
1 Check 1, 2, 3, 4, 5, 8, 10, 12, 13, 14, 15 and 16 in (a)
2 Weak or broken valve springs

(e) Compression low
1 Check 13 and 14 in (a); 6 and 7 in (c); and 2 in (d)
2 Worn piston ring grooves
3 Scored or worn cylinder bores

(f) Engine lacks power
1 Check 3, 10, 11, 12, 13, 14, 15 and 16 in (a); 2, 3, 4 and 7 in (b); 6 and 7 in (c); and 2 in (d)
2 Leaking joint washers
3 Fouled sparking plugs
4 Automatic advance not working

(g) Burnt valves or seats
1 Check 13 and 14 in (a); 7 in (b); and 2 in (d)
2 Excessive carbon round valve seats and head

(h) Sticking valves
1 Check 2 in (d)
2 Bent valve stem
3 Scored valve stem or guide
4 Incorrect valve clearance

(j) Excessive cylinder wear
1 Check 11 in (a)
2 Lack of oil
3 Dirty oil
4 Piston rings gummed up or broken
5 Badly fitting piston rings
6 Connecting rod bent

(k) Excessive oil consumption
1 Check 6 and 7 in (c); and check (j)
2 Ring gaps too wide
3 Oil return holes in piston choked with carbon
4 Scored cylinders
5 Oil level too high
6 External oil leaks

(l) Crankshaft and connecting rod bearing failure
1 Lack of oil
2 Restricted oilways
3 Worn journals or crankpins
4 Loose bearing caps
5 Extremely low oil pressure
6 Bent connecting rod

CHAPTER 2

THE FUEL SYSTEM

2:1 Description

Giulia TI and Giulia Sprint models use a Bendix electric fuel pump, all other models being fitted with a Fispa type Super 83 mechanical pump. **FIG 2:1** shows the mechanical pump fitted to the engine crankcase and **FIG 2:3** the electric fuel pump in position beneath the car.

Two basic types of carburetter are used on these cars, dual barrel downdraught or twin choke sidedraught. The former will be a Solex, while the latter may be by Solex, Weber or Dellorto and may be used singly or in pairs. Details of jet sizes, etc., for the various carburetter types and the car models to which they may be fitted will be found in **Technical Data** in the **Appendix**.

The fuel injection system, where fitted, is designed to combine performance and economy while maintaining a low level of exhaust emission. This is obtained by improving the distribution and combustion, therefore no devices to cope with unburned exhaust gases are necessary.

2:2 Mechanical fuel pump

The mechanical fuel pump is operated by a lever moved by an eccentric on the distributor and oil pump drive shaft. From the exploded view of the pump in **FIG 2:2** it can be seen that the lever moves a diaphragm to draw fuel into the housing via the inlet valve and expel it under pressure through the outlet valve.

Removal:

Pull off the fuel hose and remove the two nuts and lockwashers securing the pump to the fixing studs. Lift out the pump together with the gasket.

Dismantling:

Mark the pump operating tappet and the upper and lower pump housings for reassembly in their original positions. Remove the attaching screws and separate the upper housing together with the gasket and funnel from the lower housing. From the upper pump body, remove the filter gauze 3, inlet valve spring seat 4, springs 5 and 14, the inlet valve 6 and outlet valve 15.

From the lower pump body, remove the diaphragm 8, the rubber cup 9 and the return spring 10. Unscrew and remove the spring seat 12 together with the spring 11. Drive out the rocker lever pivot pin 17 with a suitable drift, then remove the rocker lever arm towards the drive side of the pump.

FIG 2:1 The mechanical fuel pump fitted to the engine

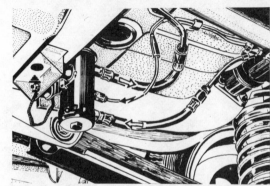

FIG 2:3 The electric fuel pump fitted beneath the car

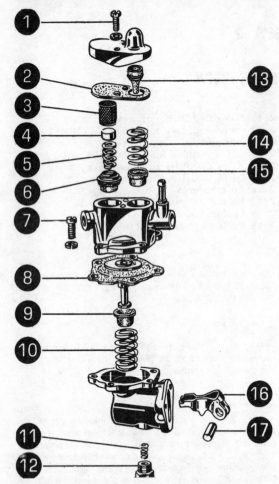

FIG 2:2 Components of the mechanical fuel pump

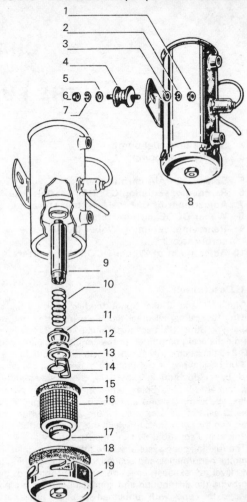

FIG 2:4 Components of the electric fuel pump

Key to Fig 2:2   1 Cover screw   2 Gasket
3 Filter gauze   4 Inlet valve spring seat
5 Inlet valve spring   6 Inlet valve   7 Body screw
8 Diaphragm   9 Rubber sealing cup   10 Diaphragm spring
11 Rocker lever spring   12 Spring seat   13 Funnel
14 Outlet valve spring   15 Outlet valve   16 Rocker lever
17 Rocker lever pin

Key to Fig 2:4   1 Nut   2 Washer   3 Washer
4 Rubber mounting   5 Washer   6 Nut   7 Washer
8 Fuel pump assembly   9 Piston   10 Return spring
11 Valve cage   12 O-seal ring   13 Washer
14 Securing clip   15 Sealing gasket   16 Fuel filter
17 Magnet   18 Gasket   19 Cover

Servicing:

Clean all parts thoroughly, using petrol and a small brush. Do not use fluffy rags for cleaning purposes as particles of lint may clog the filter or valves. Check that the diaphragm is in good condition and make sure that it is firmly in position between the two retaining discs. Inspect the rocker lever and the pivot pin for any signs of wear or damage. Springs can be checked by comparison with new springs. Renew any component found to be worn or damaged and any spring which is stretched or deformed. Always fit a new filter gauze. Blow out the filter compartment with compressed air.

Reassembling:

Reassembly and refitting is a reversal of the removal procedure, noting the following points. Index the alignment marks on the pump housing made during dismantling. Use new gaskets, coating them on both sides with non-setting jointing compound. Refit the operating tappet in accordance with the marks made on removal.

Testing:

The delivery rate of the pump may be tested on suitable bench testing equipment. When the pump is driven to an equivalent of 2500 to 3000 engine rev/min, the delivery should be 24 gall/hr with no outlet pressure. With a delivery pressure of 2.8 lb/sq in the delivered amount should be 13.2 gall/hr. With no flow, the outlet pressure should be 4.2 to 5.6 lb/sq in.

Alternatively, the pump can be checked in position by fitting a T-connection between the pump and the delivery pipe to the carburetter and connecting an accurate pressure gauge into the system. The pressure reading should be between 3 and 5 lb/sq in.

2:3 Electric fuel pump

The electrically operated fuel pump is attached to a crossmember beneath the car. When the ignition is switched on and current flows through the pump unit, the piston is lifted by a magnet. At the end of the piston stroke the magnet breaks the circuit and the piston returns to the bottom of the bore under spring action. The circuit is then reconnected and the cycle repeats. A valve controls the flow of fuel through the pump.

Removal:

Unscrew the feed and pressure pipes from the pump and disconnect the wires from their terminals. Remove the nut securing the pump to the insulated mounting and remove the pump. Plug the pipes to prevent loss of fuel.

Dismantling:

Refer to **FIG 2:4**. Remove the cover 19 by twisting it anticlockwise, then withdraw the internal components into the order shown.

Servicing:

Clean all parts thoroughly, using petrol and a small brush. Do not use fluffy rags for cleaning purposes as particles of lint may clog the filter or valves. Check the piston 9 for wear or scoring and the return spring for serviceability. Inspect the rest of the parts for wear or damage.

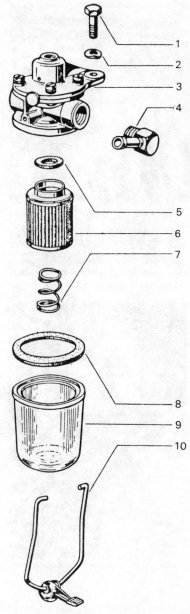

FIG 2:5 The fuel filter components

Key to Fig 2:5   1 Screw   2 Washer   3 Filter cover
4 Connector   5 Sealing washer   6 Filter element
7 Spring   8 Filter bowl gasket   9 Filter bowl
10 Retaining clip

Reassembling:

Reassembly and refitting is a reversal of the removal procedure, making sure that the feed and earth wires are correctly connected and that the fuel pipes are not buckled or obstructed.

FIG 2:6 Items to be detached for carburetter removal

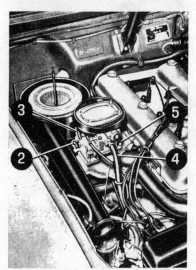

FIG 2:7 Items to be detached for carburetter removal

Testing:

With the pump installed in a suitable testing fixture a delivery pressure of 1.5 lb/sq in and a delivery rate of 13.2 to 15.4 galls/hr should be obtained. If these figures cannot be achieved on test, the pump is faulty and must be renewed complete.

2:4 Fuel filter

Giulia Sprint GT and Spider Veloce models are equipped with a bowl-type filter fitted between the fuel pump and carburetter. A pressure regulator is incorporated in the filter assembly to control the flow of fuel to the carburetter. **FIG 2:5** shows the components of the fuel filter assembly. About every 8000 miles the retaining clip should be sprung off and the bowl and element removed,

cleaned in petrol and replaced. If the element cannot be satisfactorily cleaned, it must be renewed. When refitting, check the condition of the filter bowl gasket and the sealing washer and renew them if necessary.

2:5 Solex C32 PAIA carburetter

The Solex C32 PAIA carburetter is a dual-barrel two-stage downdraft instrument and is fitted to various Giulia, Sprint and Spider models in one of two types; C32 PAIA 5 or C32 PAIA 7. The throttle linkage operates directly on the first barrel of the carburetter, the second barrel being controlled from the first barrel. When the vacuum in the first barrel reaches a certain maximum, the second stage is brought into operation through a diaphragm and linkage arrangement. This ensures high acceleration values and top speed performance, while reducing fuel consumption in the low and middle ranges. A diaphragm accelerator pump is incorporated in the first barrel and is directly operated from the throttle linkage. As the two carburetters mentioned are similar in design and operation, reference will be made only to the C32 PAIA 7 in the following instructions.

2:6 Removing, servicing C32 PAIA carburetter

Removal:

Remove the wingnut on the air cleaner cover and loosen the clamp on the carburetter. Lift off the air cleaner cover. Refer to **FIGS 2:6** and **2:7** and disconnect the choke control 1 and the throttle control 2. Remove the vacuum pipe 3 and the fuel pipe 4. Remove the fixing nuts 5 and lift off the carburetter and gasket. **FIG 2:8** shows section and exploded views of the C32 PAIA 7 carburetter.

Dismantling:

1 Refer to **FIG 2:9** and remove the accelerator pump outlet valve 1 and the cover screws 2. Lift off the cover and remove the float from its chamber. Unscrew the filter seat 3 and remove the filter.

2 Refer to **FIG 2:10** and remove from both barrels the jet carriers 1 with the main jets 2, idle jets 3, air correction jets 4 and the mixture tubes 5. Refer to **FIGS 2:11** and **2:12** and remove the pump bypass jet 1, carefully inverting the carburetter to shake out the ball into the palm of the hand. Loosen the six screws 2 securing the pump to the carburetter body and remove the splitpin 3. Remove the diaphragm assembly.

3 Refer to **FIGS 2:13** and **2:14** and loosen the screws 1 securing the choke assembly to the carburetter. Remove the stop 2 and plunger 3 and withdraw the spring 4. Unscrew the choke jet 5 from the bottom of the float chamber.

4 **FIG 2:15** shows the location of the throttle valve securing screws. It is not advisable to remove the throttle valves unless it is absolutely essential. If, however, there is excessive play between the throttle valve shafts and the bearings the valves can be removed and new shafts and bushes fitted. It must be pointed out that, should this operation be necessary, it may well prove more economical to renew the complete lower part of the carburetter.

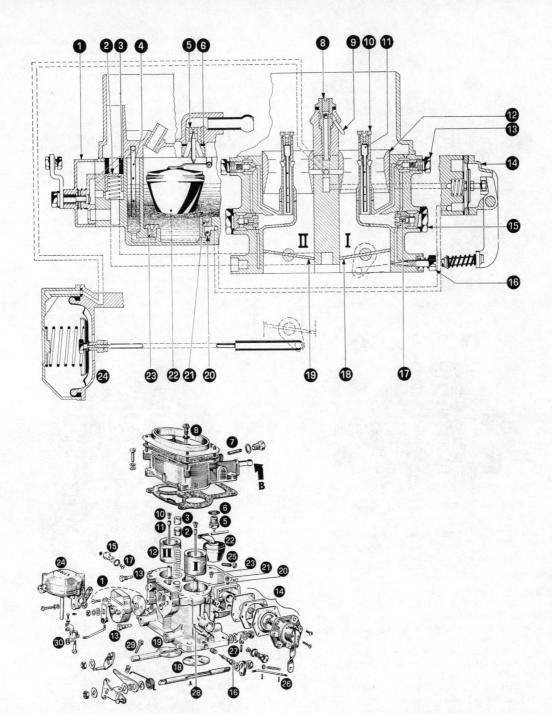

FIG 2:8 Section and exploded views of the Solex C32 PAIA carburetter

Key to Fig 2:8   **B** Fuel inlet   **1** Choke assembly   **2** Choke plunger   **3** Choke plunger stop   **4** Choke air jet
5 Needle valve seat   **6** Needle valve gasket   **7** Filter gauze   **8** Accelerating pump outlet valve   **9** Accelerating pump nozzle
10 Air correction jet   **11** Mixture tube   **12** Choke tube   **13** Idling jet   **14** Accelerating pump   **15** Main jet carrier
16 Idling mixture adjusting screw   **17** Main jet   **18** First barrel throttle   **19** Second barrel throttle
20 Accelerating pump inlet valve   **21** Accelerating pump bypass jet   **22** Float   **23** Choke jet   **24** Vacuum chamber
25 Setscrew and locknut for securing choke tube   **26** Accelerating pump linkage   **27** Second barrel throttle adjusting screw
28 Distributor vacuum connection   **29** First throttle idle adjusting screw   **30** Choke control lever

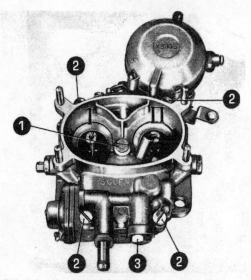

FIG 2:9   Removing the pump valve and fuel filter

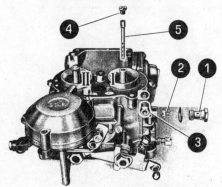

FIG 2:10   Removing the jets and mixture tubes

5 Refer to **FIG 2:16** and loosen the setscrews 1 and slide out the choke tubes. The choke tubes are dowelled to ensure correct refitting.

Servicing:

Clean and inspect all parts carefully. Clean out all sediment from the float chamber, fuel filter, jets and passages. Use compressed air, clean petrol and a small stiff brush. **Do not use cloth or a wire probe.** Renew the idle adjustment screw if the conical tip is not in perfect condition. Check the float for dents or leaks and the float needle valve for wear or damage. If the contact point for the needle valve on the top of the float is worn the float must be renewed. The float, float spindle and needle valve should always be renewed as an assembly.

A repair kit, containing replacements for all wearing parts is obtainable from Solex. If the carburetter is completely dismantled, fit all new parts contained in the kit irrespective of the condition of the original parts.

Reassembly:

Reassembly and refitting of the carburetter is a reversal of the removal and dismantling instructions, noting the following points. When refitting the vacuum unit check that the tube between the choke tube and vacuum unit is free from obstruction. Note that no gasket is used between the choke assembly and the carburetter body. When refitting the accelerator pump assembly (14 in **FIG 2:8**), make sure that the holes in the diaphragm are exactly in line with the holes in the housing before the cover is screwed down. The pump lever spring is fitted with the wider end toward the lever. Make sure that the needle valve gasket washer 6 is correctly installed as this determines the float level. The specified thickness for this washer is 1 mm (.039 inch). Ensure that the second barrel throttle linkage works freely without binding. Screw the idle control screw right home, then unscrew it $1\frac{1}{2}$ turns. This setting serves as a basic adjustment until the carburetter is properly tuned. Refit the accelerator pump valve and check its action by blowing through it. Air should pass through the valve in one direction only.

When reassembly is complete the accelerator pump delivery can be checked by filling the float chamber with fuel and, with the carburetter held over a measuring vessel, operating the pump linkage by hand. The flow should be 4 to 6 cc per 20 pump strokes. By inserting thin washers between the control lever and the splitpin the delivery amount can be altered.

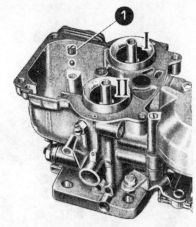

FIG 2:11   Removing the pump bypass jet and ball

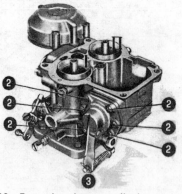

FIG 2:12   Removing the pump diaphragm assembly

2:7 Adjustment of C32 PAIA carburetter

The carburetter slow-running adjustments must be carried out with the engine at normal operating temperature. Refer to **FIG 2:17**.

Release the locknut, tighten screw 11 a quarter of a turn then retighten the locknut. This prevents binding of the second throttle unit. With the engine idling, slowly screw in adjusting screw 4 so that engine speed is increased. Now loosen screw 5 until the engine begins to 'hunt', then gradually screw it in until the engine runs smoothly.

Loosen screw 4 very slowly until an engine speed of 500 to 600 rev/min is obtained. If the engine begins to 'hunt' with this adjustment, slightly tighten screw 5 to correct it. **On no account should screw 5 be tightened to its maximum extent.**

2:8 Weber DCOE carburetter

The Weber carburetters fitted to various models in the Alfa-Romeo range are twin-choke instruments and are fitted in pairs. This arrangement gives a separate intake passage for each cylinder. Each carburetter has two separate intake passages which operate simultaneously

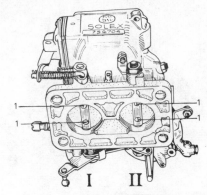

FIG 2:15   The throttle valve securing screws

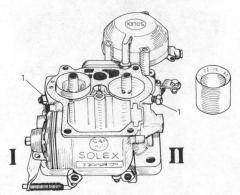

FIG 2:16   Removing the choke tubes

from a common linkage, one float chamber and fuel supply system being provided for the pair of intakes. Each barrel has its own main and slow-running jet system, but both throttle valves are operated from a single shaft actuated by a lever connected to the accelerator linkage. As the whole range of Weber DCOE carburetters are basically similar in design and operation, only the basic type is dealt with in the following instructions. Settings and jet sizes for the various alternative models are given in **Technical Data** in the **Appendix**.

2:9 Removing, servicing Weber DCOE carburetter

Removal:

Remove the wingnuts on the air cleaner cover and the bolt from the bracket between the cover and engine. Lift off the cover. Refer to **FIG 2:18**. Take out the four securing bolts and lift the air intake box 5 from the carburetter. Remove the choke cable 2, throttle control 4 and the fuel pipe 3. Remove the attaching bolts 1 and lift the carburetters from the manifold **FIG 2:19** shows the components of the Weber DCOE carburetter.

Dismantling:

1 Remove the wingnut and lift off the inspection cover and gasket. Undo the five screws and remove the top cover, using care to avoid damage to the float mechanism. Unscrew the hexagonal bolt and remove the fuel filter gauze from the top cover. Push out the

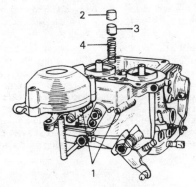

FIG 2:13   Removing the choke control components

FIG 2:14   The choke jet in the float chamber

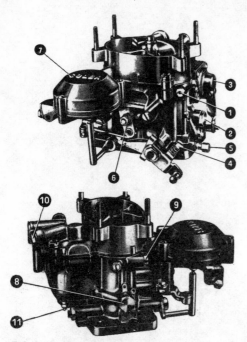

FIG 2:17   Carburetter jets and adjustment screws

Key to Fig 2:17
1 Idle jet, first barrel
2 Main jet, first barrel
3 Accelerator pump
4 Adjustment screw for minimum opening of first throttle
5 Idle mixture adjustment screw
6 Choke control lever
7 Vacuum chamber
8 Main jet, second barrel
9 Idle jet, second barrel
10 Fuel filter
11 Adjustment screw for minimum of second throttle

FIG 2:18   Items to be detached for carburetter removal

Key to Fig 2:18
1 Carburetter attaching nuts
2 Choke control cable
3 Fuel pipes
4 Throttle control
5 Air intake box

float spindle and remove the float. Unscrew the float needle valve assembly making sure that the needle remains in the valve.

2 Refer to **FIG 2:20** and remove the following parts from the carburetter housing: The idle jet holders and jets 1, the main jets 2, the inlet valve 3 from the accelerator pump, collecting the screw plugs, ball seats and balls;

the accelerator pump delivery valves 4, pump jets 5, choke jets 6, inspection screws 7, idle mixture adjusting screws 8 and the choke assembly 9.

3 Refer to **FIG 2:21** and remove the spring plate 11, using a screwdriver. Remove the accelerator pump 10 from its seat. Release the circlips from the carburetter housing and remove the choke valves 12 complete with their springs and spring seats.

4 Remove the float chamber coverplate from the lower carburetter housing. Remove the locating screws and withdraw the mixture and choke tubes as shown in **FIG 2:22**.

It is inadvisable to remove the throttle valve shaft unless it is absolutely necessary. If removal is essential, due to a suspected deformed valve or shaft, the removal procedure is as follows. Refer to **FIG 2:23**. Remove the small coverplate shown and disengage the shaft return spring after removing the retainer 1. Mark the relative positions of the throttle valves to the shaft and the shaft to the carburetter body. Detach the throttle valves from the shaft. Refer to **FIG 2:24** and remove the locking pin 2 from the pump control lever. Unscrew the nut 3 and withdraw from the shaft the control lever and shim, spring retaining cover, spring and the dust cover. Withdraw the shaft from the opposite side, removing at the same time the accelerator pump lever, spring and retaining cover.

Servicing:

Clean and inspect all parts carefully. Clean out all sediment from the float chamber, fuel filter, jets and passages. Use compressed air, clean petrol and a small stiff brush. **Do not use cloth or a wire probe.** Check the float for dents or leaks and the needle valve for wear or damage. Renew any components found to be unserviceable. A repair kit for Weber carburetters is available from Weber or Alfa-Romeo dealers, containing the parts needed for servicing.

Reassembly:

Reassembly and refitting of the carburetter is a reversal of the removal and dismantling instructions, noting the following points. If the throttle valves and shaft were removed, smear the ballbearings with high melting point grease and index the alignment marks made during dismantling when the shaft assembly is refitted. Fit one throttle valve at a time and carefully centre it in the barrel, checking the fit by holding the carburetter against the light to check the gap between the valve and the bore. When the alignment is correct, secure the throttle valve screws by peening the heads with a punch. Check the shaft for smooth operation.

When refitting the accelerator pump, press on the spring plate with a screwdriver until the plate snaps into its groove on the housing. Use a screwdriver to press the retaining rings into their grooves when refitting the two plungers of the choke assembly. All jets should be firmly tightened. **The slow-running mixture adjustment screws must never be screwed fully home or the seatings will be damaged.**

Securely tighten the float needle valve into the top cover and ensure that the damper ball valve is free to

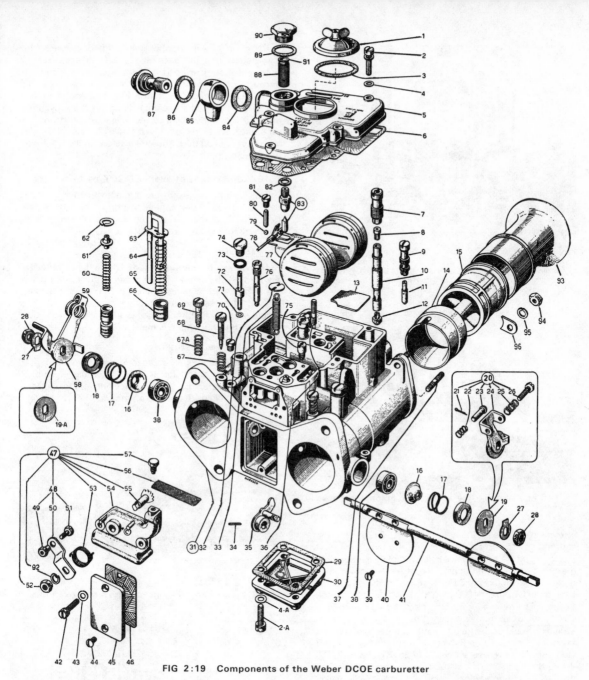

FIG 2:19   Components of the Weber DCOE carburetter

Key to Fig 2:19   1 Inspection cover   2 Securing screw   3 Gasket   4 Washer   5 Carburetter top cover   6 Gasket
7 Emulsion tube carrier   8 Air correction jet   9 Slow-running jet carrier   10 Emulsion tube   11 Slow-running jet   12 Main jet
13 Plate   14 Choke tube   15 Auxiliary choke tube   16 Dust cover   17 Spring   18 Spring plate   19 Distance washer
20 Throttle lever   21 Splitpin   22 Spring   23 Pin   24 Lever   25 Spring   26 Screw   27 Locking plate   28 Nut
29 Gasket   30 Cover   31 Carburetter flange   32 Spring plate   33 Spring   34 Spring pin   35 Pump operating lever
36 Stud   37 Stud   38 Ballbearing   39 Throttle valve screw   40 Throttle valve plate   41 Throttle valve shaft
42 Securing screw   43 Washer   44 Securing screw   45 Plate   46 Gasket   47 Choke control   48 Choke control lever
49 Nut   50 Lever   51 Clamp screw   52 Nut   53 Return spring   54 Cover   55 Choke valve shaft   56 Filter gauze   57 Screw
58 Throttle lever   59 Starter fuel valve   60 Spring guide   61 Spring   62 Spring washer   63 Spring plate
64 Pump operating lever   65 Spring   66 Pump plunger   67 Spring   68 Slow-running screw   69 Throttle screw
70 Inspection screw   71 Gasket   72 Pump jet   73 Seal ring   74 Screwed plug   75 Inlet valve   76 Starter fuel jet
77 Float   78 Float spindle   79 Ball valve   80 Plunger   81 Screw   82 Float needle valve gasket   83 Needle valve
84 Gasket   85 Link   86 Gasket   87 Screw   88 Filter gauze   89 Gasket   90 Filter plug   91 Protection sleeve
92 Spring washer   93 Air intake   94 Nut   95 Spring washer   96 Securing plate

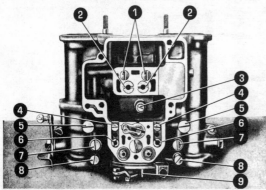

FIG 2:20 Parts to be removed for carburetter servicing

Key to Fig 2:20
1 Slow-running jet holders
2 Main jets   3 Inlet valve   4 Pump outlet valves
5 Accelerator pump jet   6 Starter fuel jets
7 Inspection screw   8 Slow-running volume screws
9 Choke assembly

FIG 2:21   Removing the accelerator pump and choke valves

operate in the needle valve. Refer to **FIG 2:25**. With the carburetter in a vertical position and the tab of the float just touching the needle valve ball, the distance A between the two floats and the upper face of the top cover with gasket fitted should be .33 inch (8.5 mm) for all models except the GT Junior 1600 for which if should be .28 inch (7 mm). The free travel B of the float should be .26 inch (6.5 mm) for all models except the GT Junior 1600 for which it should be .31 inch (8 mm). In order to obtain the correct values for A and B the position of the float tab and stop can be altered as shown in **FIGS 2:26** and **2:27**. When this adjustment is carried out, make sure that the float tab is in line vertically with the float needle valve. Check the float for free operation on the spindle. Fit the top cover assembly to the carburetter body, making sure that the float cannot contact the sides of the float chamber before tightening the cover attaching screws.

Insert the filter gauze and closing plug and fit the jet inspection cover. Set the basic slow-running adjustment by tightening the slow-running volume control screws until they are just home, then unscrewing them two turns. Screw in the throttle valve stop screws until they are just home, then tighten them a further half turn. The positions of these screws can be seen in **FIG 2:28**.

Check the eight rubber joints fitted between the carburetters and the inlet manifold. **It is essential to renew these joints if they show any signs of damage or deformation to avoid air leaks at this point.** Air leakage at this point will cause irregular running and could result in the engine firing on three cylinders only. Fit the carburetters to the manifold and do up the securing nuts finger tight. Assemble the air intake box and properly align the carburetters before finally tightening the securing nuts.

2:10 Adjustment of Weber DCOE carburetters

The carburetter slow-running adjustments must be carried out with the engine at normal operating temperature. Check that the sparking plugs and ignition system are in good working order. Refer to **FIG 2:28**.

Throttle alignment:

Disconnect the control linkage T from the carburetters. Slacken off the screws F and S almost fully and operate the throttles a few times to ensure they are not binding.

Fully depress the throttle control lever of the rear carburetter so that the throttles are fully closed, then screw in S until contact is made.

Idling speed adjustment:

Undo the screws M about one turn from the closed position. From the point at which it is just in contact, screw in the screw F one half turn. Connect the accelerator control linkage T to the carburetters.

FIG 2:22   Removing the mixture and choke tubes

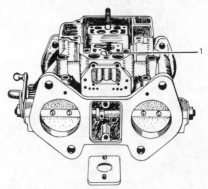

FIG 2:23   The coverplate and the shaft return spring retainer

Start the engine and when it is at working temperature, screw in screws M until the engine runs smoothly, adjust screw F to obtain an engine speed of 600 to 700 rev/min.

If the engine runs unevenly, adjust the screws M alternatively until even running is obtained. Reset the engine speed if necessary. **Never screw the screws M fully home or the seats will be damaged.**

Control linkage adjustment:

When the throttles have been aligned and the idling speed adjusted, the control linkage should be connected and adjusted as follows. Slacken the locknut on the adjustable throttle rod and alter the length of the rod so that there is a slight preload on the lever itself when the accelerator pedal is in the rest position. Retighten the locknut.

Checking the carburetter fuel level:

If it is necessary to carry out this check, ensure that the car is standing on level ground and carry out the following operations on each carburetter.

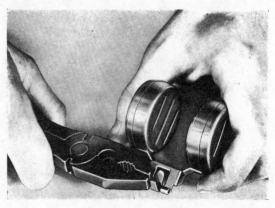

FIG 2:26 Bending the float pivot tail to adjust the float level

FIG 2:24 Removing the throttle control shaft

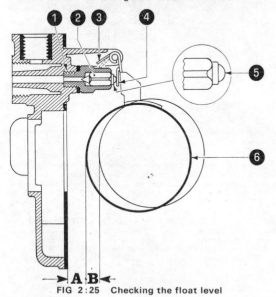

A B

FIG 2:25 Checking the float level

Key to Fig 2:25
1 Needle valve 2 Needle
3 Float pivot tail 4 Float tongue 5 Ball valve
6 Float

FIG 2:27 Bending the float tongue to adjust the float level

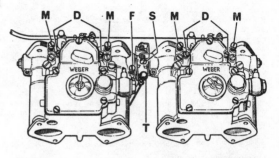

FIG 2:28 Weber DCOE throttle linkage and adjustment screws

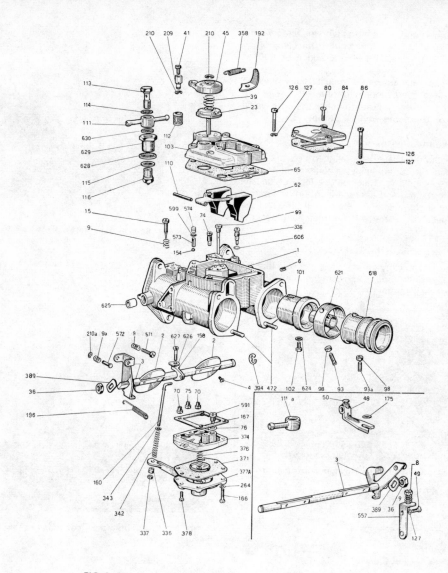

FIG 2:29   Components of the Solex C40 DDH carburetter

Key to Fig 2:29   1 Carburetter assembly   2 Throttle valve   3 Throttle valve shaft with lever   4 Screw   6 Adjusting screw
9 Spring   15 Slow-running volume screw   23 Starter rotary valve   36 Nut   39 Starter spring   41 Screw for choke control cable
45 Starter cover   62 Twin float   65 Gasket   70 Main jet   74 Slow-running jet   75 Starter fuel jet   76 O-seal ring   80 Screw
84 Coverplate   86 Gasket   93 Tube locating screw   98 Nut   99 Air correction jet   101 Venturi   102 Locating screw
103 Float chamber cover   110 Float spindle   111 Filter housing   112 Filter gauze   113 Hollow bolt   114 Sealing ring
115 Seal ring for needle valve   116 Float needle valve   126 Screw   127 Spring washer   154 Ball   158 Override lever
160 Connecting link   166 Screw   167 Gasket   196 Return spring   209 Starter cable plug   210 Securing clip
264 Spring washer   336 Nut   337 Nut   338 Injector tube   342 Spring   343 Plain washer   371 Diaphragm
374 Lower cover   376 Diaphragm spring   377 Pump cover   378 Screw   389 Securing clip   394 Spring clip
472 Stud   573 Weight   574 Closing plug   591 Valve   599 O-seal ring   606 O-sealing ring   618 Air horn
621 Pre-atomizer   624 Sealing washer   625 Sealing washer   626 Securing clip   627 Securing screw   628 Gasket
629 Seat   630 Gasket

For carburetter No. 1
9a Spring   192 Holder for starter return spring   210a Securing clip   358 Return spring   571 Adjusting screw   572 Pin

Only for carburetter No. 2
8 Slow-running screw   48 Holder for starter control cable   49 Screw   50 Clamping screw   127 Spring washer
175 Plain washer   557 Retainer

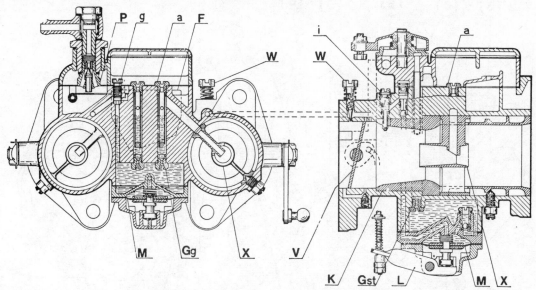

FIG 2:30 Sections of the Solex C40 DDH carburetter

Key to Fig 2:30   **a** Air correction jet   **F** Float   **g** Slow-running jet   **Gg** Main jet   **Gst** Starter fuel jet   **K** Venturi
i Injector tube   **L** Pump lever   **M** Diaphragm pump   **V** Throttle valve   **P** Float needle valve   **W** Slow-running volume screw
X Pre-atomizer

Remove the jet inspection cover and unscrew both main jets. By means of a syringe, draw off from the wells a sufficient quantity of fuel to cause a substantial lowering of the fuel level. Refit the cover and run the engine at idling speed for a few seconds. Again remove the cover and, using an accurate gauge, measure the fuel level between the upper face of the float chamber and the surface of the fuel in the chamber. The measurement should be 1.14 inch ± .02 inch (29 ± .5 mm). There may be a slight variation on GT Junior models, but if other models do not match this figure, the top cover must be removed and the float level checked as described in the reassembly instructions of **Section 2:9**. Also check the needle valve assembly for correct sealing, renewing it if there is any sign of leakage.

2:11 Solex C40 DDH carburetters

The Solex C40 DDH carburetters are twin-choke instruments and are fitted in pairs.

Each barrel of the carburetter has its own main and slow-running jet system, but both throttle valves are operated from a single shaft actuated by a lever connected to the accelerator linkage. A single float chamber serves both barrels. The accelerator pump is a diaphragm-type unit directly operated by the throttle linkage.

2:12 Removing, servicing C40 DDH carburetters

As the design and operation of these carburetters is similar to the Weber DCOE models previously described, reference should be made to that section and carburetter removal and servicing carried out as instructed therein.

The carburetter should be dismantled into the order shown in **FIG 2:29** and the components marked and stored in the correct order for reassembly. A repair kit is available from Solex containing replacements for all wearing parts. When reassembling the carburetter, use new

gaskets throughout. On completion, refit the carburetters to the engine and adjust the slow-running as described in the next section.

2:13 Adjustment of C40 DDH carburetters

FIG 2:30 shows the sectioned views of the carburetter and **FIG 2:31** the layout of the adjustment screws and linkage with the carburetters and air intake box installed. The slow-running adjustments must be carried out with the engine at normal operating temperature. Check that the sparking plugs and ignition system are in good working order.

Throttle alignment:

Refer to **FIG 2:31** and disconnect the throttle valve lever at T. Unscrew the screw F for the minimum opening of the throttle valves and check that the valves and linkage

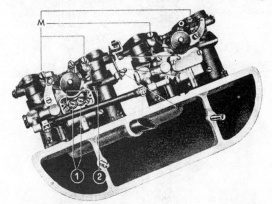

FIG 2:31 Solex C40 DDH throttle linkage and adjustment screws

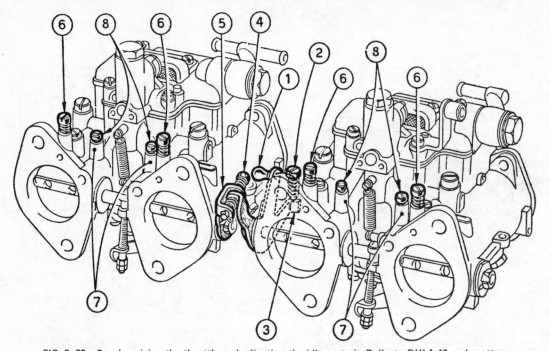

FIG 2:32 Synchronizing the throttle and adjusting the idle on twin Dellorto DHLA 40 carburetters

Key to Fig 2:32 1 Front throttle control lever   2 Throttle stop screw   3 Throttle stop   4 Coupling screw   5 Throttle control lever (rear)   6 Mixture adjustments screws   7 Vacuum take off unions   8 Plugs

move freely without binding. Press down the control lever of the rear carburetter as far as it will go to completely close the throttle valves. Now screw in the screw S until it makes contact. This will synchronize the throttle valves. Finally, screw in screw F until it makes contact then screw it in a futher one turn.

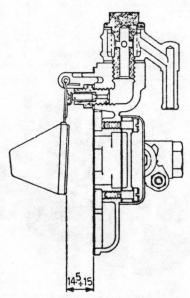

FIG 2:33 Setting the float level

Idling speed adjustment:

Screw in the mixture control screws M until they reach their stops, then loosen them half a turn each. Reconnect the throttle lever T then start the engine and warm it up. Turn the adjusting screw F very slowly to obtain a smooth idling speed of 600 to 700 rev/min. If the engine 'hunts' screw in the screws M slightly then correct the engine speed with screw F.

Checking the float level:

If it is necessary to carry out this check, ensure that the car is standing on level ground and carry out the following operations on each carburetter.

Run the engine at idling speed for about two minutes then switch off the ignition. Unscrew the coverplate and remove one of the main jet carriers. Use a gauge inserted in the main jet carrier bore to measure the fuel level between the upper face of the carburetter housing and the surface of the fuel. The measurement should be .590 to .630 inch (15 to 16 mm) for a 1300, or .610 to .650 inch (15.5 to 16.5 mm) for a 1600, 1750 or 2000 model.

If the level is incorrect, change the thickness of gasket washer under the float needle valve assembly to obtain the figure quoted. **Do not bend the float arm.**

2:14 Solex C40 PHH/2 carburetters

These horizontal two-stage carburetters are no longer supplied by Alfa-Romeo as complete assemblies, but replacement parts can be obtained and repair kits are available. The carburetters were fitted to certain Giulia Super and Sprint GT models. Servicing is as previously described for Solex carburetters, and details of settings and jet sizes are given in **Technical Data** in the **Appendix.**

2:15 Dellorto DHLA 40 carburetters

These carburetters, which are used in pairs on the 1750 and 2000 engines, are similar to the Weber DCOE and are in fact interchangeable with these. Details of the calibrated parts are given in **Technical Data** and these settings should be adhered to if ever replacement parts are required.

Dismantling and cleaning the carburetter presents no difficulty and the only other operations which the owner may wish to undertake are the idle speed adjustment and checking the float level.

Throttle synchronization and idle speed adjustment:

Refer to **FIG 2:32**. Disconnect the link rod from the lever 1 on the rear carburetter and unscrew the throttle stop screw 2 until it ceases to contact the lever 3.

Turn back the screw 4 on the throttle lever 5 until the throttle butterflies close completely when lever 1 is pressed.

Hold the throttles in the closed position by means of lever 1 and screw in the screw 4 until it **just** touches the lever again.

Tighten the throttle stop screw 2 by one complete turn and turn the four mixture regulating screws 6 two full turns out from their fully closed position.

Connect the link rod to lever 1.

Start up the engine and run it until it has reached its full operating temperature, then use the throttle stop screw to give an idle speed of 600 to 700 rev/min.

If the engine now runs irregularly, use the mixture regulating screw on each unit to obtain smooth running, noting that clockwise rotation of the screw weakens the mixture and anticlockwise rotation richens it.

If this last adjustment has altered the engine speed bring it back to 600 to 700 rev/min by using the throttle stop screw.

More precise synchronization is obtainable with vacuum gauges connected to the take-off points at 7 if they are available. These points are normally sealed with the plugs 8. Connect the vacuum gauges and adjust until equal depression is registered on each barrel.

It is claimed that the correct use of the mixture regulating screws in this manner will ensure an exhaust in conformity with current European requirements.

Checking the float level:

This should only be necessary if the carburetter has been dismantled or if the quality of the engine running suggests an incorrect fuel level.

Ensure first that the seat of the needle valve is screwed in tightly and that the valve moves correctly to shut off the fuel supply.

See that the float is in good condition and is of the correct weight.

Refer to **FIG 2:33**. Hold the float cover assembly vertically as shown and see that the float arm is in light contact with the base of the valve needle.

The distance shown between the two halves of the float and the face of the cover joint must be between .57 and .59 inch (14.5 and 15 mm) for 1750 models or .65 and .67 inch (16.5 and 17 mm) for 2000 models.

2:16 Air cleaner

The air cleaner elements should be removed and cleaned at 4000 mile intervals and renewed at 12,000 mile intervals, both operations being carried out more frequently if the vehicle is operated under dusty conditions. To remove the element, unscrew the wingnut(s) securing the air cleaner cover and remove the cover and the element.

Paper elements should be cleaned by blowing through from the inside with compressed air. Felt elements should be washed in petrol then blown through from the inside with compressed air.

2:17 Fault diagnosis (carburetters)

(a) Leakage or insufficient fuel delivered

1 Air vent to tank restricted
2 Fuel pipes blocked
3 Air leaks at pipe connections
4 Pump filter blocked
5 Pump gaskets faulty
6 Pump diaphragm defective
7 Pump valve sticking or seating badly
8 Fuel vaporizing in pipelines due to heat

(b) Excessive fuel consumption

1 Carburetters require adjustment
2 Fuel leakage
3 Sticking mixture control
4 Dirty air cleaner
5 Excessive engine temperature
6 Brakes binding
7 Tyres under-inflated
8 Idling speed too high
9 Car overloaded

(c) Idling speed too high

1 Rich fuel mixture
2 Carburetter control sticking
3 Incorrect slow-running adjustment
4 Worn throttle valves

(d) Noisy fuel pump

1 Loose mountings
2 Air leaks at suction side or at diaphragm
3 Obstruction in fuel pipe
4 Clogged pump filter

(e) No fuel delivery

1 Float needle stuck
2 Tank vent blocked
3 Connections to electric pump faulty
4 Pipeline obstructed
5 Pump diaphragm stiff or damaged
6 Pump inlet valve stuck open
7 Bad air leak on suction side of pump

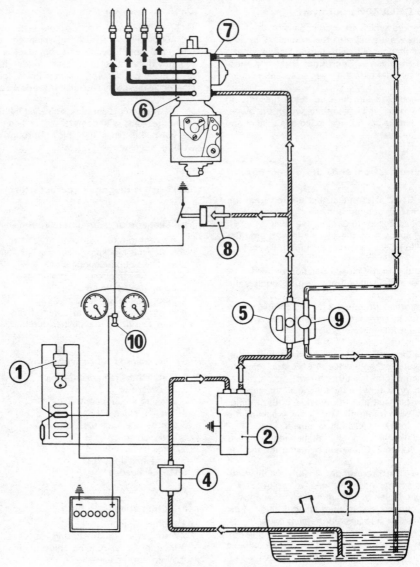

FIG 2:34 The fuel injection system

Key to Fig 2:34   1 Ignition switch   2 Fuel pump   3 Tank   4 Tank filter   5 Main filter   6 Injection pump   7 Pressure control   8 Pressure switch   9 Relief valve   10 Warning light

2:18 Fuel injection

Description:

FIG 2:34 shows the general arrangement of the fuel system. Fuel is pumped from the tank through the line filter 4, main filter 5 and injection pump 6. Excess fuel acts as a coolant for the injection pump and is passed through a calibrated orifice 7 which regulates the fuel pressure. A pressure relief valve 9 is incorporated to bypass fuel to the recovery pipe at 16 to 18 psi. A pressure switch in the delivery pipe will switch on a dash light should the pressure drop to 7 psi.

The air induction system is shown in FIG 2:35. When the throttle valves are closed, idling air is taken from the air cleaner 2 and the crankshaft ventilating circuit through the equaliser 9.

The accelerator pedal 5 is connected to the throttle lever 4 and the control unit lever 6 so that any pedal position corresponds to an exact position of throttle valve and control unit levers.

Also incorporated are a solenoid operated cold start device and an initial running device, controlled by a thermostat which ensures smooth running soon after a cold start.

Crankshaft ventilation:

Gases and vapours developed in the engine are taken off into the combustion chambers to be burned. The system ensures that these emissions are dealt with both at idle and normal running engine speeds (see **FIG 2:36**).

The vapours pass through the separator 2 where the oil is returned through the pipe 8. Under normal running conditions the vapours then pass through the pipe 3 to the manifold chamber 4. At idling speeds, the vapours are taken from the separator through the secondary circuit 9.

Maintenance:

To maintain a constant fuel/air ratio as seasonal temperatures change, the control unit is fitted with a temperature setting lever as shown in **FIG 2:37**. This lever should be moved to the correct position as follows:

F (freezing) for ambient temperatures below 0°C;
C (cold) for temperatures between 0°C and 15°C;
N (normal) for temperatures exceeding 15°C.

Every 6000 miles the air cleaner elements must be changed (see **FIG 2:36**). Detach the two upper anchoring straps at the manifold. Loosen, at the engine side, the four clamps on the intake hoses. Free the crankshaft ventilation hoses 3 and 9 from the separator. Disconnect the four idle hoses 10 from the equalisers 6 on the cleaner body. The cover of the cleaner can now be removed and the elements replaced after having cleaned the inside of the housing.

The throttle valve throats should be cleaned every 12,000 miles by removing the air filter, holding the throttles fully open and using a brush soaked in petrol. Rub clean with non-fluffy cloth. Clean the valve edges in a similar fashion taking care not to strain the spindles.

The tank filter, 4 in **FIG 2:34**, should be replaced every 12,000 miles. Slacken the bolt on the clamp securing the filter to the rear underbody. Loosen the hose clamps at the filter and remove. Fit the new filter in the reverse order.

The main filter element as fitted to these cars is shown in **FIG 2:38** and should be changed every 6000 miles. Remove the air filter and disconnect the battery and starter positive cable. Clean the exterior of the filter body

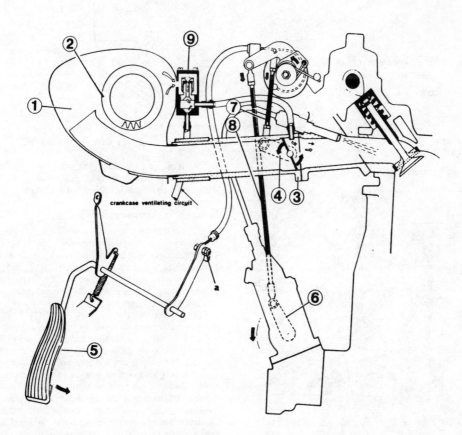

FIG 2:35   The air induction system

Key to Fig 2:35   1 Silencer   2 Air cleaner   3 Throttle   4 Throttle lever   5 Pedal   6 Control unit lever   7 Relay to throttle valve rod   8 Relay to control unit rod   9 Idle equaliser   a Cable adjustment

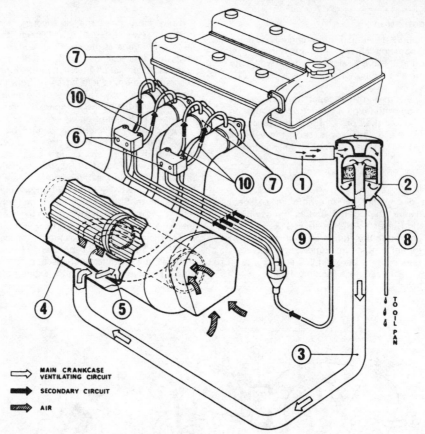

FIG 2:36 The crankcase ventilating system

Key to Fig 2:36   1 Hose   2 Separator   3 Hose   4 Manifold chamber   5 Inlet port   6 Equalisers   7 Throttles
8 Oil return pipe   9, 10 Secondary circuit

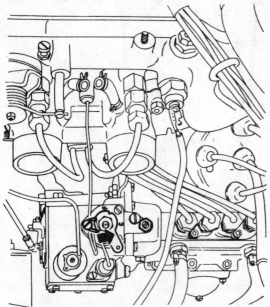

FIG 2:37 The temperature setting lever (arrowed)

before removal to prevent the entry of dirt. Remove the bolt to release the filter bowl. Before fitting the new filter, make sure the bowl is cleared of sediment.

Linkage adjustments:

To check the linkage adjustment the engine must be at operating temperature with the air cleaner removed. The clearance between the control unit input lever and its reference screw must be between .012 and .024 inch (.3 and .6 mm), when the relay crank is resting against the idle limit stop. If adjustment is required, allow the engine to cool before proceeding.

Disconnect the rods 7 and 8 in **FIG 2:35**, and the throttle cable and clamps. Obtain the maker's tool No. A.4.0121 and fit it onto the studs as shown in **FIG 2:39**. Adjust the idle stop screw until the ball joint just touches the reference plane on the tool and lock in this position. If the linkage assembly has been removed or strained check also the full throttle setting and make the adjustment as necessary at the full throttle limit stop screw.

Now the 'actuator' section of the thermostatic control can be removed from the control unit; to do so, remove the two screws retaining the actuator mounting flange and the two screws clamping the actuator pipe anchoring grommet (do not remove the thermostat bulb). Withdraw the actuator taking care not to distort the pipe excessively.

Fit the dummy actuator, such as tool No. A.4.0120 shown in **FIG 2:40**, in place of the original. At this point refit the relay crank/control unit lever rod and, if necessary, adjust the rod length so that the linkage is at rest against the idle limit stop when, between the control unit lever and its reference screw, there is a clearance of .035 to .050 inch (0.9 to 1.3 mm).

Reconnect the relay crank/throttle valve rod and, if necessary, adjust the rod length so that the throttle valves are just closed when the linkage rests against the idle limit stop ('just closed' means such a position that, when slightly opening the throttle valves and then releasing them, definite contact of the linkage and the idle stop is felt).

Remove the dummy actuator, carefully fit the original and tighten into place. Again check that, with the engine

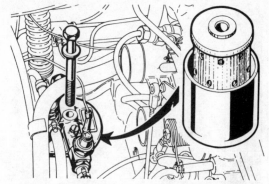

FIG 2:38   Replacing the main fuel filter element

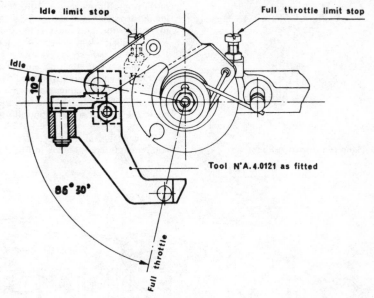

FIG 2:39   Adjusting the linkage

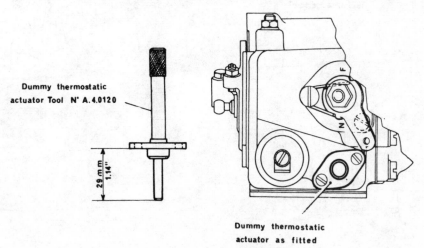

FIG 2:40   Fitting the dummy actuator

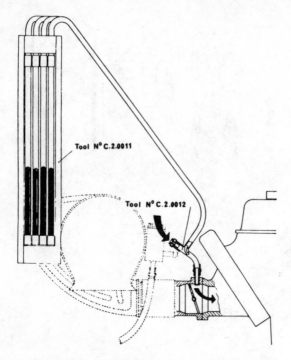

FIG 2:41　Checking the throttle alignment

at operating temperature, the clearance between the control unit input lever and its reference screw is .012 to .014 inch (.30 to .35 mm).

Never disturb the reference screw of the control unit input lever.

Equalising the throttles:

Remove the air cleaner body, equalisers, and pipes from the warm engine and fit the four adaptors connected to the four columns of mercury as shown in **FIG 2:41**.

Start the engine and, making sure that the engine is at operating temperature, check that the height difference of the columns in the gauge is no greater than .4 inch (10 mm). If readings show that the vacuum in the front pair of cylinders is greater than that in the rear pair, unscrew the throttle adjusting screw to close the rear pair of throttles. If the vacuum in the front pair of cylinders is lower than that in the rear pair, disconnect the relay crank to throttle rod and set the throttle coupling adjusting screw in such a way as to close the front pair of throttles (screw in the adjusting screw).

Reconnect the relay rod and adjust its length so that the throttle valves are just closed (as already described).

If, before these adjustments, the engine was running unevenly (lean mixture), make sure that throttle valves are in the 'just closed' position; if not, the relay rod must be shortened.

Reinstall the air cleaner assembly with the checking equipment fitted as shown in **FIG 2:42**. Start the engine

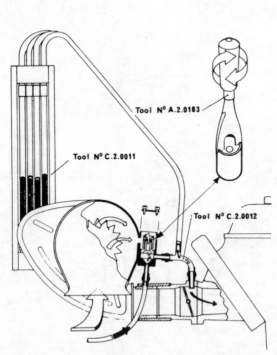

FIG 2:42　Adjusting the equalisers

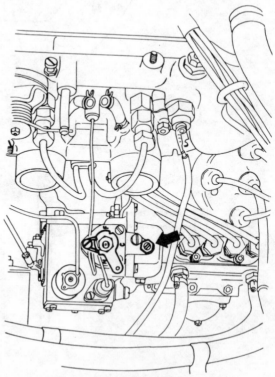

FIG 2:43　The delivery adjusting screw

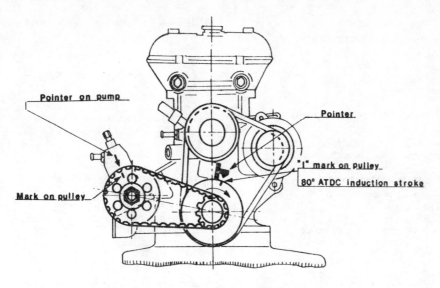

FIG 2:44 Timing the injection pump

and, when at operating temperature, check that the vacuum readings are the same. If necessary adjust using the tool shown after removing the equaliser cover plates. After each adjustment replace the cover plate before taking the reading. During this adjustment ensure that the engine is running smoothly at 720 rev/min using an electronic tachometer of proven accuracy.

If too lean a mixture results from increasing the adjuster orifice and the engine begins to hunt, screw in, at the same time, the injection pump delivery adjusting screw after slackening the locknut (see **FIG 2:43**).

Whilst making these adjustments avoid any sudden increase in engine speed as too great a vacuum may cause the mercury to be sucked out at the gauge columns.

Injection pump:

The injection pump must never be dismantled for any reason. A pump that has been tampered with may lose its exchange value. If it becomes necessary to renew the pump, proceed as follows:

Remove the air cleaner and disconnect the battery. Disconnect the lead from the cold starting solenoid. Remove the two screws from the thermostat actuator mounting flange and the two screws clamping the actuator pipe anchoring grommet (do not remove the thermostat bulb). Withdraw the actuator from the control unit, taking care not to distort the pipe.

Disconnect the fuel hoses from the pump and detach the connecting rod from the control unit. Bring No. 1 cylinder to the induction stroke with the mark 'I' (80 deg. ATDC) on the pulley aligned with the pointer on the crankcase. This will facilitate the installation of the new pump.

Unscrew the three attaching nuts and remove the drive belt cover. Take the drive belt off the injection pump pulley.

Fully slacken the injection pipe nuts on the pump outlet fittings, without removing the pipes (use tool No. A.5.0164). Unscrew the nuts on the two bolts attaching the pipe cluster plate and the injection pump slanting bracket. Loosen the two screws attaching the control unit to its bracket at the engine mount. From under the car, unscrew the four nuts (use tool No. A.5.0167 for the front ones) attaching the pump support to the engine front cover.

Withdraw the pump and its support. Fit the new pump in the reverse order. The new injectors supplied with the pump have location numbers and must be installed accordingly.

Owing to the special construction of the injection pump the plungers must on no account be operated directly with a lever.

On re-installation align the reference marks on the pump and the drive pulley (with the engine previously timed for injection on No. 1 cylinder), then fit the drive belt onto the pulley avoiding the use of tools that might damage the belt (see **FIG 2:44**).

Fuel cut-off regulator:

This device regulates the rate of fuel cut-off during deceleration with a fully released accelerator pedal, thus minimising exhaust emissions and preventing detonations from taking place due to incomplete combustion.

The device is adjustable by the knurled nut located at the bottom of the unit and accessible from under the car.

If denotations occur during deceleration, progressively screw in the knurled nut until the trouble is remedied.

If, however, the engine stalls when decelerated rapidly from 4000 rev/min in neutral the adjustment must be reversed until a satisfactory medium is obtained.

2:19 Fault diagnosis (injection)

(a) Excessive fuel consumption

1 Fuel leakage
2 Thermostatic actuator defective
3 Defective injection pump
4 Idling speed too high

(b) Exhaust detonations on deceleration

1 Throttle not returning fully
2 Control unit lever out of adjustment
3 Fuel cut-off regulator out of adjustment

(c) Unsatisfactory performance

1 Control linkage out of adjustment
2 Fuel pressure too low
3 Injector defective
4 Injection pump or control unit defective

(d) Low fuel pressure (light stays on)

1 Faulty fuel pump
2 Pressure switch faulty
3 Fuel line or filter blockage
4 Pressure relief valve stuck open·

(e) Engine stops on deceleration

1 Fuel cut-off regulator out of adjustment

(f) Rough idle and misfiring

1 One injector defective
2 Injection pipe fittings leaking
3 Injection pipes cracked
4 Lean mixture

CHAPTER 3

THE IGNITION SYSTEM

3:1 Description

Conventional coil ignition is employed, with a distributor of Bosch or Marelli manufacture. All distributors have a centrifugal advance and retard mechanism which advances the ignition timing progressively as engine speed rises. Some units additionally have a vacuum control unit which advances the timing in response to inlet manifold depression.

All Bosch and some Marelli units have the centrifugal mechanism beneath the base plate which carries the contact breaker. In this case the rotor arm is a push fit on the top of the contact breaker cam. An alternative type of Marelli distributor has the centrifugal mechanism above the contact breaker, with a larger circular rotor arm held in place by two screws (**FIG 3:6**).

Certain models such as the Giulia Sprint GTA are equipped with a dual-ignition system, using twin plugs and coils. The distributor contains two contact breaker units and a twin arm insulated rotor system which fire both sparking plugs in a given cylinder simultaneously, through separate wiring. The circuit configuration of a dual-ignition system is shown in **FIG 3:1**. It will be appreciated that, for this type of ignition system, the following instructions for maintenance and servicing must be

carried out in duplicate where necessary, to cover both ignition circuits.

In all cases the firing order is 1–3–4–2, the cylinders being numbered 1–2–3–4 starting from the front of the engine.

3:2 Routine maintenance

About every 3750 miles, pull off the two spring clips and remove the distributor cap to gain access to the contact breaker points. If the rotor arm is of the pull off type, remove it from the cam spindle. Refer to **FIG 3:2** for standard ignition systems and soak the felt 1 with oil and apply a few drops of oil through the lubrication hole 3. Apply a thin smear of grease to the cam. Refer to **FIG 3:3** for dual-ignition systems and soak the felt 3 with oil. When lubricating the distributor, ensure that no oil or grease contaminates the contact breaker points.

Adjusting the contact breaker points:

Standard ignition systems:

Refer to **FIG 3:2** and turn the engine until one of the cams has opened the points to the full extent, then check the gap at S with a feeler gauge. The gap should be

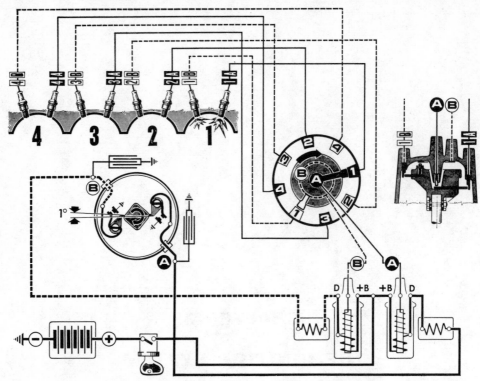

FIG 3:1 Dual ignition system wiring and components

as specified in **Technical Data** for the version in question. To adjust the gap, loosen the screw or screws securing the fixed contact (2 in **FIG 3:2**) and insert a small screwdriver between the pins on the contact breaker plate and in the slot at the end of the fixed contact point. Turn the screwdriver in the required direction to obtain a gap as specified. If the contact breaker plate is provided with an eccentric screw for adjustment, turn the screw until the correct gap is obtained. Tighten the locking screw and recheck the gap.

Dual-ignition systems:

Refer to **FIG 3:3** and turn the engine until the cams have opened both sets of contact breaker points to the full extent, then check the gaps at S with a feeler gauge. Each gap should be between .012 and .016 inch (.30 and .40 mm). To adjust a gap, loosen the screw 1 then turn the eccentric screw 2 until the specified gap is obtained. Tighten the screw 1 and recheck the gap.

Cleaning the contact breaker points:

Use a fine carborundum stone or a contact breaker file to polish the contact points if they are dirty or pitted, taking care to keep the faces flat and square. Afterwards, wipe away all dust with a cloth moistened in petrol. The contact points may be dismantled to assist cleaning by referring to **Section 3:4**.

3:3 Ignition faults

If the engine runs unevenly, pull back the rubber covers to expose the sparking plug lead connectors. Start the engine and set it to idle at about 1000 rev/min and, taking care not to touch any metal part, earth each plug in turn by placing the shaft of an insulated-handle screwdriver between the plug connector and the camshaft cover. Doing this to a plug which is firing properly will accentuate the uneven running but will make no difference if the plug is not firing. Having located the faulty cylinder, stop the engine and remove the plug lead. Start the engine and hold the lead carefully to avoid shocks so that the metal end is about $\frac{1}{8}$ inch away from the cylinder head. A strong regular spark confirms that the fault lies with the sparking plug which should be cleaned as described in **Section 3:6** or renewed if defective.

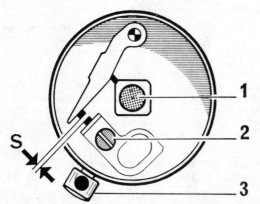

FIG 3:2 Distributor lubrication points and contact point adjustment, standard ignition system

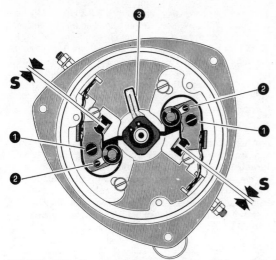

FIG 3:3 Distributor lubrication points and contact point adjustment, dual ignition systems

If the spark is weak or irregular, check the condition of the lead, and, if it is perished or cracked, renew it and repeat the test. If no improvement results, check that the inside of the distributor cap is clean and dry, that the carbon brush can be moved freely against its internal spring and that there is no 'tracking', which can be seen as a thin black line between the electrodes or to some metal part in contact with the cap. 'Tracking' can only be rectified by fitting a new cap.

Testing the low-tension circuit:

Check that the contact breaker points are clean and correctly set, then proceed as follows. Disconnect the thin wire from the coil that connects to the distributor. Connect a test lamp between these terminals, turn on the ignition and turn the engine slowly. If, when the contacts close the lamp lights, and goes out when they open, the circuit is in order. If the lamp fails to light there is a fault in the low-tension circuit. Remove the test lamp and re-connect the cable to the coil and distributor.

If the fault lies in the low-tension circuit, use the test lamp to carry out the following tests with the ignition switched on.

Remove the wire from the ignition switch side of the coil and connect the lamp between the end of this wire and earth. If the lamp fails to light a fault in the wiring or connections between the battery and coil is indicated. Reconnect the wire if the lamp lights.

Disconnect the wire from the coil that connects to the distributor and connect the test lamp between the coil terminal and earth. If the lamp fails to light it indicates a fault in the primary winding and a new coil must be fitted. Reconnect the wire if the lamp lights and disconnect its other end from the distributor. If the test lamp does not light when connected between the end of the wire and earth it indicates a fault in that section of wire.

Capacitor:

The best method of testing a capacitor (condenser) is by substitution. Disconnect the original capacitor and connect a new one between the low-tension terminal on the side of the distributor and earth for test purposes. If a new capacitor is proved to be required, it may then be properly fitted. The capacitor is of .23 to .33 microfarad capacity.

3:4 Removing and dismantling distributor

Removal:

Pull off the two spring clips and remove the distributor cap. Refer to FIG 3:7 and turn the engine until the timing marks on the crankshaft pulley and reference plate are aligned as shown and the distributor rotor is pointing towards the front. This will facilitate the refitting of the distributor.

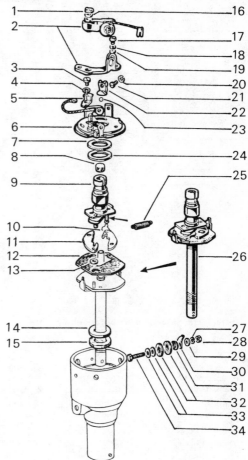

FIG 3:4 Bosch distributor components

Key to Fig 3:4
1 Retaining clip
2 Contact breaker points   3 Securing screw
4 Spring washer 5 Connector tongue 6 Contact breaker plate
7 Fibre washer   8 Lubrication felt   9 Cam
10 Spring clip   11 Flyweights   12 Intermediate plate
13 Insulating washer   14 Shim   15 Fibre washer
16 Shim   17 Securing screw   18 Spring washer
19 Plain washer   20 Spring washer   21 Securing screw
22 Spring   23 Ball   24 Shim   25 Flyweight spring
26 Distributor shaft   27 Spring washer   28 Securing nut
29 Plain washer   30 Retainer   31 Insulating bush
32 Insulating washer   33 Washer   34 Screw

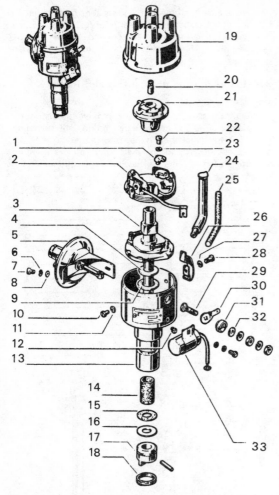

FIG 3:5 Marelli distributor components

Key to Fig 3:5 1 Retainer 2 Contact breaker plate
3 Distributor shaft 4 Thrust washer 5 Vacuum unit
6 Circlip 7 Securing screw 8 Plain washer
9 Plastic washer 10 Securing screw 11 Spring washer
12 Securing screw 13 Distributor housing 14 Felt ring
15 Plastic washer 16 Spacing washer 17 Driving dog
18 Locking spring 19 Distributor cap
20 Centre carbon brush 21 Distributor rotor
22 Securing screw 23 Spring washer 24 Oiler
25 Oil wick 26 Spring clip 27 Spring washer
28 Securing screw 29 Clamp screw 30 Insulating lug
31 Insulating bush 32 Washer 33 Capacitor

Remove the vacuum hose from the distributor connection and disconnect the low-tension cable. Loosen the clamp bolt on the distributor mounting bracket at the crankcase and withdraw the distributor and drive shaft.

Dismantling:

Refer to **FIG 3:4** for Bosch distributors or **FIG 3:5** for Marelli distributors. Remove the securing screws and detach the vacuum unit. Pull off the rotor from the top of the cam. Using a suitable punch, drive out the retaining

pin from the drive dog and remove the drive dog and washers. Withdraw the contact breaker plate complete with the centrifugal advance mechanism from the distributor body. Collect the thrust washers from beneath the plate. Loosen the terminal screw on the contact breaker and disconnect the leads, then remove the contact breaker assembly. Remove the securing clip from the moving contact point arm and separate the contact breaker points.

Servicing:

Check all parts for wear, the moulded cap for 'tracking', the condition of the points and the moving contact spring for satisfactory tension. The contact breaker points should be cleaned as described in **Section 3:2** or renewed if they are badly burned or pitted. Renew any parts found to be unserviceable. Clean the inside and outside of the distributor cap and make sure it is dry and free from grease and oil.

Reassembly:

Reassembly is a reversal of the dismantling procedure, noting the following points. Make sure that the thrust washers are positioned onto the drive shaft before it is fitted to the distributor body. Refit the thrust washers to the bottom of the drive shaft before securing the drive dog with the retaining pin.

Refitting:

This is the reverse of the removal instructions. On completion, check the contact breaker points gap as described in **Section 3:2** and the ignition timing as described in **Section 3:5**.

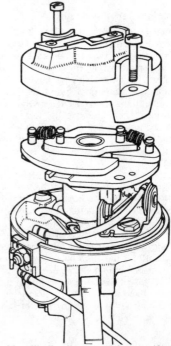

FIG 3:6 Marelli distributor with centrifugal mechanism above contact breaker. The rotor arm is shown removed

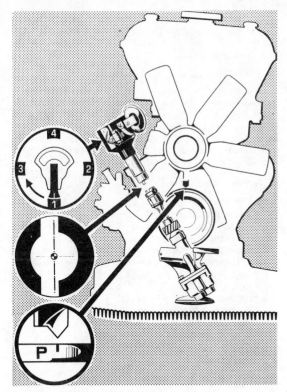

FIG 3:7 Alignment of the engine and distributor timing marks

FIG 3:8 Alignment of the static timing marks on the crankshaft pulley and reference plate

FIG 3:9 Alignment of the maximum advance marks when using a stroboscopic lamp

3:5 Timing the ignition

Make sure that the contact points are correctly adjusted then align the timing marks on the crankshaft pulley and reference plate as shown in **FIG 3:7** with the distributor rotor pointing towards the front. Loosen the distributor clamp bolt and connect a 12-volt test lamp in parallel with the contact points. One lead will go to the terminal on the side of the distributor and the other to earth. Turn the engine until the static timing mark F on the crankshaft pulley is in alignment with the reference mark on the crankcase as shown in **FIG 3:8**. Switch on the ignition and turn the distributor body in an anticlockwise direction until the test lamp goes out. Now turn the distributor body back very slowly until the lamp lights, which indicates that the points are just opening. Carefully tighten the distributor clamp bolt without disturbing the setting.

Stroboscopic timing:

This method is used to check the timing with the engine running. Set the static timing as just described, then connect a stroboscopic lamp into the ignition circuit in accordance with the instructions supplied with the lamp. An accurate tachometer is also required. Disconnect the distributor vacuum pipe, if there is one, run the engine and direct the lamp beam at the timing marks. At 800 to 900 rev/min, the timing mark F should appear in line with the reference mark. At a higher speed, 5100 rev/min for 1300 and 1600 models, 5300 rev/min for early 1750

versions, or 4600 rev/min for later 1750 and 2000 models, the M mark (for maximum advance) should appear aligned as shown in **FIG 3:9**. If necessary, slacken the distributor clamp bolt and carefully turn the distributor body, a little at a time, to align the marks. Then retighten the clamp. Always adjust the maximum advance timing correctly, even if it means disturbing the original static setting, as the timing is most criticial at higher engine speeds.

3:6 Sparking plugs

To maintain peak engine performance, sparking plugs should be inspected and cleaned at regular intervals. Before removing plugs, ensure that the recess around each one is clean and dry so that nothing can fall into the cylinder. The most effective way to clean sparking plugs is to use an abrasive blasting machine. Failing that, deposits can be gently scraped or wire brushed off, taking care not to damage the ceramic insulator, provided that the plug is not too heavily fouled. It is anyway a false economy to continue to use the same set of plugs for a high mileage.

Some models use Lodge 2HL plugs which have four earth electrodes; on this type the electrode gap cannot be adjusted. Lodge HLN plugs should be set to .020 to .024 inch (.50 to .60 mm), Lodge RL 47 plugs to .015 to .018 inch (.35 to .46 mm) and Bosch plugs to .020 inch (.50 mm). For other types, refer to the plug manufacturer's recommendation. The gap must always be set by bending the earth electrode. Do not try to bend the centre electrode. Lightly file the electrodes until they are bright and smooth to facilitate setting the gap accurately.

Before refitting the plugs, clean the threads with a wire brush. Clean the threads in the cylinder head with a tap if the plugs cannot be screwed in by hand. Failing a tap, use an old sparking plug with crosscuts down the threads. Plugs should be tightened to a torque of 18 to 25 lb ft. Do not exceed the torque figure quoted, due to the possibility of stripping the threads in the light alloy cylinder head.

Inspection of the deposits on the electrodes can be helpful when tuning. Normally, from mixed periods of high and low-speed driving, the deposits should be powdery and range in colour from brown to greyish tan. There will also be slight wear of the electrodes. Long periods of constant speed driving or low-speed city driving will give white or yellowish deposits. Dry, black fluffy deposits are due to incomplete combustion and indicate running with a rich mixture, excessive idling and possibly defective ignition. Overheated plugs have a white, blistered look about the centre electrode and the side electrode may be baldy eroded. This may be caused by poor cooling, incorrect ignition or sustained high speeds with heavy loads.

Black, wet deposits result from oil in the combustion chamber from worn pistons, rings, valve stems or guides. Sparking plugs which run hotter may alleviate the problem but the cure is an engine overhaul.

Sparking plug leads:

Renew high-tension leads if they are defective in any way. Inspect for broken, swollen or deteriorated insulation which can be the cause of 'tracking', especially in wet weather conditions. Check the condition of the rubber covers on the sparking plugs and the terminal nuts and renew them if perished. Thread the new lead through the rubber covers and the terminal nuts before refitting the lead and connections.

3:7 The distributor drive shaft

The distributor drive shaft is removed with the distributor as described in **Section 3:4**. The distributor drive dog can then be renewed if it is worn or damaged. The drive slot into which the drive dog engages is at the end of the oil pump shaft and, if wear at this point is suspected, reference must be made to **Section 1:9** for oil pump removal and servicing instructions.

3:8 Fault diagnosis

(a) Engine will not fire

1 Battery discharged
2 Distributor contact points dirty, pitted or maladjusted
3 Distributor cap dirty, cracked or 'tracking'
4 Carbon brush inside distributor cap not touching rotor
5 Faulty cable or loose connection in low-tension circuit
6 Distributor rotor arm cracked
7 Faulty coil
8 Broken contact breaker spring
9 Contact points stuck open

(b) Engine misfires

1 Check 2, 3, 5 and 7 in (a)
2 Weak contact breaker spring
3 High-tension plug and coil leads cracked or perished
4 Sparking plug(s) loose
5 Sparking plug insulation cracked
6 Sparking plug gap incorrectly set
7 Ignition timing too far advanced

CHAPTER 4

THE COOLING SYSTEM

4:1 Description

The cooling system is pressurized and thermostatically controlled. The water circulation is assisted by a centrifugal pump which is mounted at the front of the cylinder block and the cooling fan, which draws air through the radiator, is fitted to the same shaft as the pump impeller. The pump and fan and the generator are driven from a pulley on the crankshaft by a common belt. The tension of this belt is adjustable at the generator mounting.

The pump takes coolant from the bottom of the radiator and delivers it to the cylinder block from which it rises to the cylinder head. At normal operating temperatures the thermostat is open and the coolant returns from the head to the top of the radiator. At lower temperatures the thermostat is closed and the coolant bypasses the radiator and returns to the pump inlet. This provides a rapid warm-up.

On later models a modified system incorporating a compensating reservoir is used (see **Section 4:8**).

4:2 Maintenance

The cooling system should periodically be drained, flushed to remove sediment and refilled. If antifreeze is in use, the coolant may be collected for re-use but should be discarded after two winters. Check that the clips are tight on all hoses including the heater inlet and outlet pipes.

Draining:

Remove the filler cap and open the radiator drain tap shown at 20 in **FIG 4:1**. To drain the cylinder block open the drain tap on the left side of the engine. Turn the heater control to the MAX position.

Flushing:

Tighten the drain taps and fill the radiator with a solution consisting of approximately $1\frac{3}{4}$ gallons of water and $10\frac{1}{2}$ oz of sodium bicarbonate. Refit the filler cap and run the engine slowly for 10 to 15 minutes. Drain off the solution. Allow the engine to cool, then use a water hose to circulate clean water with the drain taps open. Close the drain taps, refill the system with clean water and run the engine slowly for a few minutes then again drain the system. When the flushing procedure has been carried out, the system should be finally filled with coolant as follows.

Refer to **FIG 4:2** and loosen the bleed screw R. Make sure that the heater control is in the MAX position. Fill the cooling system, making sure that all air in the system is expelled through the bleed screw. When water flows freely from the bleed screw, tighten the bleed screw and top up the radiator to the correct level.

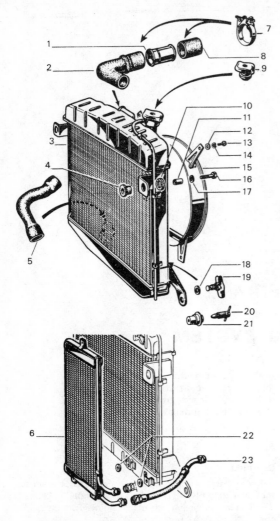

FIG 4:1   The radiator and water hoses

Key to Fig 4:1   1 Cooling flow regulator
2 Top hose   3 Radiator   4 Rubber bush   5 Bottom hose
6 Oil cooler   7 Hose clip   8 Hose   9 Radiator cap
10 Rubber ring   11 Spacer   12 Washer   13 Screw
14 Lockwasher   15 Fan cowl   16 Screw   17 Washer
18 Sealing washer   19 Radiator drain tap
20 Alternative drain tap   21 Threaded insert   22 Spacers
23 Flexible hose

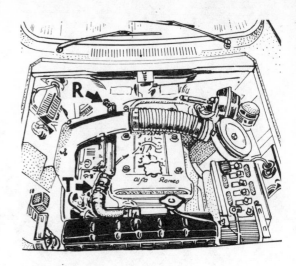

FIG 4:2   The cooling system bleed valve R and the thermostat position T

FIG 4:3   Checking the fan belt tension

FIG 4:4   Adjusting the fan belt tension

4:3 Removing the radiator

Drain the radiator as described in **Section 4:2** and disconnect the top and bottom hoses. Remove the mounting bolts, spacers and rubber rings shown in **FIG 4:1**, then lift out the radiator using care to avoid damaging the radiator matrix on the cooling fan.

Refitting is a reversal of the removal procedure. On completion, refill and bleed the cooling system as described in **Section 4:2**.

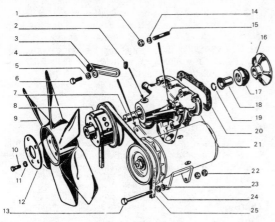

FIG 4:5 Components of the fan and water pump assembly

Key to Fig 4:5 1 Nut 2 Locating screw 3 Washer
4 Generator bracket 5 Spring washer 6 Screw
7 Pump shaft 8 Pump pulley 9 Fan 10 Screw
11 Spring washer 12 Fan retaining plate
13 Dynamo pivot bolt 14 Spring washer 15 Stud
16 Impeller 17 Seal 18 Bush 19 Retaining ring
20 Gasket 21 Pump body 22 Nuts 23 Lockwasher
24 Washer 25 Fan belt

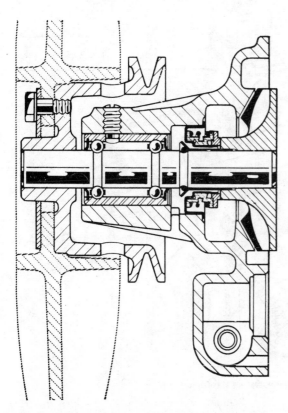

FIG 4:6 A section through the water pump

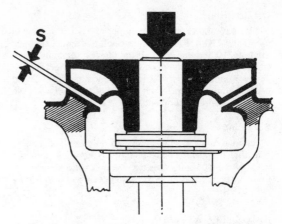

FIG 4:7 Water pump impeller clearance in the pump housing

FIG 4:8 Removing the thermostat

4:4 Adjusting fan belt

The fan belt tension is correct when the belt can be deflected about $\frac{1}{2}$ inch when pressed manually as shown in **FIG 4:3**. To adjust the tension, loosen the generator hinge pin nut which can be seen in **FIG 4:3**, then loosen the generator adjusting nut and lever the generator outwards to increase the tension as shown in **FIG 4:4**. Tighten the generator mounting bolts and recheck the tension.

The belt may be removed by slackening the generator mounting bolts as just described and pushing the generator inwards until the belt can be removed from the pulleys.

A tight fan belt will cause undue wear on the belt, pulleys and pump and generator bearings. A slack belt will cause slip and, possibly, overheating and reduced generator output.

4:5 The fan and water pump

Removal:

Remove the radiator as described in **Section 4:3**. The tachometer cable is connected to the water pump housing on some models, in which case it must be disconnected. Remove the fan belt as described in **Section 4:4**. Remove the fixing nuts and lift off the water pump and fan assembly.

Dismantling:

FIG 4:5 shows the components of the fan and water pump and **FIG 4:6** a section through the pump. Remove the bolts 10 and then pull off the fan and retaining plate. Using a suitable puller such as tool A.3.0147 remove the pulley 8 from the shaft. Remove the locating screw 2 and press the impeller and shaft assembly together with the seal from the pump housing.

Servicing:

Remove rust and scale deposits from the parts, making sure that none enters the bearings. Check all parts for wear or damage and renew any found unserviceable. If the bearing is faulty it must be renewed as an assembly with the shaft.

Reassembly and refitting:

Fit the retaining ring and bush onto the shaft with the aid of tools A.3.0155 and A.3.0137. Heat the pump body to 80°C and insert the shaft assembly into the body, making sure that the hole in the bearing is aligned with the threaded hole for the locating screw as shown in

FIG 4:6. Fit a new seal to the shaft with tool A.3.0177. Heat the impeller to 80°C and shrink it onto the shaft with the aid of a press. Continue pressing until the clearance between the impeller vanes and the pump body is .02 inch. The clearance is shown at **S** in **FIG 4:7**. Heat the pulley to 80°C and refit it to the shaft.

Refitting the pump to the engine is a reversal of the removal procedure.

4:6 The thermostat

The position of the thermostat is at the inlet manifold water outlet and access to it is by removing the top hose connection at the manifold. The removal of the thermostat can be seen in **FIG 4:8**.

Testing:

Clean the thermostat and immerse it in a container of cold water together with a zero to 100°C thermometer. Heat the water, keeping it stirred and check that the thermostat opens at about 82°C to 87°C. If the operation is satisfactory, the thermostat may be refitted, if not, a new unit must be obtained.

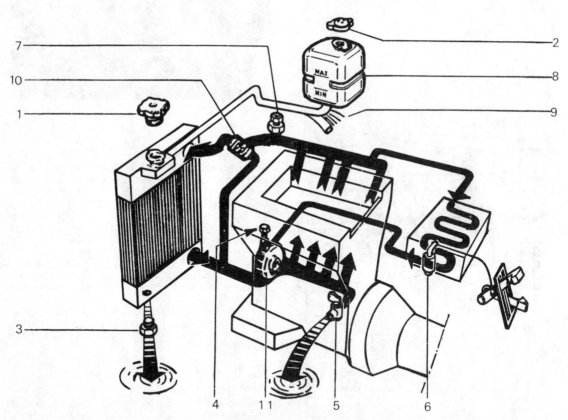

FIG 4:9   Reservoir type cooling system (later models)

Key to Fig 4:9   1 Radiator cap   2 Reservoir filler cap   3 Radiator drain plug   4 Bleed screw on pump
5 Bleed cock on crankcase   6 Heater cock   7 Bleed screw on manifold   8 Reservoir   9 Supply line from reservoir
10 Thermostat   11 Centrifugal pump

4:7 Frost precautions

If antifreeze is to be used the system should first be drained and flushed as described in **Section 4:2**. Ethylene-glycol type antifreeze must be added to the cooling system in the correct proportion recommended by the manufacturer, to give protection from freezing in the lowest temperatures in which the vehicle is to be operated. After the second winter, drain and flush the system and refill with fresh solution.

4:8 Reservoir system—later models

This system is illustrated in **FIG 4:9** and it is recommended that an antifreeze mixture be used at all times, with the system being drained and refilled once a year.

The level of the coolant should always be checked with a cold engine as the level may vary considerably when hot. It should always be between the 'min' and 'max' lines.

The radiator cap should never be removed unless absolutely necessary and then only after the coolant has returned to ambient temperature.

Draining:

Remove the radiator filler cap 1. Unscrew the drain plug 3 and the bleed screw 7 on the manifold. Turn on the heater cock 6.

Turn on the drain cock 5 and let the liquid drain off. Empty the reservoir 8 by removing the pipe 9.

When draining is finished, turn off the cock 5, reconnect the pipe 9 and tighten drain plug 3.

Refilling:

Remove the caps from both radiator and reservoir and see that the heater cock is on. Bleed screw 7, on the manifold, should be open, and if a bleed screw is fitted at 4, on the pump, that also should be open.

Pour the coolant mixture in the top of the radiator until it comes out of the aperture at 4 which should then be screwed in. Continue to pour in until it appears at the bleed screw 7, then with this screw open and radiator cap off, run the engine for a few seconds to expel any air and tighten screw 7.

Add more liquid to the radiator until it is full, then pour in to the reservoir up to the max level. Replace both filler caps.

To check that the system is correctly filled, run the engine for a short time at working temperature and then allow it to cool down. Remove the cap and check that the radiator is full. Top up the reservoir to the max mark.

The purpose of running the engine in this check is to bleed any air in the circuit and cause it to collect in the top of the radiator or reservoir.

4:9 Fault diagnosis

(a) Internal water leakage

1 Cracked cylinder wall
2 Loose cylinder head nuts
3 Cracked cylinder head
4 Faulty head gasket

(b) Poor circulation

1 Radiator matrix blocked
2 Engine water passages restricted
3 Low water level
4 Slack fan belt
5 Defective thermostat
6 Perished or collapsed radiator hoses

(c) Corrosion

1 Impurities in the water
2 Infrequent draining and flushing

(d) Overheating

1 Check (b)
2 Sludge in crankcase
3 Faulty ignition timing
4 Low oil level in sump
5 Tight engine
6 Choked exhaust system
7 Binding brakes
8 Slipping clutch
9 Incorrect valve timing
10 Retarded ignition
11 Mixture too weak

NOTES

CHAPTER 5

THE CLUTCH

5:1 Description

A single dry plate clutch is fitted to the rear face of the flywheel. Operational pressure is provided by either a series of coil springs (as shown in **FIG 5:1**), or a diaphragm spring, in the pressure plate assembly. When the clutch is engaged, the driven plate which is splined to the gearbox primary shaft is nipped between the pressure plate and the flywheel, so that it rotates with the flywheel and transmits torque to the gearbox. The clutch is disengaged when the pressure plate is withdrawn from the driven plate by a mechanical linkage, or a hydraulic system, transferring clutch pedal movement to the release bearing.

Sections 5:2, 5:3 and **5:4** cover the coil spring type clutch and mechanical operating linkage. The diaphragm spring type, which cannot be dismantled, and the hydraulic operating system are detailed in **Section 5:5**.

5:2 Removing and dismantling clutch

1 Remove the gearbox as described in **Chapter 6**. Mark both the clutch cover flange and the flywheel so that the clutch will be refitted in its original position. Remove the clutch securing bolts diagonally and evenly and lift out the pressure plate and the driven plate, ensuring that the faces of the driven plate are kept clean.

2 Screw down the pressure plate assembly in the service tool C.6.0104 or alternatively place the plate under a press to compress the clutch springs. Refer to **FIG 5:2** and unhook the release plate springs and remove the release plate. Remove the stakings which lock the nuts to the release lever bolts, then unscrew the bolts without turning the nuts. Lift off the release levers.

3 Mark the relative positions of the clutch cover and pressure plate so that they can be reassembled correctly to retain clutch unit balance. Unscrew the service tool screws or release the press slowly and evenly to relieve the spring pressure gradually. Remove the individual parts of the unit.

Servicing:

Inspect the flywheel and pressure plate friction surfaces for scoring or roughness. Slight roughness can be smoothed with fine emerycloth, but if the surface is deeply scored the part should be reground. Check that the pressure plate is smooth and flat, using a straightedge as shown in **FIG 5:3**. If the plate is distorted it must be reground.

Check the driven plate for loose rivets and broken or very loose torsional springs. The friction linings should be well proud of the rivets and have a light colour, with a

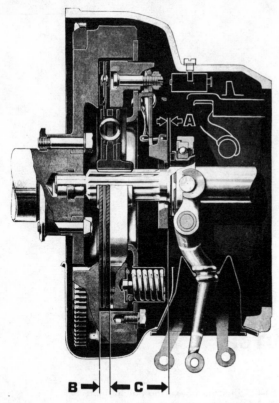

FIG 5:1 Layout of the clutch assembly and release mechanism

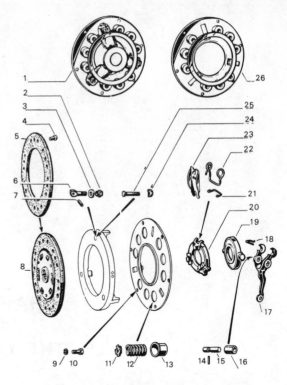

FIG 5:2 Components of the clutch assembly

Key to Fig 5:2   1 Clutch assembly   2 Nut   3 Washer
4 Rivet   5 Friction lining   6 Eye bolt   7 Pivot bolt
8 Clutch driven plate   9 Spring washer
10 Clutch securing screw   11 Spring seat
12 Clutch thrust spring   13 Pressure spring cap
14 Retaining pin   15 Pivot bolt   16 Bush
17 Clutch release fork   18 Spring clip
19 Clutch release bearing   20 Clutch release plate
21 Anti-rattle spring   22 Release lever spring
23 Release lever   24 Locknut   25 Release lever bolt
26 Pressure plate assembly

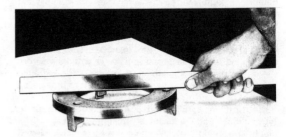

FIG 5:3 Checking the pressure plate for distortion with a straightedge

5:3 Assembly and refitting clutch

Reassembly and refitting is a reversal of the removal and dismantling procedures, noting the following points.

Index the alignment marks made during dismantling when refitting the clutch cover to the pressure plate. Adjust the release levers to the same heights, measuring the clearance S in FIG 5:7 between the surface of the

polished glaze through which the grain of the material is clearly visible. A dark, glazed deposit indicates oil on the facings and, as this condition cannot be rectified, a new plate will be required. Any signs of oil on the clutch will call for examination of the rear main bearing oil seal. Check the condition of the guide bush and felt washer at the rear of the crankshaft as described in **Chapter 1, Section 1:12.** Check the driven plate for a smooth sliding fit on the constant pinion shaft and smooth any possible burrs on the splines with a fine carborundum stone. **FIG 5:4** shows the clutch driven plate components. Refer to **FIG 5:5** and check the clearance between the driven plate splines and the gearbox constant pinion shaft, using a feeler gauge. The clearance should be between .0012 and .0043 inch, with a maximum wear limit of .0118 inch. Check the driven plate runout at the rim and, if it exceeds .02 inch, true the plate by applying pressure to the side faces until the runout is within the limit stated.

Check the clutch release bearing shown in **FIG 5:6** for roughness or excessive play. Make sure that the graphite ring is not worn down to the inner ring. If there is any doubt about the condition of the release bearing, it should be renewed. Check the clutch springs for distortion or loss of tension by comparing them with new springs. Spring free length should be 1.71 to 1.79 inches and should be not less than 1.14 inches under a load of 100 lbs.

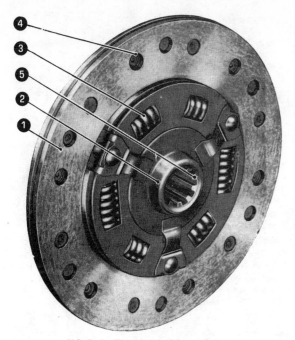

FIG 5:4   The clutch driven plate

Key to Fig 5:4   1 Friction lining   2 Hub
3 Torsion springs   4 Rivets   5 Hub splines

FIG 5:6   The clutch release bearing

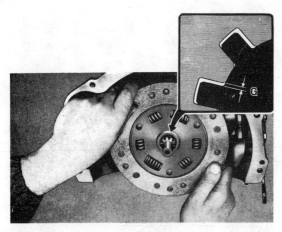

FIG 5:5   Checking the clearance of the driven plate hub splines

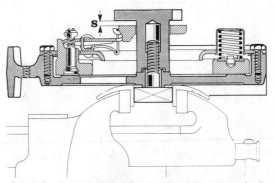

FIG 5:7   Adjusting the clutch release levers to obtain the correct pressure plate clearance

service tool C.6.0104 and the release plate or between the release plate and a fixed reference surface if a press is used for clutch assembly. Adjust the mounting bolts of the individual levers until the dimension **S** is .039 inch.

Place the clutch driven plate and pressure plate assembly against the flywheel and index the alignment marks previously made. Centre the clutch driven plate with a spare constant pinion shaft or tool A.4.0103 as shown in **FIG 5:8**. With the tool in position, tighten the securing bolts diagonally and evenly then remove the tool. Refit the gearbox as described in **Chapter 6**.

FIG 5:8   Refitting and aligning the clutch assembly

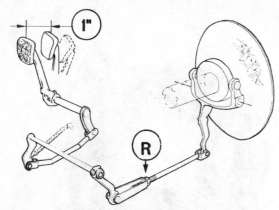

FIG 5:9 Adjusting the clutch pedal free play. Free travel=23 mm (1 inch)

5:4 Adjusting operating mechanism

The clutch pedal free play depends on the clearance between the release bearing and the clutch release plate. The clearance A in FIG 5:1 should be .079 inch to obtain a clutch pedal free play of 1 inch. As the friction linings wear down, the clearance is reduced. When the thickness of the clutch linings B has worn down to the extent that the free play at the pedal is $\frac{1}{2}$ inch or less, the linkage must be adjusted to compensate. To do this, refer to FIG 5:9 and adjust the length of the clutch operating rod to obtain a free play of 1 inch at the clutch pedal by loosening and turning the nuts at R. When the adjustment is correct, retighten the nuts.

5:5 Diaphragm spring clutch
Early system:

A hydraulically-operated clutch is fitted to later cars, at first using the system shown diagrammatically in FIG 5:10.

The clutch pedal is coupled directly to a master cylinder similar to that used in the braking system and so actuates the piston in the slave cylinder 4. This in turn moves the clutch operating lever 5, acting on the diaphragm spring clutch as shown.

Adjustment:

The clutch pedal free travel at A should be about $1\frac{1}{4}$ inch (30 to 32 mm). This dimension is not critical, but when, owing to wear on the friction facing, it is reduced to $\frac{3}{4}$ inch (17 to 19 mm) the free travel must be restored as follows:

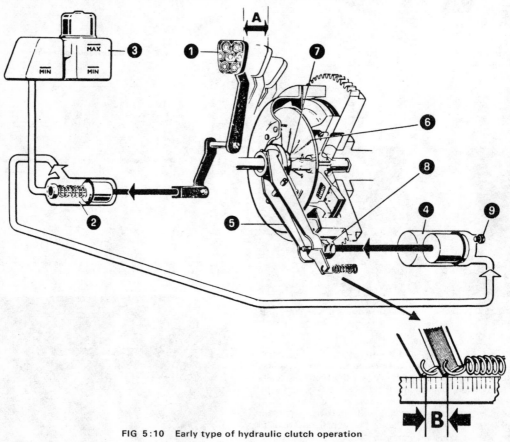

FIG 5:10   Early type of hydraulic clutch operation

Key to Fig 5:10   A Pedal free travel   B Disengagement lever free travel   1 Pedal   2 Master cylinder   3 Clutch and brake fluid reservoir   4 Slave cylinder   5 Disengagement lever   6 Diaphragm spring   7 Throwout bearing   8 Adjusting nuts   9 Air bleed screw

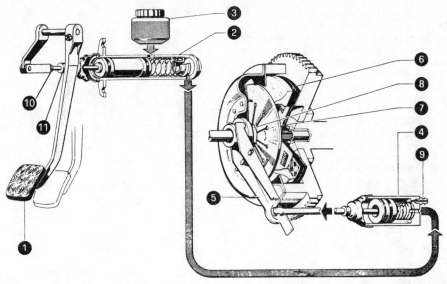

5:11   Self-adjusting clutch mechanism

Key to Fig 5:11   1 Pedal   2 Master cylinder   3 Clutch fluid reservoir   4 Operating cylinder   5 Disengagement lever
6 Driven plate   7 Diaphragm spring   8 Throwout bearing   9 Air bleed screw   10 Locknut   11 Pushrod

Measure the free travel B at the end of the lever 5, pushing the lever by hand until the release bearing 7, contacts the diaphragm spring 6. This should be about .08 inch (2 mm) corresponding to a clearance of .04 inch (1 mm) between the release bearing and the diaphragm. Should it be any less, the clearance must be restored by turning the adjusting nuts 8 as necessary.

At the same time make sure that with full pedal movement, the actuating rod can move through a total distance of $\frac{3}{4}$ inch (18 to 19 mm). Bleeding the system is only necessary if any components in the system have been removed.

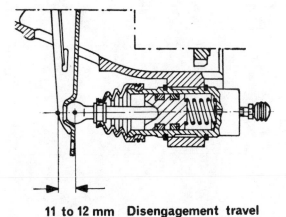

11 to 12 mm   Disengagement travel

FIG 5:12   Showing movement of slave cylinder piston

Later system:

In 1970 a modified system was introduced in which the hydraulic mechanism is self-adjusting. This is shown in **FIG 5:11**. It will be seen that the clutch master cylinder has now its own individual fluid reservoir 3.

With this system the release bearing is constantly in contact with the diaphragm spring. There is no free travel in any part of the system and any wear is automatically taken up by the addition of extra fluid from the reservoir.

Adjustment:

If in the course of time any difficulty in disengagement is experienced a check should be made to ensure that when the clutch pedal is fully depressed the pushrod in the slave cylinder has a total travel of .45 inch (11 to 12 mm) (see **FIG 5:12**).

Should an adjustment be necessary, slacken the locknut 10 on the master cylinder pushrod and then screw in or unscrew the pushrod 11 to increase or decrease its travel until the total movement of the slave cylinder piston is as specified. When correctly set the travel on the master cylinder pushrod should be $1.06 \pm .06$ inch (27 ± 1.5 mm).

Clutch servicing:

The diaphragm spring clutch assembly can be removed from the flywheel, after marking clutch cover and flywheel to ensure refitting in the same relative position, by loosening and removing the securing bolts in a progressive, diagonal sequence. No further dismantling of the pressure plate and cover assembly is possible, and the assembly should be renewed complete if it is badly worn, damaged or otherwise faulty.

Inspect the flywheel and pressure plate friction surfaces and examine the condition of the driven plate in the same manner as for a coil spring clutch, as described in **Section 5:2**. The driven plate should be renewed if wear has reduced its total thickness to, or close to, the minimum of $\frac{1}{4}$ inch (6.5 mm).

To refit the clutch, centralise the driven plate on the flywheel spigot bearing, using a spare gearbox shaft, a universal clutch centralising tool or other suitable mandrel, as shown in **FIG 5:8**. Then place the cover assembly in position, aligning the marks made before removal if the original unit is to be refitted and, with the centralising tool still in place, fit the securing bolts and tighten them progressively in a diagonal sequence to the specified torque. Remove the centralising tool, and the gearbox can then be refitted.

5:6 Fault diagnosis

(a) Drag or spin

1 Oil or grease on driven plate linings
2 Misalignment between engine and splined shaft
3 Driven plate binding on splined shaft
4 Distorted driven plate
5 Warped or damaged pressure plate or clutch cover
6 Broken driven plate linings
7 Dirt or foreign matter in clutch
8 Incorrect clutch pedal free travel

(b) Fierceness or snatch

1 Check 1, 2 and 8 in (a)
2 Worn driven plate linings

(c) Slip

1 Check 1, 2 and 8 in (a)
2 Check 2 in (b)
3 Weak clutch springs
4 Seized operating linkage

(d) Judder

1 Check 1 and 2 in (a)
2 Pressure plate not parallel with flywheel face
3 Contact area of driven plate linings not evenly distributed
4 Bent or worn splined shaft
5 Badly worn splines in driven plate hub
6 Buckled driven plate
7 Faulty engine or gearbox mountings

(e) Rattle

1 Check 3 in (c)
2 Check 4 and 5 in (d)
3 Broken springs in driven plate
4 Worn release mechanism
5 Excessive backlash in transmission
6 Wear in transmission bearings
7 Release bearing loose on fork

(f) Tick or knock

1 Check 4 and 5 in (d)
2 Release plate out of line
3 Loose flywheel

(g) Driven plate fracture

1 Check 2 in (a)
2 Drag and distortion due to hanging gearbox in driven plate hub

CHAPTER 6

THE GEARBOX

6:1 Description
6:2 Removing and refitting gearbox
6:3 Dismantling and reassembling gearbox

6:4 The gearchange mechanism
6:5 Fault diagnosis

6:1 Description

Models in the Giulia, 1750 and 2000 ranges are provided with gearboxes having five forward speeds and reverse, synchromesh operating on all five forward gears. **FIG 6:1** shows a section through the five-speed gearbox. Gear selection is by means of either a floor-mounted lever or a steering column lever and linkage, both of which are covered in **Section 6:4**. The light-alloy gearbox case consists of two main casing halves, a front bellhousing which encloses the clutch assembly, and a rear cover. An exploded view of the gearbox case assembly is shown in **FIG 6:2**. Gearbox oil level should be maintained to the level of the filler plug, and should be checked and, if necessary, topped-up to the correct level at 4000 mile intervals. Every 10,000 miles the gearbox should be drained while the oil is hot, then refilled with fresh SAE.90 gear oil.

6:2 Removing and refitting the gearbox

Removal:

1 On cars equipped with floor-mounted gearlevers, remove the floor carpet, slacken the clamp and remove the rubber boot from the gearlever. Unscrew and remove the gearlever, collecting the two balls from the inside of the gearlever.

2 Refer to **FIGS 6:3** and **6:4** and detach the following items from beneath the car. The propeller shaft at the intermediate joint flange 1, marking both flanges for correct refitting; the propeller shaft centre bearing support 2, the cross-plate 3, speedometer drive cable 4, exhaust pipe bracket 5, clutch cover 6, gear selector lever 7, reversing light leads 8, clutch operating lever 9 and the gear engagement lever 10.

3 Remove the bolts shown in **FIG 6:5** securing the gearbox crossmember to the car body, then remove the bolt securing the gearbox to the crossmember as shown in **FIG 6:6** and remove the crossmember. Remove the bolts securing the gearbox to the engine crankcase and remove the gearbox towards the rear. **Do not allow the weight of the gearbox to rest on the splined shaft during removal, or serious damage to the clutch driven plate will result.** Drain the oil from the gearbox and remove the front section of the propeller shaft from the rear of the gearbox, using tool A.2.0124.

Refitting:

Refitting the gearbox is a reversal of the removal procedure, noting the following points. Index the alignment marks at the intermediate joint flange when refitting the propeller shaft. If the clutch was removed, refer to

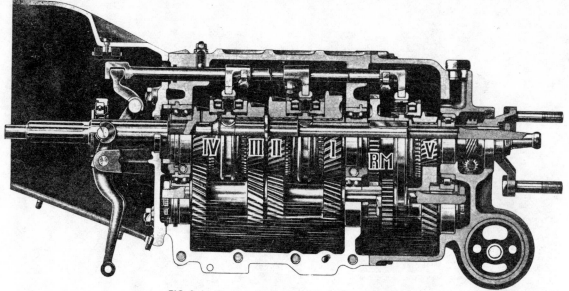

FIG 6:1   Section through the fivespeed gearbox

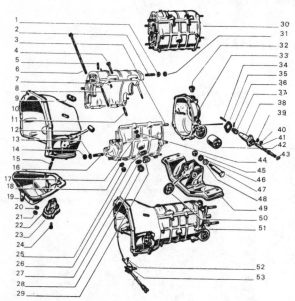

FIG 6:2   Exploded view of gearbox casing

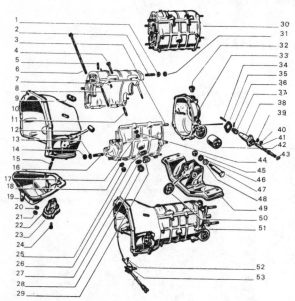

FIG 6:3   Items to be detached for gearbox removal

Key to Fig 6:2 1 Washer 2 Stud 3 Dowel 4 Bolt 5 Stud
6 Bolt   7 Dowel   8 Stud   9 Inspection cover   10 Clutch
housing   11 Stud   12 Bush   13 Washer   14 Nut   15 Stud
16 Stud   17 Nut   18 Washer   19 Bottom cover   20 Washer
21 Nut   22 Cover plate   23 Rubber cap   24 Self tapping
screw   25 Nut   26 Gasket   27 Gasket   28 Magnetic drain
plug   29 Closing plug   30 Gearbox casing halves   31 Nut
32 Vent plug   33 Rear cover   34 Stud   35 Gasket   36 Pin
37 Speedometer pinion   38 Pinion housing   39 Washer
40 Nut   41 Speedometer cable   42 Rubber banded mounting
43 Sealing washer   44 Washer   45 Nut   46 Washer
47 Bolt   48 Washer   49 Cross member   50 Washer
51 Gearbox assembly   52 Screw   53 Reversing lamp switch

Chapter 5 for clutch driven plate alignment procedure.
Support the gearbox when refitting to the engine
to avoid straining the clutch driven plate. Refill the
gearbox with oil.

6:3 Dismantling and reassembling gearbox

Dismantling:

1 Mount the gearbox in a suitable stand. Refer to FIG
  6:7 and remove the gearbox drive flange, screwing
  in one of the flange bolts as shown to prevent the

FIG 6:4 Items to be detached for gearbox removal

mainshaft from turning. Unscrew the nuts securing
the rear cover and remove the cover, noting that for
floor-change gearboxes it will be necessary to engage
third gear to do this.

2 Refer to **FIG 6:8** and remove the bolt securing the
fifth and reverse gear selector fork in order to remove
the selector shaft. Remove the reversing light switch,
if fitted. Detach the spring clips and remove the clutch
release bearing from the clutch release lever. Remove
the nut arrowed in **FIG 6:9** and remove the gearchange lever. Using suitable circlip pliers, remove the
retaining ring shown in **FIG 6:10** from the groove
in the shaft. Remove the large retaining ring which
secures the seat for the reverse gear return spring from
the groove in the boss. Remove the spring seat and
withdraw the shaft.

3 Unscrew the nuts securing the gearbox bellhousing
to the gearbox case and remove the bellhousing.
Unscrew the nuts fastening the gearbox case halves
together and separate the halves as shown in **FIG
6:11**, tapping the case lightly with a soft mallet if
necessary. **Do not try to lever the case halves
apart or the joint faces will be damaged.** The
joint faces are machined to fit together without gaskets
so care must be used to avoid damage to any gearbox
joint face during servicing.

4 Remove the selector shaft plunger retaining plate as
shown in **FIG 6:12** and withdraw the plungers,
springs and balls. Loosen the setscrews shown in
FIG 6:13 which lock the selector forks to the
selector shafts, then slide out the shafts and forks
together with the interlock. If only one of the selector
shafts is to be removed, push out the shaft with a
dummy shaft as shown in **FIG 6:14** to hold the interlock plunger and ball in position. Push the dummy
shaft out with the selector shaft when refitting. If
necessary, remove the outer race of the layshaft rear
bearing with puller A.3.0101. The race should be
refitted with a suitable punch and the aid of a press.
FIG 6:15 shows the method of removal.

5 Lift the constant pinion shaft and mainshaft from the
gearbox case and separate the two shafts. Lift out the
layshaft assembly. Remove the reverse idler gear from
the upper gearbox case half. **FIG 6:16** shows the
mainshaft and constant pinion shaft assemblies.

The dismantling of the internal parts of the gearbox is
best carried out with access to suitable press equipment.
If such equipment is not available, a suitable puller can
be employed to remove the various components from
their shafts. **FIGS 6:16** and **6:17** show the components
of the mainshaft and constant pinion shaft assemblies.

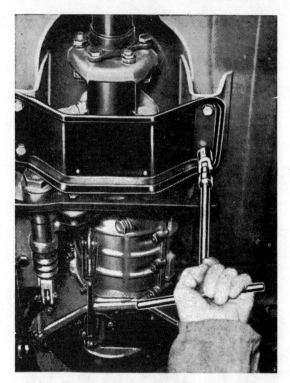

FIG 6:5 Removing the crossmember mounting bolts

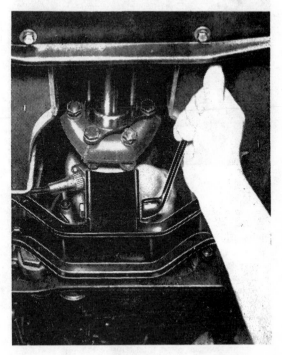

FIG 6:6 Removing the gearbox to crossmember bolt

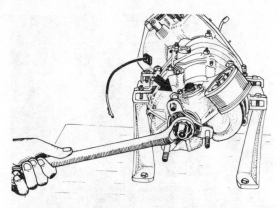

FIG 6:7   Removing the gearbox drive flange

FIG 6:8   Removing the fifth and reverse gear selector bolt

FIG 6:9   Removing the gearchange lever

FIG 6:10   The reverse gearshaft retaining rings

Dismantling the mainshaft:

1 With the press plates behind reverse gear, press off the reverse gear together with the synchronizer unit, fifth-speed gear and the rear bearing. Remove the securing keys.

2 Press off the intermediate bearing and withdraw the shims, the first-speed gearwheel with its bush, and the operating sleeve for the first- and second-speed synchronizer unit. Press off the synchronizer hub for first and second gears then remove the keys and slide off the second-speed gearwheel.

FIG 6:11 Separating the gearbox case halves

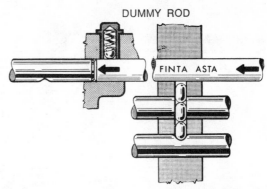

DUMMY ROD

FINTA ASTA

FIG 6:14 Inserting a dummy shaft for the removal of one selector shaft

FIG 6:12 Removing the selector shaft plunger retaining plate

FIG 6:15 Removing the layshaft rear bearing outer race

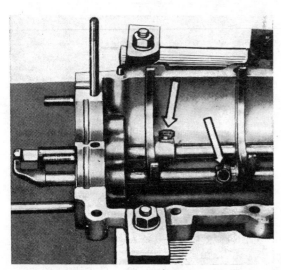

FIG 6:13 The selector fork setscrews

3 Remove the retaining ring from the third- and fourth-speed synchromesh hub then press off the hub. Slide off the third-speed gear and remove the keys.

Dismantling the constant pinion shaft:

After removing the retaining ring and the shim beneath it, press off the constant pinion shaft bearing.

Dismantling the layshaft:

The dismantling of the layshaft is only necessary if one or more of the layshaft bearings are to be renewed (see **FIG 6:18**).

FIG 6:16   The mainshaft and constant pinion shaft assembly

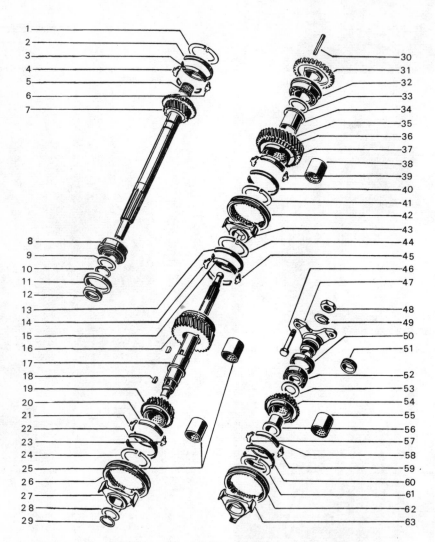

FIG 6:17   Components of the mainshaft and constant pinion shaft assemblies

Key to Fig 6:17   1 Retaining ring   2 Synchronizing ring   3 Locking band   4 Stop   5 Roller bearing   6 Segment
7 Constant pinion shaft   8 Bearing   9 Shim   10 Retaining ring   11 Spacer   12 Oil seal   13 Synchronizing ring
14 Stop   15 Locking band   16 Second-speed gearwheel   17 Mainshaft   18 Key   19 Third-speed gearwheel
20 Locking band   21 Stop   22 Synchronizing band   23 Segment   24 Retaining ring   25 Bushes   26 Operating sleeve
27 Synchromesh hub   28 Shim   29 Retaining ring   30 Retaining key   31 Gearwheel   32 Bearing   33 Shim   34 Spacer bush
35 First-speed gearwheel   36 Stop   37 Locking band   38 Bush   39 Segment   40 Synchronizing ring   41 Retaining ring
42 Operating sleeve   43 Synchromesh hub   44 Retaining ring   45 Segment   46 Bolt   47 Drive flange   48 Nut   49 Lockplate
50 Oil seal   51 Speedometer drive gear   52 Bearing   53 Shim   54 Fifth-speed gearwheel   55 Bush   56 Spacer bush
57 Stop   58 Locking band   59 Segment   60 Synchronizing ring   61 Retaining ring   62 Operating sleeve
63 Synchromesh hub

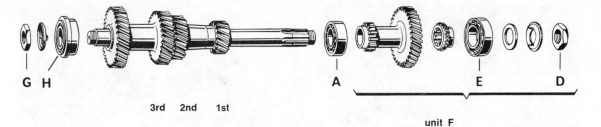

G H   A   E   D

3rd   2nd   1st

unit F

FIG 6:18   Components of the layshaft assembly

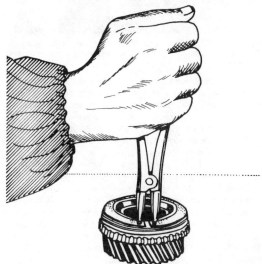

FIG 6:19   Removing the retaining ring from a synchro-mesh unit

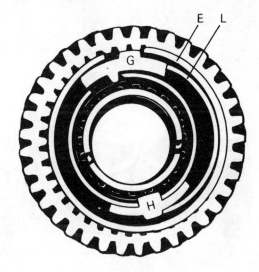

FIG 6:20   First gear synchromesh assembly

Clamp the layshaft into a vice, using soft vice jaws or suitably padding the layshaft to prevent damage, then remove the nut **D**. Pull off the roller bearing **E** and the gear assembly **F** for fifth and reverse gears. Press off the bearing **A**.

With the layshaft again held in the vice, remove the nut **G** and the washer then press off the front bearing **H**.

Inspection and servicing:

Clean all parts with the exception of the clutch release bearing in paraffin and dry them off. **The clutch release bearing must not be cleaned with a solvent of any kind as this would destroy the internal lubrication.** Wipe the bearing clean with a cloth. Lubricate all the ball and roller bearings after cleaning and turn them between the fingers to check for roughness or side play. If there is any doubt about the condition of a bearing it must be renewed. The clutch release bearing is sealed and lubricated for life and must be renewed if not in good condition.

Clean the inside and outside of the clutch bellhousing, gearbox half casings and the rear cover with paraffin. Remove all traces of old sealing compound from the joint faces, using care to avoid damaging the surfaces. Do not use sharp or pointed tools for cleaning the joint faces as the gearbox case joints fit together without gaskets and oil leakage will result from damaged faces.

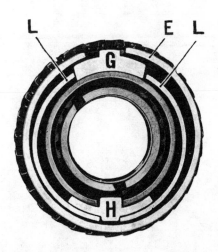

FIG 6:21   Second, third, fourth and fifth-speed synchromesh assembly

FIG 6:22 Checking the clearance between the selector fork and the operating sleeve

FIG 6:26 Fitting a shim of the correct thickness to take up end play between the retaining ring and the synchronizer hub

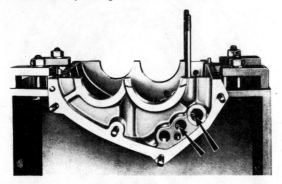

FIG 6:23 Checking the free movement of the selector shaft interlock pins

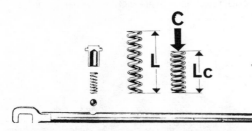

FIG 6:24 Checking the dimensions of the selector lockball springs

FIG 6:25 Renewing the gearbox silentbloc mounting pad with the special tool

Dismantle and inspect the synchromesh units. Refer to **FIG 6:19** and remove the retaining ring as shown and check the engaging teeth for signs of wear or seizure. Check that the operating sleeves move freely on the synchromesh hub. Refer to **FIGS 6:20** and **6:21** and check for excessive wear on the rings **E** and that the stop **G** and segment **H** show no signs of scoring where they contact strips **L**. Renew any parts found unserviceable. Reassemble the synchromesh units in the reverse order of dismantling, taking care that the components are installed in the correct original positions (see **FIGS 6:20** and **6:21**). Check the side clearance between the selector forks and the synchromesh operating sleeves as shown in **FIG 6:22**. The correct clearance is .006 to .013 inch (.150 to .340 mm), with a wear limit of .033 inch (.850 mm).

Inspect all gearwheels for wear and chipped or damaged teeth. Mount the mainshaft between the centres of a lathe and use a dial gauge to check the runout at the centre of the shaft. Carry out the same operation on the constant pinion shaft. In either case shaft runout should not exceed .002 inch (.05 mm). If runout exceeds this figure a new shaft must be fitted.

Check that the interlock pins arrowed in **FIG 6:23** slide freely in their grooves and that the working surfaces of the pins and the selector rods are perfectly smooth. If one of the interlock pins should stick, round off the fillet on the notch in the selector shaft slightly, using a very fine file. Refer to **FIG 6:24** and check the locking balls, springs and caps for wear or damage, renewing parts as necessary. Check that the notches in the selector shafts are in good condition. For earlier boxes, the free length of the springs **L** should be .598 inch (15.2 mm) and the length **Lc** under a load **C** of 11 to 12 lb (4.77 to 5.45 kg) should be .394 inch (10 mm). For later boxes, **L** = 1.41 inch (35.8 mm), **C** = 17 to 18 lb (7.68 to 8.32 kg) and **Lc** = .68 inch (17.2 mm).

Remove the old oil seals from the front and rear gearbox covers. Drive in new oil seals, preferably with mandrel A.3.0180, keeping them square. If necessary, renew the Silentbloc mounting pad which supports the gearbox and engine unit. Use tool A.3.0118 for mounting block removal and installation as shown in **FIG 6:25**. The Silentbloc mounting pad can be renewed without the need for complete gearbox removal but, in this case, it will be necessary to carry out all operations previously detailed

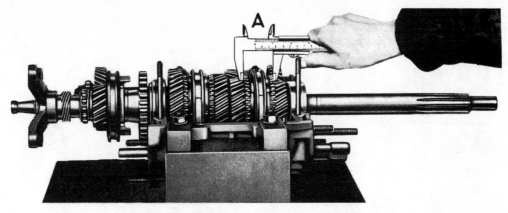

FIG 6:27   Checking for correct shim thickness between the first gear bush and the mainshaft bearing inner race

for gearbox removal except the removal of the gearbox to engine fixing bolts. The engine and gearbox assembly can then be tilted downwards to gain the necessary access to the mounting pad.

Reassembly:

Reassembling the layshaft:

This is a reversal of the dismantling instructions given earlier. Tighten the layshaft nuts to a torque of 57.8 lb ft.

Reassembling the constant pinion shaft:

Press the bearing onto the shaft and refit the shim and retaining ring.

Reassembling the mainshaft:

1 Place the mainshaft in tool A.3.0185 and slide on the third-speed gearwheel and the keys. Heat the third- and fourth-speed synchronizer hub to a temperature of 150°C in a hot oil bath or an oven, then fit it to the shaft. Fit the retaining ring and check that there is no end play between the retaining ring and the hub. Any clearance must be taken up by fitting a shim of the correct thickness as shown in **FIG 6:26**.

2 Turn the mainshaft over and slide the second-speed gearwheel over the shaft with the synchronizing mechanism facing downwards. Heat the first- and second-speed synchronizer hub in the manner previously described then drive it onto the shaft until it abuts against the shaft shoulder. Fit the operating sleeve over the synchronizer hub. Fit the first-speed gearwheel together with the bush and shims. The shims must be of sufficient thickness to ensure that there is no end play when the retaining rings are fitted.

3 Heat the intermediate bearing as previously described and fit it to the shaft, then insert the key. Heat the reverse-speed gearwheel and drive it onto the shaft until it abuts against the face of the bearing. Heat up and fit the fifth-speed synchronizer hub and fit the operating sleeve over the hub. Fit the fifth-speed gearwheel and bush over the shaft. Fit the rear main-shaft bearing, speedometer drive gear and the gearbox drive flange to the shaft, tightening the mainshaft nut

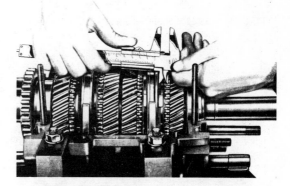

FIG 6:28   Measuring the distance between the operating sleeves and the engagement teeth abutment faces

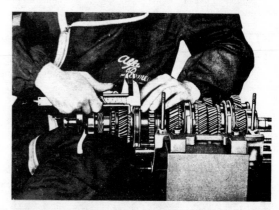

FIG 6:29   Measuring the distance between the fifth-speed operating sleeve and the engagement teeth abutment faces

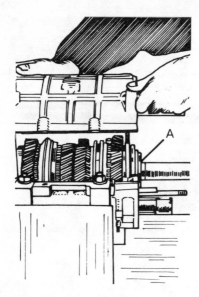

FIG 6:30　Fitting the centralizing ring A to its seat

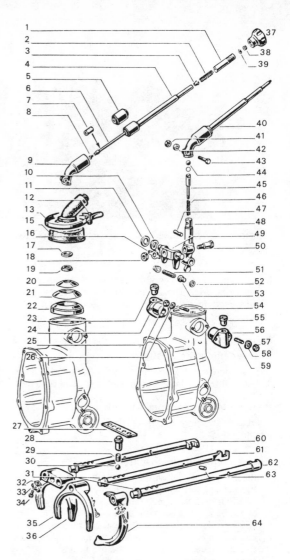

FIG 6:32　The components of the floor-mounted gear-change mechanism

Key to Fig 6:32　1 Sleeve　2 Spring　3 Rubber grommet
4 Gearchange lever　　　　　5 Bonded rubber block
6 Retaining rod　　7 Rubber sleeve　　8 Rubber plug
9 Adaptor　11 Washer　12 Retaining pin　13 Clamp
15 Rubber gaiter　16 Retainer　17 Cup washer　18 Nut
19 Sealing washer　20 Dished washer　21 Dished washer
22 Cap　23 Bleeder plug　24 Bearing block　25 Nut
26 Washer　27 Retaining plate　28 Bush　29 Spring
30 Ball　31 Sealing washer　32 Adjusting plate
33 Locking plate　34 Securing screw　35 Selector fork
for third and fourth-speed　　36 Selector fork for first and
second-speed　37 Gearchange lever knob　38 Locknut
39 Spring washer　40 Gearchange lever　41 Nut
42 Washer　43 Securing screw　44 Ball
45 Operating plunger　46 Spring　47 Locking pin
48 Inner selector lever　49 Selector head　50 Bolt
51 Spring　52 Retaining ring　53 Spring seat　54 Stud
55 Bleeder plug　56 Bearing block　57 Nut　58 Washer
59 Stud　　60 Selector shaft for first and second-speed
61 Selector shaft for third and fourth-speed　62 Selector
shaft for fifth and reverse-speed　63 Interlocking plunger
64 Selector fork for fifth and reverse-speed

FIG 6:31　The oil seal protection sleeve in position

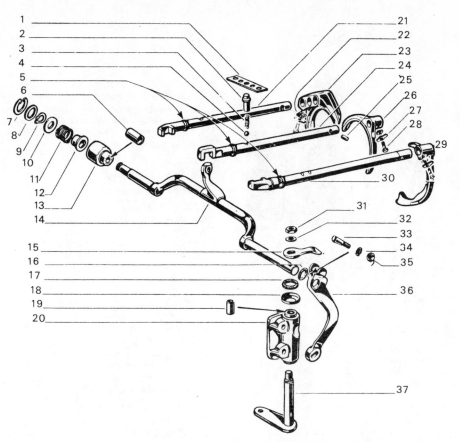

FIG 6:33 The selector shaft mechanism

Key to Fig 6:33 1 Retaining plate   2 Bush   3 Spring   4 Ball   5 Sealing washers   6 Bush   7 Retaining ring   8 Washer
9 Retaining ring   10 Spring seat   11 Spring   12 Spring collar   13 Spring housing   14 Selector cross-shaft
15 Inner engagement lever   16 Seal ring   17 Seal washer   18 Seal retainer   19 Bush   20 Bracket
21 First and second selector shaft   22 Adjusting plate   23 First and second selector fork   24 Third and fourth selector shaft
25 Interlock plunger   26 Third and fourth selector fork   27 Lockplate   28 Securing screw   29 Fifth and reverse selector fork
30 Fifth and reverse selector shaft   31 Nut   32 Washer   33 Lever securing bolt   34 Washer   35 Nut   36 Gear engagement
lever   37 Selector lever

to a torque of 56 lb ft. The end clearance of the first-speed gearwheel, which is determined by the first-speed gearwheel bush, should not exceed .0095 inch (.24 mm). The clearance between the second- and third-speed gearwheels, determined by the second-speed gearwheel bush, should not exceed .0083 inch (.21 mm).

4 Fit the roller bearing into the counterbore in the constant pinion shaft and assemble the mainshaft and constant pinion shaft as shown in **FIG 6:16**. Fit the layshaft into the gearbox casing half and check that the locking device is positioned correctly. Place the mainshaft and constant pinion shaft assembly into the gearbox casing half and, using an accurate measuring caliper, check that the dimension **A** in **FIG 6:27** is between 1.654 and 1.661 inch (42 and 42.19 mm). If not, the shim thickness between the first-gear bush and the mainshaft bearing inner race must be changed accordingly. Remove the gearbox drive flange and speedometer drive gear from the mainshaft.

5 Place the gearbox in neutral and check that the operating sleeves of third- and fourth-speed and first- and second-speed are equally spaced between the abutment faces of the engaging teeth on the gearwheels as shown in **FIG 6:28**. Refer to **FIG 6:29** and check that the rear edge of the fifth-gear operating sleeve is .394 inch (10 mm) on earlier models or .508 inch (12.9 mm) on 1750 and later models away from the engaging teeth when the gearwheel is in the neutral position. When these checks have been made, correctly adjust the positions of the selector forks on the selector shafts and tighten the selector forks securing screws and tab the lockplates. Engage third gear.

6 Refer to **FIG 6:30** and insert the centring ring **A** in its seat as shown. Fit the reverse idler gear onto the reverse idler shaft. When reassembling the gearbox case the joint faces must be smeared with Permatex No. 3 jointing compound. No gaskets are used. Fit the two gearbox case halves together, then fit the rear cover. When refitting the clutch bellhousing to the

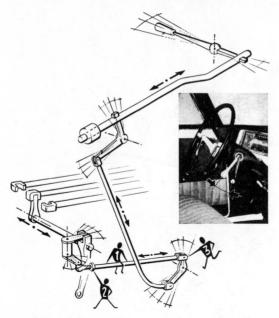

FIG 6:34   Checking and adjusting gear selector control linkage

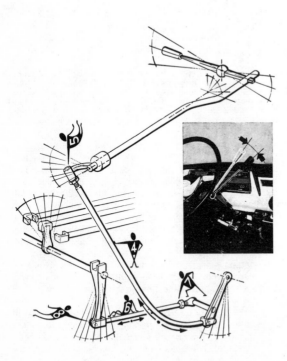

FIG 6:35   Checking and adjusting gear engaging control linkage

gearbox case halves it is recommended that tool A.3.0114 be used to protect the oil seal as shown in **FIG 6:31**. On cars fitted with floor mounted gearchange, check that the finger of the inner swivel is engaged with the third- and fourth-speed selector shaft. Engage each gear in turn and check that the operation is smooth and light. Refit the selector lever end cover with a new O-ring seal. Fit the speedometer drive gear and the gearbox drive flange and tighten the securing nut to the torque specified in **Technical Data** and tab the lockplate.

6:4 The gearchange mechanism

Floor mounted gearchange:

FIG 6:32 shows an exploded view of the floor mounted gearchange mechanism and the selector shaft assemblies. The removal and refitting of the selector shafts and forks is described in **Section 6:3**. If overhaul of the gearlever mechanism is necessary it should be dismantled into the order shown in **FIG 6:32** and faulty components renewed.

Steering column gearchange:

FIG 6:33 shows the selector shaft mechanism, the removal and refitting of these components being covered in **Section 6:3**. After gearbox overhaul or if there has been difficulty in changing gear, the linkage should be checked and, if necessary, adjusted as follows.

Checking and adjusting:

Gear selector control:

Refer to **FIG 6:34**. Engage first or second gear and check that the gearlever can be moved still further towards the steering wheel as shown in the inset. Engage fifth or reverse gear and check that the gearlever can be moved still further towards the dashboard. The extra travel should be approximately the same in both cases. If there is no travel towards the steering wheel or it is shorter than the travel towards the dashboard, **lengthen** the pushrod 1 by acting on the adjuster 2. If, alternatively, there is no travel towards the dashboard or it is shorter than the travel towards the steering wheel, **shorten** the pushrod 1 by acting on the adjuster 2. To adjust the rod, free it from the lever 3 by removing the pivot pin.

Gear engaging control:

Refer to **FIG 6:35**. Engage first, third or fifth gear and check that the gearlever can be moved still further after engagement. Engage second, fourth or reverse gear and check that the gearlever can be moved still further after engagement. The extra travel should be approximately the same in both cases. If there is no further travel after engaging an odd gear or it is shorter than the travel with an even gear engaged, **shorten** the pushrod 4 by acting on adjuster 5. If, alternatively, there is no further travel after engaging an even gear or reverse or it is shorter than the travel with an odd gear engaged, **lengthen** the pushrod 4 by acting on adjuster 5.

If the correct travel adjustments cannot be obtained by the method just described, adjust the lower pushrod 6 by acting on the adjuster 7. To do this, detach the rod 6 from the lever 8 by removing the pivot pin.

6:5 Fault diagnosis

(a) Jumping out of gear

1 Broken spring behind selector rod locating ball
2 Excessively worn groove in selector shaft
3 Worn synchromesh units
4 Fork to selector shaft securing screw loose

(b) Noisy transmission

1 Insufficient oil
2 Worn or damaged bearings
3 Worn or damaged gearwheels

(c) Difficulty in engaging gear

1 Incorrect clutch pedal adjustment
2 Worn synchromesh assemblies
3 Worn or loose selector forks

(d) Oil leaks

1 Worn or damaged oil seals
2 Damaged faces on gearbox casing components

NOTES

CHAPTER 7

PROPELLER SHAFT, REAR AXLE AND SUSPENSION

PART 1   THE PROPELLER SHAFT

7:1 Description

The tubular steel propeller shaft shown in **FIG 7:1** consists of a front section connected to the gearbox drive flange by means of a flexible coupling and a rear section connected to the rear axle drive pinion by means of a flanged universal joint. The front section is supported in a rubber-mounted intermediate bearing attached to the underside of the car. The two sections are connected by a flange coupling which incorporates a universal joint and a splined sliding joint. At about 3750 mile intervals the propeller shaft universal joints and sliding joint should be greased at the nipples indicated in **FIG 7:1**, using Shell Retinax G grease.

The propeller shafts, on vehicles equipped with limited slip differentials, cannot be turned with only one wheel clear of the ground as with conventional differentials. If the propeller shaft is forced to turn either manually, or driven from the engine, with only one wheel jacked up, the grounded wheel will take up the drive and force the vehicle off the jack. Ensure that both wheels are clear of the ground and the vehicle is well supported with additional stands.

7:2 Removing and refitting

Removing:

Refer to **FIG 7:2** and remove the centre crossmember 1. Hold the flexible coupling 2 with a clamp such as

A.2.0124 shown at 3 then remove the bolts securing the coupling to the gearbox drive flange. Remove the nuts 4 holding the intermediate bearing support to the car frame. Mark the flanges on the propeller shaft rear yoke and drive pinion for correct refitting then remove bolts 5 and remove the propeller shaft assembly from the car.

Refitting:

Refitting is a reversal of the removal procedure, noting the following points. Pack the end of the propeller shaft with grease and fit the shaft yoke flange to the drive pinion flange in accordance with the alignment marks previously made. Tighten the nuts and bolts to the torque given in **Technical Data**.

7:3 Dismantling and reassembly

Dismantling:

Refer to **FIGS 7:3** and **7:4**. Mark the relative positions of the yoke flanges 1 and 2 then remove the bolts 3 and separate the two sections of the shaft. Undo the bolts 4 and remove the flexible coupling. Mark the yoke flange 1 in relation to the shaft end then unscrew the nut and locknut and remove the flange, keys 6, spring 7 and the deflector 8. If the intermediate bearing is to be renewed the bearing support must be pressed off then the bearing removed from the support with the aid of a drift. Unscrew the ring nut 9 and seal 10 to release the yoke 2.

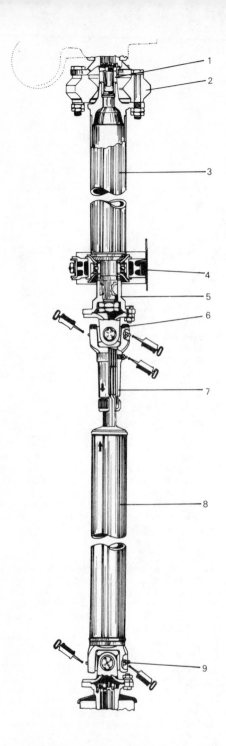

FIG 7:1 The propeller shaft

Key to Fig 7:1
1 Grease seal
2 Hardy-Spicer coupling   3 Propeller shaft front section
4 Intermediate bearing   5 Shaft yoke   6 Universal joint
7 Sliding joint   8 Propeller shaft rear section
9 Universal joint

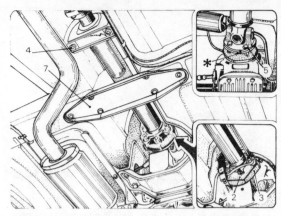

FIG 7:2 Items to be detached for propeller shaft removal

Servicing:

With the exception of the rubber parts of the intermediate bearing assembly, clean all parts thoroughly in petrol. Inspect the intermediate bearing and check that bearing play is not beyond the permissible limit of .008 inch. Renew the bearing support if it shows any signs of distortion. Fit the bearing into the support and stake in place as shown in **FIG 7:5**, using a suitable punch. Check all other components and renew any that show signs of wear or damage. Check the splined shaft and the sliding joint for serviceability as shown in **FIG 7:6** and check that the play between the splines at G in **FIG 7:7** does not exceed the wear limit of .0078 inch. Check the rear section of the propeller shaft for runout as shown in **FIG 7:8** at the centre point A and the sliding joint shaft B. The runout E should not exceed .016 inch at A or .004 inch at B. If these figures are exceeded it is possible for the shaft to be straightened under an hydraulic press but, if this cannot be carried out successfully or if the shaft is damaged in any way it must be renewed.

Reassembly:

Reassembly is a reversal of the removal procedure, indexing the alignment marks made when dismantling. Tighten the intermediate bearing support mounting bolts to a torque of 32.6 to 39.7 lb ft.

PART 2   THE REAR AXLE

7:4 Description

The rear axle assembly is attached to the car body by means of two rubber-bushed radius arms, a reaction trunnion mounted on rubber bushes and two vertical coil springs secured to the radius rods. The differential assembly, with the hypoid final drive is housed in an aluminium carrier to which the two steel axle tubes enclosing the semi-floating axle shafts are connected. The axle shafts carry the wheel hubs at their outer ends, the inner ends being splined to fit into the differential side gears. A magnetic drain plug in the differential carrier serves to collect any metallic particles suspended in the oil. Some later models are optionally fitted with a limited slip differential.

Check the rear axle oil level every 3750 miles and

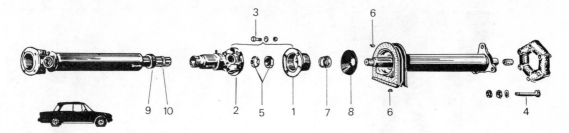

FIG 7:3   Components of the propeller shaft assembly

change the oil every 11,250 miles. The oil level should be maintained to the level of the filler plug at the rear of the differential housing.

7:5 Hubs and axle shafts

The removal and refitting of the hubs and axle shafts can be carried out with the rear axle fitted to the car but, in order to service the differential assembly it will be necessary to remove the rear axle assembly.

Removal:

1 Chock the front wheels and loosen the rear wheel nuts. Jack up the car under the rear axle and support the car with floor stands placed under the jacking brackets. Remove the road wheels and lower the jack so that the car rests on the floor stands.

2 **On cars equipped with disc rear brakes,** refer to **FIG 7:9** and free the friction pad retaining plate 1 at one end only and remove the pads. Disconnect the handbrake cable 3 and remove the return spring 4. Remove the screws 5 attaching the brake caliper to its bracket 6 and remove the caliper by withdrawing the pushrod from the slave cylinder. By removing the attaching screws detach the brake disc 8 and the shield 11. On cars fitted with Dunlop brake systems it is necessary to remove the wheel brake cylinder. Pull out the axle shaft using tool A.3.0109 as shown in **FIG 7:10**.

   On cars equipped with drum rear brakes, loosen the attaching screws and remove the brake drum then remove the nuts attaching the brake backing plate to the axle tube. Pull out the axle shaft using tool A.3.0109 as shown in **FIG 7:11**.

3 Remove the axle shaft bearing retaining ring nut by releasing the lockplate and unscrewing the ring nut with tool A.5.0120. Pull off the bearing with tool A.3.0109 or similar puller.

Refitting:

Refitting is a reversal of the removal procedure. Use a dial gauge to check that axle shaft runout does not exceed .0039 inch. It may be possible to straighten a bent shaft under an hydraulic press, but if not, the shaft must be renewed. Check the condition of the oil seal in the axle tube and renew it if unserviceable. Tap the axle shaft in until it bottoms, using a hammer and suitable drift against the hollow in the shaft flange. On completion, the brakes must be bled as described in **Chapter 10.**

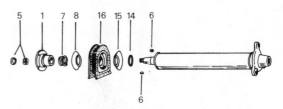

FIG 7:4   Components of the front propeller shaft section

Key to Figs 7:3 and 7:4   1 Flange   2 Sliding joint
3 Securing bolts   4 Coupling bolt   5 Nut and locknut
6 Key   7 Spring   8 Deflector   9 Ring nut   10 Seal
14 Seal   15 Deflector   16 Intermediate bearing

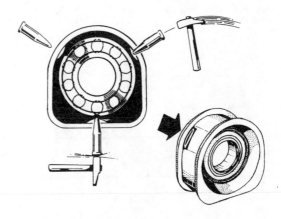

FIG 7:5   Staking the intermediate bearing into the support

7:6 Axle removal and refitting
Removal:

1 Chock the front wheels and loosen the rear wheel nuts. Jack-up the car under the rear axle and support the car with floor stands placed under the jacking brackets. Remove the road wheels and lower the jack so that the car rests on the floor stands.

FIG 7:6 Checking the condition of the sliding joint splines

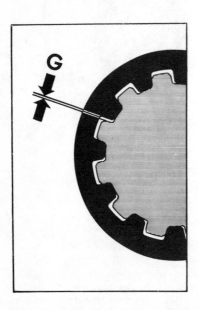

FIG 7:7 Checking the clearance G between the sliding joint splines

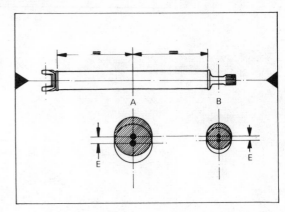

FIG 7:8 Checking the propeller shaft for runout

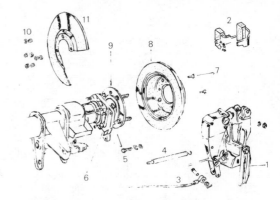

FIG 7:9 Removing the rear disc brake assembly. The numbers are referred to in the text

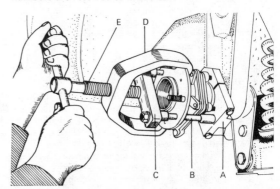

FIG 7:10 The withdrawal of the axle shaft on cars fitted with disc rear brakes

2 Refer to **FIGS 7:12** and **7:13** and proceed as follows. Disconnect the brake pipes from the union 1, plugging or taping the pipes to prevent fluid loss. Remove the bolts 2 attaching the propeller shaft to the pinion flange, marking the flange for correct refitting. Remove the cotterpin and castellated nut 3 from the reaction trunnion mounting then remove the pins fixing the handbrake cables to the shackles 4. Dis-

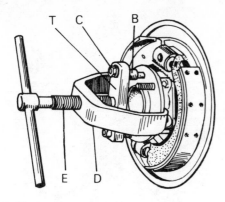

FIG 7:11 The withdrawal of the axle shaft on cars fitted with drum rear brakes

Key to Figs 7:10 and 7:11   **A** Abutment plate
B Pins   **C** Puller plate   **D** Puller   **E** Centre bolt
T Pressure plate

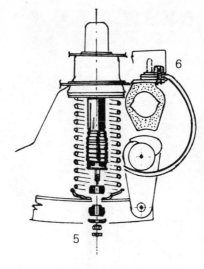

FIG 7:13 Items to be detached for rear axle removal

FIG 7:12 Items to be detached for rear axle removal

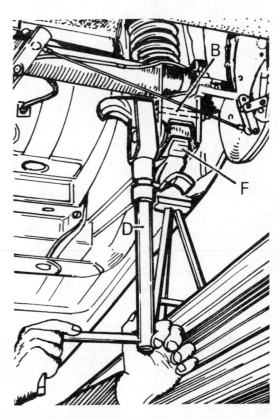

FIG 7:14 Using the special tool when disconnecting the radius rods on cars fitted with disc rear brakes

connect the cables from the brake units. Remove the nuts and rubber pads from the damper lower attachments and fully compress the dampers. Raise the axle assembly slightly with the jack to ease the load on the rebound straps and remove the strap fixing screws 6.

3 Refer to **FIG 7:14** for cars with disc rear brakes or **FIG 7:15** for cars with drum rear brakes and install tool A.2.0143 as shown to take the tension of the coil

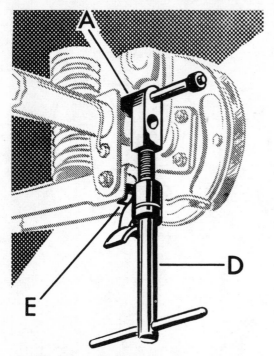

FIG 7:15 Using the special tool when disconnecting the radius rods on cars fitted with drum rear brakes

Key to Figs 7:14 and 7:15   A Tool head
B Radius rod bracket   D Tightening handle   E Bracket
F Radius rod

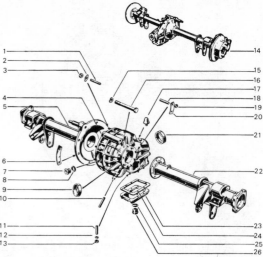

FIG 7:16 Components of the differential carrier and axle tubes

Key to Fig 7:16   1 Stud   2 Washer   3 Nut
4 Rear axle casing   5 Rear axle tube   6 Retaining plate
7 Oil filler plug   8 Sealing washer   9 Bearing race
10 Stud   11 Stud   12 Washer   13 Nut
14 Rear axle assembly   15 Washer   16 Mounting bolt
17 Rubber insert   18 Stud   19 Nut   20 Retaining plate
21 Bearing race   22 Rear axle tube   23 Bottom cover
24 Gasket for bottom cover   25 Sealing washer
26 Oil drain plug

springs when the radius rods are disconnected from the axle. With the tool firmly tightened in position, disconnect the nut and bolt attaching the radius rod to the axle. Loosen and remove the tool. Move the axle sideways on the jack to free it from the reaction trunnion mounting then lower the axle assembly and remove it to the rear of the car.

Refitting:

Refitting is a reversal of the removal instructions, but check the condition of the rear axle rubber buffers and the rebound straps and renew them if necessary. On completion, bleed the brakes as described in **Chapter 10**.

7:7 Differential assembly

It is not recommended that the owner operator should dismantle and reassemble the differential unless he is experienced in this type of operation, and has the correct precision gauges and tools. The torque loads on the 2000 limited slip differential must be checked with equipment not readily available to the average DIY operator, and it is strongly recommended that this work is carried out by an establishment having the necessary equipment.

Dismantling and pinion removal:

1 Remove the axle and axle shafts as described in **Sections 7:5** and **7:6** and drain the axle. **FIG 7:16**

shows the components of the differential carrier and axle tubes and **FIG 7:17** the components of the differential assembly. Undo the attaching nuts and remove the axle tubes from the differential housing, collecting the retaining plates. Dismantle the differential housing, using care to avoid damaging the joint faces of the light alloy castings. Lift out the differential assembly.

2 If necessary, remove the bearing outer races from the differential housing using puller A.3.0115 as shown in **FIG 7:18** and remove and retain the shims.

3 Untab the lockplate from the drive pinion ring nut. Remove the ring nut with tool A.5.0104, using tool A.2.0144 or other suitable means to prevent the shaft from turning when unscrewing the ring nut as shown in **FIG 7:19**. Refer to **FIG 7:20** and withdraw the pinion by tapping with a soft mallet. Slide out the spacer 1 and retain the shims 2. Remove the oil seal 5, deflector 4 and the front bearing 3 from the housing. If necessary, pull or press off the rear bearing from the pinion shaft, and remove the bearing outer races from the housing.

4 Pull the bearings from the differential case using a puller as shown in **FIG 7:21**, if it is necessary to renew them. Mark the position of the crownwheel to the differential case, free the tabwashers and remove the crownwheel from the case. Refer to **FIG 7:17** and drive out the bevel pinion shafts 18 from the side opposite the key, then remove the pinions and side gears together with their shims.

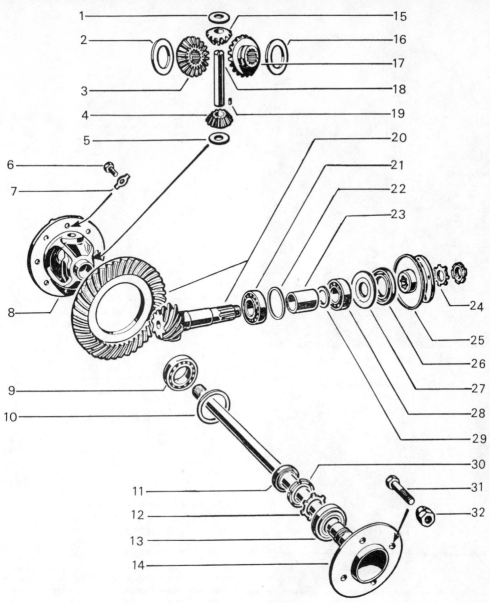

FIG 7:17   Components of the differential assembly

Key to Fig 7:17   1 Thrust washer   2 Thrust washer   3 Differential side gear   4 Differential bevel pinion
5 Thrust washer   6 Crownwheel securing bolt   7 Lockplate   8 Differential case   9 Drive shaft inner bearing   10 Shim
11 Oil seal   12 Lockplate   13 Drive shaft outer bearing   14 Rear axle drive shaft   15 Differential bevel pinion
16 Thrust washer   17 Differential side gear   18 Differential bevel pinion shaft   19 Key   20 Crownwheel and drive pinion assembly
21 Drive pinion inner bearing   22 Shim   23 Bearing spacer   24 Lockplate   25 Drive flange   26 Oil seal   27 Oil deflector
28 Drive pinion outer bearing   29 Shim   30 Pinion shaft nut   31 Wheel stud   32 Wheel nut

5 Check all parts for binding, excessive wear and damage
and renew any part found to be unserviceable. Note
that crownwheel and pinion assemblies are supplied
only as matched sets and are not available separately.

Assembling the differential:

Insert the differential side gears and pinions together
with shims into the differential case and fit the differential

pinion shaft. Check that the backlash between the pinion
and side gears does not exceed .002 inch. Adjust the
backlash if necessary by changing the shim thickness
until it is within the figure stated, then check for free gear
movement. **The gears must rotate freely by hand.**
Refit the crownwheel to the differential case in accordance
with the alignment marks made previously, tighten the
attaching bolts to the torque specified in **Technical Data**
and tab the lockwashers.

ARG1600

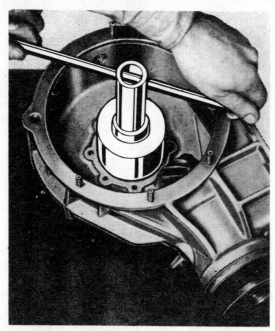

FIG 7:18 Using the special puller to remove the bearing outer races

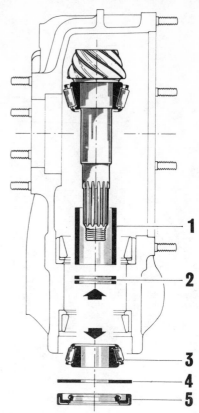

FIG 7:20 Drive pinion assembly details

Key to Fig 7:20   1 Spacer   2 Shims   3 Bearing
4 Deflector   5 Oil seal

FIG 7:19 Removing the ring nut from the pinion shaft

Assembling the drive pinion:

Fit the pinion front and rear bearing outer races into the differential housing. Drive the rear bearing onto the pinion shaft and refit the pinion to the housing together with the spacer and the shims previously retained, in the order shown in **FIG 7:20**. Press in the pinion front bearing and fit the deflector. **Do not install the oil seal at this stage.** Tighten the pinion ring nut to a torque of 58 to 100 lb ft, holding the pinion shaft as previously described in the removal procedure.

Checking the pinion preload:

Install the tool C.5.0100 onto the pinion flange as shown in **FIG 7:22** and rotate the tool in both directions to settle the bearings. Position the weight in the slot marked 105 P. If the lever drops from the horizontal position through approximately 30 deg. as shown in the figure, the preload is correct. If the preload is too low, the lever will rotate freely or, if the preload is too high, the lever will not move under the action of the weight. To correctly adjust the pinion preload the thickness of shims between the pinion spacer and front bearing must be altered. Add shims to decrease the preload, remove shims to increase the preload. The shims are item 2 in **FIG 7:20** and are available in many different thicknesses, final selection being by trial and error until the correct preload is obtained under the test conditions described.

Checking and adjusting the distance of the pinion to the crownwheel centre line:

Refer to **FIG 7:23**. The distance B from the pinion face to the crownwheel centre line should be 57 mm plus or minus the value stamped on the face of the pinion. This value is in hundredths of a millimeter and will be preceded by either a plus or a minus sign. If the value is preceded by a plus sign the distance B should be 57 mm plus the value

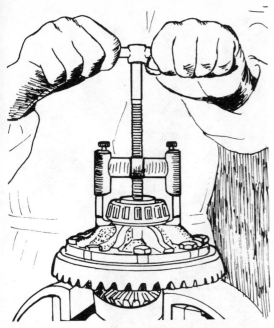

FIG 7:21 Removing the differential side bearings

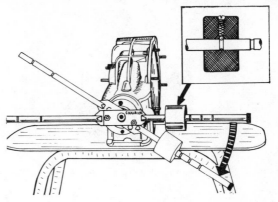

FIG 7:22 Using the special tool to check the pinion preload

indicated or, if the value is preceded by a minus sign the distance B should be 57 mm minus the value indicated. Check the dimension B as follows.

Remove the righthand bearing race from the housing and insert the dummy shaft U, which is tool C.6.0114, into the bearing seat. Tighten the nut C to retain the tool in position. Mount a dial gauge on a support V and set the gauge to the zero position by means of gauge block C.6.0101 so that a dimension of 70 mm is obtained at D. This dimension corresponds to the distance between the face of the pinion and the upper edge of the dummy shaft. Rest the dial gauge support on the front face of the pinion and check that the reading obtained (positive or negative in respect to D) is in accordance with the figure stamped on the pinion face. If this is not the case, alter the thickness of the shims S1 between the rear pinion bearing and the housing. Shims are available in many different thicknesses. If the shim thickness is changed to correct the meshing depth of the pinion, then it will be necessary to alter the thickness of shims S2 accordingly to retain the pinion preload already obtained.

Refitting the differential:

Drive the differential side bearing outer race into position fitting the shims previously retained. Refit the side bearings to the differential case and fit the differential case assembly into the housing. Place the outer race of the lefthand bearing on to the tool C.6.0115 and bolt the tool to the differential housing. Tighten the centre bolt of the tool until the crownwheel is pushed against the drive pinion. Install the tool C.5.0100 onto the pinion flange in the same manner as described for checking pinion preload as shown in FIG 7:22. Rotate the tool in both directions to settle the bearings, then position the

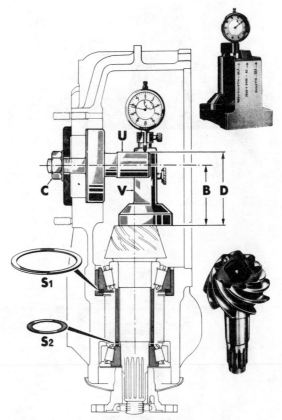

FIG 7:23 Checking and adjusting the distance of the pinion face to the crownwheel centre line. The inserts show the use of the gauge block and the marking on the pinion face

weight in the slot marked 105 T. If the lever drops from the horizontal position through 30 deg. the preload is correct. Adjust the centre screw of the tool until this condition is obtained and the lever moves freely. If the lever does not move freely, remove the bearing outer race and fit a thinner shim. Check and repeat this operation until the correct preload is obtained.

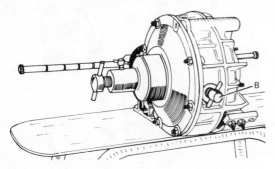

FIG 7:24 Locking the crownwheel with the screw B

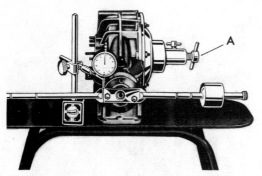

FIG 7:25 Checking the crownwheel and pinion backlash

FIG 7:27 Checking the clearance in the axle tube to determine shim thickness

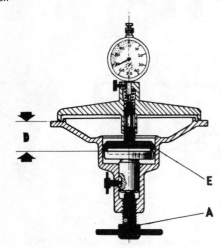

FIG 7:26 Checking the clearance obtained with the special tool fitted

When the preload is correctly set, the backlash between the teeth of the pinion and crownwheel must be checked. Refer to **FIG 7:24** and tighten the screw B into the drain plug boss to lock the crownwheel in position. Mount a dial gauge as shown in **FIG 7:25** and, by swinging the

tool in both directions, check that the backlash is between .006 and .009 inch (.15 and .23 mm) for earlier models or .002 and .004 inch (.05 and .10 mm) for 1750 and later models. Change the thickness of shims between the righthand bearing outer race and its seat to obtain the stated backlash. Fitting a thinner shim will decrease the backlash, fitting a thicker shim will increase it.

When the backlash setting is correct, check the thickness of shims required between the lefthand bearing and its seat as follows. Remove the tool C.6.0115 from the differential housing without disturbing the setting of the adjusting screw and remove the outer race previously fitted. Measure the dimension D shown in **FIG 7:26**, using a dial gauge and tool E which is C.6.0102. Record the figure obtained. Now take a similar measurement in the lefthand axle tube as shown in **FIG 7:27** and record the figure obtained. The difference between the two, minus .002 inch (.05 mm) for preload, will give the thickness of shims to be fitted between the outer bearing race and the bearing seat in the axle tube.

Fit the shims in the axle tube and refit the outer bearing race to the lefthand differential side bearing. Attach the lefthand axle tube to the differential housing but do not tab the lockwashers. Now recheck the backlash and preload of the differential. If the preload is correct and the backlash is too low, add shims at the righthand bearing and remove shims of the same thickness at the lefthand bearing. If the backlash is too high add shims at the left bearing and remove the same thickness from the right

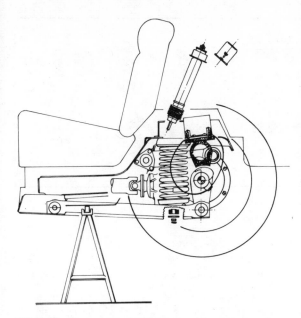

FIG 7:28 The rear suspension assembly, showing the mounting of the damper, rebound strap and rubber buffers

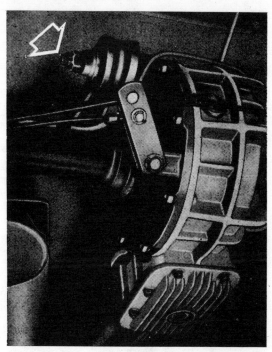

FIG 7:30 The reaction trunnion to rear axle attachment point

FIG 7:29 The reaction trunnion to car body attaching bolt location

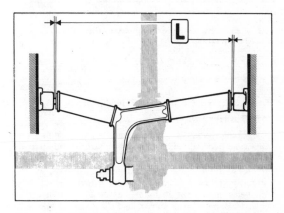

FIG 7:31 Checking the clearance between the rubber bushes and plastic washers when refitting the reaction trunnion

bearing. If the backlash is correct and the preload is wrong, add or remove the same number of shims at both bearings. Add shims to increase the preload, remove shims to reduce the preload. When the adjustments are correct, tighten the axle tube nuts and tab the lockwashers.

Remove the drive pinion flange and drive in the pinion oil seal. Refit the flange and tighten the pinion shaft nut to a torque of 58 to 101 lb ft in the manner previously described. Refit the axle assembly to the car as described in **Section 7:6** and fill the housing with oil to the correct level.

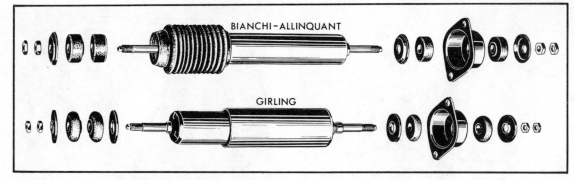

FIG 7:32   The two alternative types of damper which may be fitted

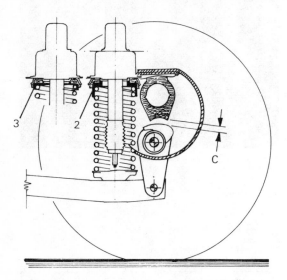

FIG 7:33   Checking the alignment of the rear suspension after reassembly

PART 3   THE REAR SUSPENSION

7:8 Description

The rear suspension is by means of coil springs and telescopic hydraulic dampers. The action of the suspension is controlled by two rubber-bushed radius rods which counteract tractive and braking forces, and a rubber-mounted reaction trunnion which counteracts transverse movement of the axle assembly. The layout of the rear suspension is shown in **FIG 7:28**. Suspension movement is limited in an upward direction by rubber buffers and in a downward direction by a rebound strap. Refer to **Section 7:12** for suspension alignment details.

7:9 Spring removal and refitting

The removal of the rear springs is carried out by removing the rear axle assembly as described in **Section 7:6**, refitting being a reversal of the removal procedure. Renew both springs even if one of them appears to be satisfactory.

7:10 The reaction trunnion

Removal:

Remove the rear section of the exhaust pipe, then loosen the trunnion to car body bolts shown in **FIG 7:29**. Unscrew the nut shown in **FIG 7:30** which attaches the trunnion to the pin on the rear axle and remove the trunnion from the car. Check the condition of the trunnion rubber mountings and renew them if necessary.

Refitting:

This is a reversal of the removal instructions. On completion, check the dimensions L in **FIG 7:31** between the rubber bush and plastic washer do not exceed .004 inch. If necessary add shims between the trunnion and plastic washers until the clearance is correct. The shims selected must then be electrically welded to the trunnion. The bolts attaching the trunnion to the car body and the nut securing the trunnion to the rear axle should be tightened to the torque specified in **Technical Data**.

7:11 Rear dampers

The telescopic hydraulic dampers are the sealed type and require no maintenance. Should a damper become unserviceable a replacement must be fitted. Renew both dampers even if one of them appears to be satisfactory.

Removal and refitting:

Disconnect the damper from the radius rod and fully compress the damper. Remove the damper upper attachment from inside the luggage compartment and withdraw the damper upwards. This operation may be facilitated by removing the rear seat backrest. Refitting is the removal procedure in reverse, referring to **FIG 7:32** for assembly details of Bianchi and Girling dampers.

7:12 Suspension alignment

The rear suspension must always be checked for correct alignment after any dismantling operations have been carried out. The dimension C in **FIG 7:33** between the axle tube and the rubber buffer must be within the limits stated in the following table. If this is not the case, shims must be added at 2 between the spring and seat to increase the dimension or the spring seat 3 removed to reduce the dimension.

Model	Dimension C*
1300, 1600:	
Giulia TI, Giulia Super	.4 inch (10 mm)
Giulia TI Super	.8 inch (20 mm)
Giulia Sprint GT, Giulia Sprint	
GTV	.6 inch (15 mm)
Giulia GTC	.48 inch (12 mm)
Spider	1.3 inch (33 mm)
1750, 2000:	
Berlina	1.4 inch (36 mm)
GTV	1.6 inch (41 mm)
Spider Veloce	1.3 inch (33 mm)

All dimensions to a tolerance of ± .2 inch (± 5 mm)

PART 4 GENERAL

7:13 Fault diagnosis

(a) Noisy axle

1 Insufficient or incorrect lubricant
2 Worn bearings
3 Worn gears

(b) Excessive backlash

1 Worn gears or bearings
2 Worn axle shaft or side gear splines
3 Worn universal joints
4 Worn sliding joint
5 Loose or broken wheel studs

(c) Oil leakage

1 Defective seals in axle tube
2 Defective drive pinion seal

(d) Vibration

1 Propeller shaft out of balance
2 Worn universal joint bearings

(e) Rattles

1 Worn intermediate bearing
2 Loose intermediate bearing mounting
3 Worn suspension rubber mountings

(f) 'Settling'

1 Weak springs
2 Suspension alignment incorrect

NOTES

CHAPTER 8

THE FRONT SUSPENSION AND HUBS

8:1 Description

The independent front suspension assemblies are mounted on a box-section steel crossmember which is welded to the car body. Unequal length upper and lower wishbones pivot on bonded rubber bushes at their attachment points on the body, and the swivel hub assemblies are connected to the wishbone outer ends by ball joints which accommodate the vertical and horizontal movement of the suspension and steering linkages. Coil springs are mounted between the lower wishbones and the car body, spring control being by means of double-acting telescopic hydraulic dampers. The upward movement of the suspension is limited by rubber buffers fitted inside the coil springs and downward movement is limited by rubber pads attached to the crossmember. To improve lateral stability during cornering, an anti-roll bar is fitted between the lower wishbones, being attached to the car body at two mounting points incorporating bonded rubber bushes. Control rods are fitted between the upper ball joint mountings and the car body, the attachment point at the body being provided with a swivel joint. **FIG 8:1** shows the layout of the front suspension components. No routine maintenance is normally needed on the front suspension, the ball joints being fitted with special seals to retain the factory lubrication for the life of the component. Grease nipples are fitted to the ball joint assemblies as a precautionary measure so that, should a faulty seal cause a loss of lubricant, a grease gun can be used.

8:2 Wheel hubs

Removal:

Remove the road wheel. On cars fitted with drum brakes, remove the drum attaching screws and pull off the drum. On cars fitted with disc brakes, refer to **Chapter 10** and dismount the caliper.

Refer to **FIG 8:2**. Remove the grease cap 3 and the splitpin and castellated nut 4 from the wheel spindle. Pull off the hub. If the bearings are to be renewed, prise out the oil seal 7 from the wheel hub and drive out the bearing outer races.

Refitting:

This is the reverse of the removal procedure. Use a suitable mandrel such as tool A.3.0120 to fit the outer bearing races into the hub. Lubricate the bearings with high melting point grease and fill the cavity in the wheel

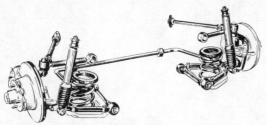

FIG 8:1   The front suspension assembly

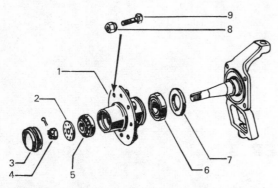

FIG 8:2   The components of the front wheel hub

Key to Fig 8:2   1 Wheel hub   2 Locating washer
3 Grease retaining cap   4 Hub securing nut
5 Outer wheel bearing   6 Inner wheel bearing
7 Oil seal   8 Wheel securing nut   9 Wheel securing stud

hub with two ounces of similar grease. Smear the outer lip of a new oil seal with grease and drive it into position, keeping it square. Refit the hub carefully to avoid distorting the swivel joint, the use of tool A.3.011 being recommended. On completion, adjust the bearing end float.

Bearing end float adjustment:

Jack up the car and remove the hub cap and the splitpin from the castellated nut 4. Leave the road wheel fitted. Turn the wheel and at the same time tighten the castellated nut to a torque of 18 lb ft to settle the bearings. Loosen the nut by half a turn then tap against the inside of the wheel swivel with a soft mallet to seat the outer bearing. Now tighten the nut to a torque of 7 lb ft. Loosen the nut by a quarter of a turn and insert a new splitpin, tightening the nut slightly if necessary to line up the hole in the wheel spindle with a slot in the nut. Check that it is possible to move the locating washer 2. If necessary, again tap against the rear of the swivel joint until the wheel can be rotated freely with no signs of binding. If a dial gauge is available to check the bearing end float, the figure obtained should be .002 to .005 inch (.05 to .13 mm). Lock the splitpin when the adjustment is satisfactory.

8:3 Removing and dismantling suspension

Removal:

Slacken the front wheel nuts, jack up the car under the front crossmember and support it on floor stands placed beneath the body sidemembers. Remove the wheels. Refer to **FIG 8:3** to identify the components of the front suspension.

1 Remove the dampers as described in **Section 8:5**. Refer to **Chapter 10** and detach the brake hose and the caliper on cars fitted with disc brakes, or the brake hose and brake backing plate on cars fitted with drum brakes.

2 Refer to **Section 8:6** and detach the anti-roll bar connections from the lower wishbones and swing the arms of the anti-roll bar out of the way.

3 Remove the bolts from the spring retainer by first compressing the spring with tool A.2.0123. If no compressor is available, use a jack placed under the spring plate to compress the spring sufficiently for the bolts to be removed. Release the spring compressor or lower the jack and remove the spring from the suspension, together with the bearing washer and the top and bottom rubber mountings. Retain any shims which are fitted as they are necessary to set the suspension angle correctly.

4 Remove the ball joint from the upper suspension arm, using tool A.3.0156 or any suitable puller. Lift out the swivel joint complete. Unscrew the two attaching bolts and remove the lower wishbone from the front axle crossmember.

5 Disconnect the control rod from the upper suspension arm and remove the pivot bolt from the top of the crossmember. Lift out the upper suspension arm. Unscrew the two bolts attaching the control rod swivel joint to the car frame and remove the control rod.

6 Remove the lower ball joint from the lower wishbone assembly and remove the wishbone arms from the pivot bolt.

Servicing:

Examine the suspension arms for signs of damage or distortion. Check the condition of the suspension mounting bushes and renew them if they are worn, using tool A.3.0159 for this operation. The ball joints must swivel smoothly but have no free play. Check all parts for good condition and serviceability and renew parts where necessary. Coil springs should preferably be renewed in pairs. If one new spring only is to be fitted, make sure that the coloured paint marking on the new spring is the same as that on the old spring.

Refitting:

Refitting is a reversal of the removal procedure. The suspension should be assembled to the vehicle with the nuts and bolts installed finger-tight only. Final tightening should be carried out with the weight of the car resting on the wheels. Take care to ensure that every nut and bolt is fully tightened and bleed the brakes as described in **Chapter 10** before road testing the car. It is always advisable to check and adjust the suspension geometry as described in **Section 8:4** after assembling the front suspension.

8:4 Adjustments

Before any checking and adjusting of the castor and camber angles is carried out the car must be standing on level ground, the tyre pressures must be correct and the

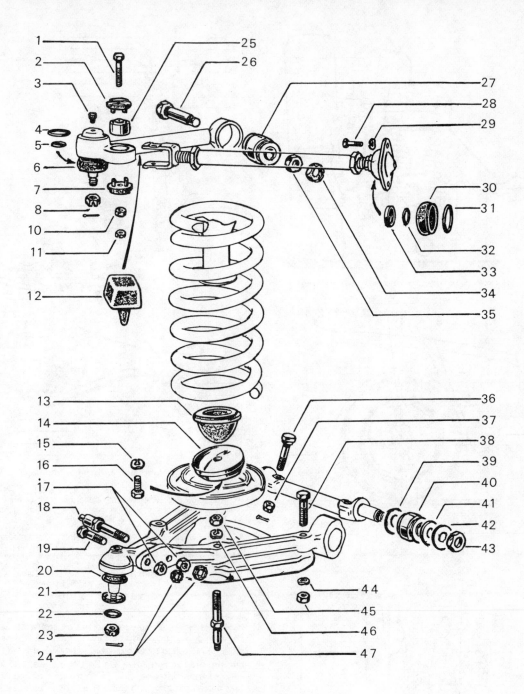

FIG 8:3   The components of the front suspension

Key to Fig 8:3   1 Bolt   2 Locating washer   3 Screwed plug   4 Retaining ring   5 Retaining washer   6 Dust cover   7 Washer
8 Slotted nut   10 Nut   11 Locknut   12 Rebound buffer   13 Rebound buffer   14 Rubber seat   15 Spring washer   16 Bolt
17 Hexagonal nut   18 Suspension arm bolt   19 Mounting bolt   20 Dust cover   21 Retaining washer   22 Retaining washer
23 Slotted nut   24 Locknut   25 Bonded rubber bush   26 Mounting bolt   27 Bonded rubber bush   28 Securing screw
29 Washer   30 Rubber dust cover   31 Sealing ring   32 Retaining washer   33 Sealing ring   34 Locknut   35 Hexagonal nut
36 Mounting bolt   37 Slotted nut   38 Mounting bolt   39 Washer   40 Rubber bush   41 Washer   42 Washer   43 Hexagonal nut
44 Washer   45 Hexagonal nut   46 Washer   47 Mounting bolt

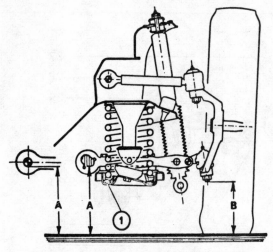

FIG 8:4   Checking the suspension adjustment

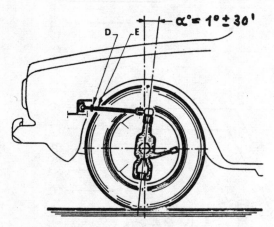

FIG 8:5   Checking and adjusting the castor angle

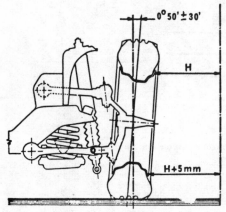

FIG 8:6   Checking the camber angle

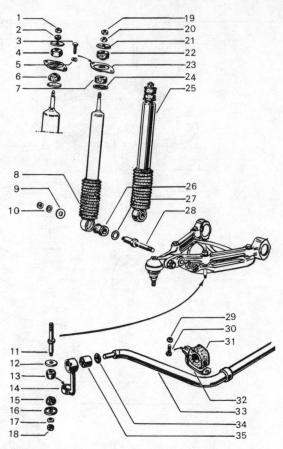

FIG 8:7   Damper and anti-roll bar components

Key to Fig 8:7   1 Locknut   2 Locknut   3 Bolt
4 Rubber ring   5 Washer   6 Rubber ring   7 Rubber bush
8 Protection gaiter   9 Plain washer   10 Spring washer
11 Mounting stud   12 Washer   13 Rubber bush
14 Anti-roll bar link   15 Rubber bush   16 Cup washer
17 Spring washer   18 Nut   19 Locknut   20 Securing nut
21 Cup washer   22 Rubber bush   23 Mounting flange
24 Cup washer   25 Damper   26 Rubber bush
27 Plain washer   28 Mounting stud   29 Spring washer
30 Bolt   31 Rubber bearing   32 Clamp bracket
33 Anti-roll bar   34 Washer   35 Bonded rubber bush

car fully loaded. Make sure that the oil and water levels are correct and that the fuel tank is full. The front seats must be occupied by two passengers or weights must be put into the car as follows. On 2-door models, 100 lb on each of the front seats and 55 lb in front of each front seat on the car floor. On Super 1.6, 110 lb on each seat, and 44 lb on each foot well, front and rear. On 4-door models, 100 lb in each seat and 55 lb in each foot well, front and rear. Detach the anti-roll bar from the lower suspension arms and disconnect one end of each damper.

Suspension alignment:

While it should be possible to carry out a suspension height check with a reasonable degree of accuracy, castor and camber angles are very difficult to measure without specialised equipment. If uneven tyre wear or unsatisfactory handling characteristics suggest that these settings, or the front wheel alignment (see **Chapter 9, Section 9:5**), may be at fault as a result of worn components or accident damage, it is probably best to leave checking to a service station. Use of the proper optical equipment makes the task a relatively simple one.

Ride height:

In order that this check may be carried out accurately, the car must be standing on a perfectly flat surface. Refer to **FIG 8:4**. Lift the front of the car 2 inches and allow it to drop to the rest position. Now measure the distance A from the lower suspension arm to the level surface and the distance B from the lower ball joint to the level surface. Deduct B from A and note the figure obtained. Push the front of the car down 2 inches and allow it to return. Now repeat the measuring procedure and again deduct B from A and note this second figure obtained. Add together both figures and divide the result by two in order to calculate an average figure. The figure should be as follows. For models equipped with round section lower suspension pivot bolts, $1.50 \pm .12$ inch (38 ± 3 mm). For Saloon and Coupé models (except GT Junior 1300) with oval section lower pivot bolts, $1.34 \pm .2$ inch (34 ± 5 mm). For Spider models and GT Junior 1300, $.95 \pm .2$ inch (24 ± 5 mm).

If the measurement is incorrect, distance washers (available in 3.5, 7 and 10.5 mm thicknesses) should be fitted below the spring at position 1.

Castor angle:

This is the angle between the vertical line through the wheel centre and the line through the two ball joint centres as shown in **FIG 8:5**. Use an approved gauge to measure the castor angle, which should be $1\frac{1}{2}$ deg. plus or minus $\frac{1}{2}$ deg. The difference in castor angle between the two wheels should not exceed 20'.

Adjustment is by slackening the locknut D and altering the length of the control rod E. Tighten the locknut when the correct setting is obtained.

Camber angle:

This is the angle of wheel inclination from the vertical when viewed from the front as shown in **FIG 8:6**. Use an approved gauge to measure the camber angle, which should be 0 deg. 50' plus or minus 30'. The camber angle is preset and non-adjustable, so if camber angle is found to be incorrect a check should be made on the components of the front suspension and any worn or damaged parts which may be causing the condition renewed. On 1750 and later models the camber angle is 20' $\pm$ 30'.

When the suspension geometry tests have been completed, reconnect the dampers and anti-roll bar and remove the loading weights.

8:5 Dampers

The telescopic hydraulic dampers which are shown in **FIG 8:7** are of the sealed type and require no maintenance. Should a damper become unserviceable a replacement must be fitted. Renew both dampers even if one of them appears to be satisfactory.

Removal:

Unscrew the nuts from the upper damper mounting and remove the cup washers and rubber bushes. Remove the nut, spring washer and plain washer from the damper lower mounting on the suspension arm and remove the damper, together with the cup washer and rubber mounting.

Refitting:

This is a reversal of the removal procedure, referring to **FIG 8:7** for details of the correct fitting of the upper and lower rubber mountings.

8:6 Anti-roll bar

Removal:

Refer to **FIG 8:7** and disconnect the anti-roll bar from the attachment points on the lower suspension arms. Remove the two rubber bush clamps from the car body attachment points and remove the anti-roll bar. If the anti-roll bar is bent it is possible to straighten it in a cold condition under a press. Check that the arms are parallel to each other when viewed from the side. Check the rubber bushes at the body and suspension arm mounting points and renew them if they are worn or damaged.

Refitting:

Refitting is a reversal of the removal instructions.

8:7 Fault diagnosis

(a) Wheel wobble

1 Worn hub bearings
2 Broken or weak front springs
3 Uneven tyre wear
4 Worn suspension linkage
5 Loose wheel fixings
6 Incorrect tracking

(b) 'Bottoming' of suspension

1 Check 2 in (a)
2 Rebound rubbers worn or missing
3 Damper(s) not working

(c) Heavy steering

1 Wheel swivels unlubricated
2 Wrong suspension geometry

(d) Excessive tyre wear

1 Check 4 and 6 in (a) and 2 in (c)

(e) Rattles

1 Check 2 in (a) and 1 in (c)
2 Worn bushes
3 Damper attachments loose
4 Anti-roll bar broken, mountings loose or bushes worn

(f) Excessive rolling

1 Check 2 in (a) and 3 in (b)
2 Check 4 in (e)

NOTES

CHAPTER 9

THE STEERING GEAR

9:1 Description

This range of models may be fitted with either ZF worm and cam steering or Burman recirculating ball steering. The components of the ZF steering box are shown in **FIG 9:1** and the Burman steering box components in **FIG 9:2**.

Steering motion is transmitted from the inner column worm, which is supported in ballraces, to the rocker shaft. The drop arm is splined to the rocker shaft. One track rod is directly connected to the drop arm, the second track rod being connected through a centre tie rod and idler lever linkage as shown in **FIG 9:3**

9:2 The ZF steering box

Removal:

1 Remove the padding from the steering wheel followed by the horn button, horn contact and cable sleeve guides. Remove the steering wheel attaching nut and retaining washer and pull the steering wheel from the tapered shaft by means of a suitable puller. Remove the key from the steering inner shaft.

2 Set the steering column lock to the 'Garage' position and detach the outer tube by removing the attaching bolts from the engine compartment and the car interior. Disconnect the cable terminals from the switch connectors.

3 Remove the ball joint from the steering drop arm and remove the steering box attaching bolts. Remove the air cleaner assembly then lift the steering box from the car.

Dismantling:

Refer to **FIG 9:1** for details of the components of the ZF steering box assembly.

1 Remove the splitpin and castellated nut from the rocker arm shaft. Mark the position of the steering drop arm to the shaft then remove the drop arm, using a suitable puller. Unscrew the plug from the top cover and drain the oil.

2 Slacken the locknut on the adjusting screw 9 then remove the top cover 6. Before removing the retaining ring 7 for the adjusting screw guide washer, check the clearance between the adjusting screw and the end of the steering rocker shaft. The correct clearance is .002 inch and, if necessary, a washer of different thickness should be fitted to obtain the specified clearance. Washers are available in six different thicknesses from 2.20 mm to 2.45 mm.

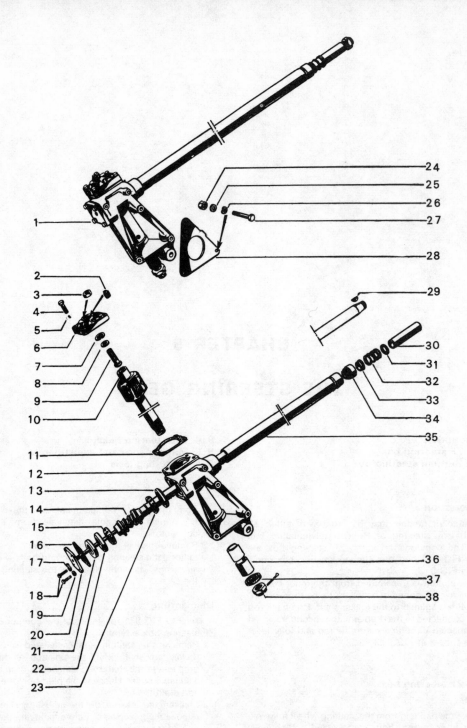

FIG 9:1   Components of the ZF steering box

Key to Fig 9:1   1 Steering box assembly   2 Oil filler plug   3 Nut   4 Top cover screw   5 Spring washer   6 Top cover
7 Retaining ring   8 Guide washer   9 Adjusting screw   10 Rocker shaft   11 Gasket   12 Housing   13 Upper bearing outer race
14 Worm   15 Lower bearing   16 End cover shim   17 Lockwasher   18 End cover screws   19 Washer   20 End cover   21 Spacer
22 Lower bearing outer race   23 Upper bearing   24 Nut   25 Washer   26 Spring washer   27 Bolt   28 Mounting plate   29 Key
30 Sleeve   31 Ring   32 Column spring   33 Inner tube bush   34 Spring seat   35 Outer tube   36 Bush
37 Oil seal   38 Castellated nut

3 Remove the steering rocker shaft, taking care to avoid damaging the lower oil seal with the splines on the shaft. Remove the end cover 20 and withdraw the steering shaft from the housing, together with the shim 16, spacer 21 and the upper and lower shaft bearing assemblies.

Servicing:

Clean all parts in petrol or paraffin and dry them off. Check the components for wear or damage, particularly the steering worm and the teeth on the rocker shaft, and renew any component found unserviceable. The normal clearance between the rocker shaft and the bush 36 is .0005 inch. If this clearance is exceeded, a new bush should be fitted and reamed to give a shaft clearance of .0003 inch. Check the condition of the oil seal 37 and renew it if necessary.

Reassembly:

Reassembly is a reversal of the dismantling procedure, noting the following points. Refit the steering shaft and worm assembly and fit the end cover with the original shim. Now check the torque required to turn the steering shaft, which should be between .10 and .5 lb ft. If necessary, alter the thickness of the shim beneath the end cover to obtain a torque reading within the limits stated. Shims are available in five different thicknesses from .10 mm to .30 mm.

Fit the steering rocker shaft and place the drop arm over the shaft splines in accordance with the alignment marks made during dismantling. Set the drop arm in the central position and tighten the adjusting screw until all perceptible clearance between the worm and the steering rocker shaft is eliminated. Now turn the drop arm through an angle of 30 deg. in each direction and check the clearance in each position, again using the adjusting screw to eliminate any free play. When this is done correctly the steering should have a clearance-free movement without any sign of binding. Fit the guide washer retaining ring and lock the adjusting screw. Tighten the drop arm securing nut to a torque of 90 to 100 lb ft and lock with a new splitpin. On completion, refill the steering housing with SAE.90 oil.

Refitting:

Refitting the steering assembly to the car is a reversal of the removal procedure.

9:3 Burman steering box

Removal:

The removal of the Burman steering box is carried out in the same manner as that previously described for the removal of the ZF assembly.

Dismantling:

Refer to **FIG 9:2** for details of the components of the Burman steering box assembly.

1 Remove the splitpin and castellated nut from the rocker arm shaft. Mark the position of the steering drop arm to the shaft then remove the drop arm, using a suitable puller. Unscrew the plug from the top cover and drain the oil.

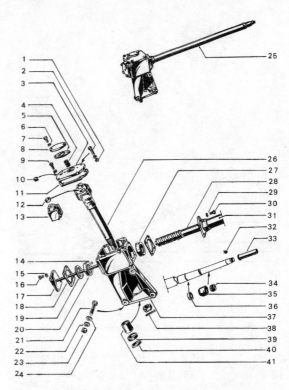

FIG 9:2   Components of the Burman steering box

Key to Fig 9:2   1 Nut   2 Bolt   3 Top cover
4 Shaft spring   5 Paper or steel shim   6 Lockwasher
7 Screw   8 Small cover   9 Screw   10 Oil plug
11 Paper shim .   12 Main nut roller   13 Main nut
14 Ball   15 Lockwasher   16 Screw   17 End cover
18 Paper or steel shim   19 Spacer   20 Lower bearing
21 Bolt   22 Spring washer   23 Nut   24 Washer
25 Steering box assembly   26 Rocker shaft
27 Upper bearing   28 Wormshaft   29 Lockwasher
30 Screw   31 Outer tube   32 Key   33 Sleeve
34 Inner tube spring   35 Ballbearing   36 Bush
37 Housing   38 Castellated nut   39 Oil seal   40 Retainer
41 Bush

2 Unscrew the four bolts attaching the top cover to the housing and remove the cover, paper shim 11 and the roller 12. Remove the bolts securing the end cover 17 and remove the cover, together with the shim 18 and the bearing spacer 19. Remove the key 32, sleeve 33 and spring 34 from the end of the steering shaft. Push on the end of the shaft to remove the bearing outer race from the housing and collect the ten steel balls. Remove the remaining thirteen steel balls which will have fallen into the housing. Remove the steering column tube.

3 Turn the steering column clockwise and remove the second bearing outer race from the housing. Remove the rocker shaft 26 and the steering main nut 13 from the housing, then withdraw the lower shaft bearing and oil seal.

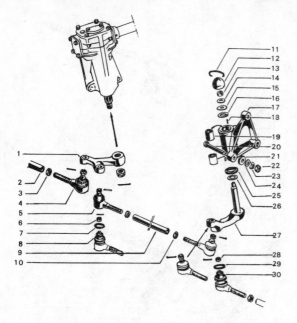

FIG 9:3   Components of the steering linkage

Key to Fig 9:3   1 Steering drop arm
2 Track rod   3 Locknut   4 Track rod end   5 Tie rod end
6 Castellated nut   7 Retaining ring   8 Rubber cover
9 Tie rod   10 Locknut   11 Securing clip
12 Protective cover   13 Nut   14 Locking plate
15 Washer   16 Thrust washer   17 Idler arm bracket
18 Pin 19 Bush 20 Mounting bolt 21 Washer 22 Nut
23 Spring washer   24 Washer   25 Oil seal
26 Thrust washer   27 Idler arm   28 Castellated nut
29 Retaining ring   30 Rubber cover

Servicing:

Clean all parts in petrol or paraffin and dry them off. Check the components for wear or damage and renew any component found unserviceable. Renew any worn bushes, noting that the steering shaft bush must be fitted with the oil groove toward the shaft. New bushes must be reamed until the shaft is a smooth sliding fit in the bush. If the steering shaft worm is worn or damaged, a new shaft must be fitted. The steering main nut and roller should be examined for signs of scoring or wear and parts renewed as required.

Reassembly:

Reassembly is a reversal of the dismantling procedure, noting the following points. Mount the steering column tube horizontally in a vice. Fit the upper bearing outer race over the steering shaft and insert the shaft a short distance into the tube. Retain the steel recirculatory balls in the steering main nut by the use of heavy grease. Insert the steering shaft into the housing and screw the worm carefully into the main nut until the nut is centrally positioned on the worm. Fit the bearing outer race on the steering shaft into the housing and refit the steering column flange to the housing, making sure that the gasket is correctly positioned. Retain the ten steel balls in the upper bearing with heavy grease, then push the bearing into the housing until it abuts against the steering column. Apply heavy grease and refit the thirteen balls in the same manner. Fit the end cover and shim and tighten the end cover attaching bolts.

There should be no perceptible end play on the steering worm with the end cover fitted. Alternative metal shims are available in .003 and .004 inch thicknesses, paper shims in .002 and .010 thicknesses. Select and fit an appropriate shim to remove end play, making sure that the steering is in the central position when making tests and adjustments.

Fit the top cover and gasket and tighten the cover attaching bolts to a torque of 16.5 to 18 lb ft and check the steering column end float in the following manner. Fit a dial gauge assembly to the top of the steering column and read off the end float measurement while applying a load of 22 lbs to the lower end of the shaft. The end play should be between .002 and .010 inch. A shim of appropriate thickness must be fitted between the small cover and the top cover to obtain the figure quoted, making sure that

FIG 9:4   The positions of the steering lockstops

the steering is in the central position when making tests and adjustments. Do not fit the spring 3 when making the adjustments.

When the adjustments have been completed, check that the steering can be turned freely from one lock to the other. Refit the steering drop arm to the rocker shaft in accordance with the marks made during dismantling, tighten the castellated nut and lock with a new splitpin.

Refitting:

Refitting the steering assembly to the car is a reversal of the removal procedure.

9:4 The steering linkage

The components of the steering linkage are shown in **FIG 9:3**.

Steering idler unit:

Removal and refitting:

Detach the tie rod and track rod ball joints from the idler arm then remove the mounting bolts from the idler arm bracket and lift the idler unit from the car. Remove the securing clip, protective cover and the pivot bolt nut and withdraw the idler arm from the bracket, collecting the washers, thrust washers and locking plate. Check the pivot bolt and bearing bushes for wear and renew parts as necessary. New bushes must be reamed out until the pivot bolt is a smooth sliding fit without side play. The pivot bolt must have no end play when it is refitted to the bracket and the nut tightened to a torque of 35 to 40 lb ft. Eliminate any end play by fitting thicker thrust washers. Tighten the mounting bolts to a torque of 35 to 40 lb ft when refitting the idler arm bracket to the car.

Tie rod:

If the tie rod ball joints are worn they should be renewed. Remove the splitpins and castellated nuts from both joints and remove the tie rod. Use a puller such as A.3.0157 to remove the ball joints. When refitting the unit to the car, tighten the ball joint castellated nuts to a torque of 35 to 40 lb ft and lock with a new splitpin.

Track rods:

Renew the track rod ball joints if they are worn, in the manner previously described for the tie rod joints. If the track rod ends are removed, count the number of turns taken to unscrew them so that they can be screwed in an equal number of turns when they are refitted. Tighten the ball joint castellated nuts to a torque of 35 to 40 lb ft and lock with a new splitpin. On completion, check the front wheel alignment as described in **Section 9:5**.

9:5 Maintenance and adjustments

Maintenance:

Steering unit:

Every 3750 miles, remove the steering box oil filler plug and top up with the recommended lubricant until no more oil will enter.

Ball joints:

The steering ball joints are lubricated and sealed for life, so no routine maintenance is necessary. If the joints

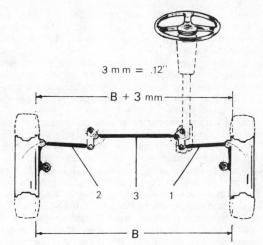

FIG 9:5 Checking and adjusting the front wheel alignment

Key to FIG 9:5   1/2 Track rods   3 Tie rod

are worn or the oil seals are damaged the complete ball joint should be renewed as described in **Section 9:4**.

Adjustments:

Steering box:

If there is any play in the steering, the steering box internal clearances should be checked and adjusted as described in **Section 9:2** for ZF units, or **Section 9:3** for Burman units. Before carrying out any adjustments to the steering box, a check should be made to ensure that worn ball joints or loose wheel bearings are not the cause of the trouble.

Lockstops:

The lockstops limit the travel of the steering drop arm in one direction and the idler arm in the other direction. Lockstops are factory set to give the correct turning circle but, if adjustment should be necessary, refer to **FIG 9:4** and slacken the locknuts and adjust the screws to obtain the desired left and right turning circles. Tighten the locknuts and recheck.

Front wheel alignment:

The car should be in a loaded condition as described in **Chapter 8, Section 8:4** and standing on level ground before any checks and adjustments are made. With the wheels in the straight-ahead position, check the wheel alignment using an approved track setting gauge. Each wheel should be toed-in .06 inch (1.5 mm), equivalent to 0° 13' with 15 inch rims or 0° 14' with 14 inch rims. Push the car forward until the wheels have turned through 180° and recheck.

If adjustment is required, lock the steering wheel in the straight-ahead position by suitable means, then slacken the locknuts at each end of the track rods and at each end of the tie rod.

Refer to **FIG 9:5**. Rotate the track rod 1 until the wheel on the steering box side is toed-in by .06 inch (1.5 mm). Accurately measure the resultant length of the track rod, then adjust track rod 2 on the other side to the same length on a righthand drive car or .20 inch (5 mm) shorter on a lefthand drive car. Now adjust tie rod 3 to set the other wheel to a toe-in of .06 inch (1.5 mm) and tighten the locknuts.

Righthand drive 2000 models with a white marked steering arm are adjusted in a similar manner to other lefthand drive cars, beginning with the side rod on the steering box side and then adjusting the other side rod to the same length + .20 inch (5 mm).

After setting, the lengths of rods measured between ball joint centres should fall between the following limits. Longer side rod, or both side rods on symmetrically adjusted righthand drive cars, 10.4 to 11 inch (264 to 280 mm). Shorter side, 10.2 to 10.8 inch (259 to 275 mm). Centre rod, 20.9 to 21.7 inch (530 to 550 mm). Failure to achieve these values probably indicates body-shell distortion resulting from accident damage.

To achieve the degree of accuracy needed for a reliable front wheel alignment setting will require very careful measurement. It may well be best to leave the job to a service station, since specialised optical equipment makes the task a simple one.

9:6 Fault diagnosis

(a) Wheel wobble

1 Unbalanced wheels and tyres
2 Slack steering connections
3 Incorrect steering geometry
4 Excessive play in steering gear
5 Broken or weak front springs
6 Worn hub bearings

(b) Wander

1 Check 2, 3 and 4 in (a)
2 Uneven tyre pressures
3 Uneven tyre wear
4 Ineffective dampers

(c) Heavy steering

1 Check 3 in (a)
2 Very low tyre pressures
3 Neglected lubrication
4 Wheels out of track
5 Steering gear maladjusted
6 Steering column bent
7 Steering column bushes tight

(d) Lost motion

1 Loose steering wheel
2 Worn steering box and idler unit
3 Worn ball joints
4 Worn suspension system and wheel swivels

CHAPTER 10

THE BRAKING SYSTEM

10:1 Description

Early Giulia models are fitted with drum brakes front and rear, disc front brakes being introduced at the end of 1964 and fitted to all models produced after that date. Later models are equipped with disc brakes on all four wheels and a vacuum servo unit. The brakes on all four wheels are hydraulically operated by the brake pedal, the handbrake operating the rear brakes only through a mechanical linkage. The brake pedal is directly connected to the master cylinder where pressure on the fluid is generated and passed to the brakes by a system of metal and flexible pipes.

Front drum brakes are of the three leading shoe type arranged in a fully-floating configuration, each shoe being operated by a separate wheel cylinder. Rear wheel drum brakes each have one leading and one trailing shoe, both being operated by a single wheel cylinder.

Disc brakes have a fixed caliper with two self-adjusting friction pads between which the disc rotates. The friction pads are applied by two pistons operated by hydraulic pressure from the master cylinder, both pistons operating simultaneously to exert equal pressure on the pads. On Dunlop braking systems, the rear disc brakes are actuated through a pair of pressed steel levers by pushrods connected to remote operating cylinders mounted on the rear axle.

10:2 Maintenance

Regularly check the level of the fluid in the master cylinder supply tank and replenish if necessary up to the MAX mark on the tank. Wipe dirt from around the filler cap before removing it and check that the vent hole in the cap is unobstructed. If frequent topping-up is required the system should be examined for leaks, but it should be noted that disc brake systems will need more frequent topping-up than all-drum systems, due to the wheel cylinder movement compensating for friction pad wear. **Never use anything but a top quality disc brake fluid.**

On cars equipped with four disc brake assemblies no adjustment is necessary, wear being automatically taken up by the brake mechanisms. Drum brakes must be adjusted when brake pedal travel becomes excessive, at all four wheels on earlier cars or at the rear wheels only when disc front brakes are fitted.

Front drum brake adjustment:

Three adjusters are provided on the drum front brake plate, one for each brake shoe. **As the shoes are fully-floating, any adjustments made to one shoe will also affect the others therefore shoe adjustments must be made carefully and accurately to ensure equal pressure on each shoe when the brakes are**

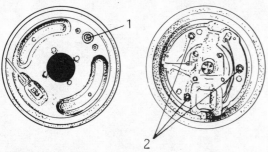

FIG 10:1 The rear and front drum brake adjusters

Key to Fig 10:1   1 Rear brake shoe adjuster
2 Front brake shoe adjusters

GAUGE

FIG 10:2 Checking that the brake shoes operate parallel to the brake drum

applied. If the brakes are adjusted in an incorrect manner it is possible for a brake shoe to be cracked under the effects of heavy braking, apart from the obvious consequence of brake inefficiency.

Jack up the car so that the front wheels can be turned freely. Refer to FIG 10:1 and slacken each of the brake shoe adjusters to its fullest extent, this operation ensuring that each shoe is in the same position relative to the others. Now tighten the adjusters equally and alternately until the shoes just contact the brake drum. This condition can be felt by turning the wheel after each adjustment is made. When resistance to turning can be felt, slacken off the adjusters equally by one to three clicks, or until the wheel just rotates freely. Press the brake pedal several times then check again for free rotation, slackening the adjusters further if necessary.

Rear drum brake adjustment:

Chock the front wheels, jack up the rear of the car and release the handbrake. Refer to FIG 10:1 and tighten the adjuster shown until the brake shoes can be felt touching the drum when the wheel is rotated, then slacken the adjuster until the wheel can just be rotated freely. If the adjuster needs to be slackened more than three-quarters of a turn to allow the wheel to rotate freely misalignment of the brake shoes could be indicated, in which case shoe alignment should be checked in the following manner. Remove the road wheel and the brake drum, then fit tool C.6.0106 to the brake assembly as shown in FIG 10:2. If the brake lining does not contact the gauge plate over the whole of its length, the brake shoe alignment screw at the rear of the brake plate should be turned until this condition is fulfilled. Repeat the operation on the second shoe. With the shoes set parallel to the drum in this manner, readjust the brake as previously described.

Preventative maintenance:

Regularly examine friction pads, brake linings and all pipes, unions and hoses. Change the brake fluid every year or 11,250 miles. Every 22,500 miles check all flexible hoses and fluid seals in the system and renew if necessary. Do not leave brake fluid in unsealed containers as it will absorb moisture which can be dangerous. It is best to discard fluid drained from the system or after bleeding. **Observe absolute cleanliness when working on all parts of the hydraulic system.**

10:3 Drum brakes

Removing and refitting brake shoes:

Front brakes:

Removal:

Jack up the car and remove the road wheel and brake drum. Refer to FIG 10:3. Mark the brake shoes 5 for

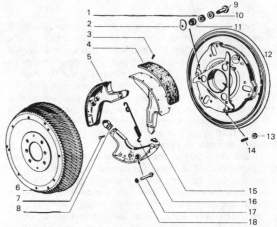

FIG 10:3 Components of the front drum brake assembly

Key to Fig 10:3   1 Spring washer   2 Adjuster cam
3 Lining rivet   4 Brake lining   5 Brake shoe
6 Brake drum   7 Rivet   8 Guide   9 Pivot pin
10 Washer   11 Bush   12 Brake backplate   13 Nut
14 Guide pin   15 Guide   16 Shoe return spring
17 Adjusting pin   18 Washer

refitting in their original positions and remove the return spring 16. Carefully lift out the brake shoes, noting that each shoe guide is slotted into the adjacent shoe.

Refitting:

Clean the brake drum and backing plate thoroughly, using care to avoid dirt entering the wheel cylinder seals or wheel bearings. Make sure that the return spring is correctly fitted and that the brake shoe guides are correctly aligned. Slacken off all three brake shoe adjusters completely before refitting the drum and, when assembly is completed, adjust the brake as described in **Section 10:2**.

Rear brakes:

Removal:

Chock the front wheels, jack up the rear wheel and release the handbrake, then remove the brake drum. Refer to **FIG 10:4**. Remove the return springs 2 and 8 and lift out the brake shoes.

Refitting:

Clean the brake drum and backing plate thoroughly, using care to avoid dirt entering the wheel cylinder seals or bearings. Make sure that the return springs are correctly refitted, noting that the waisted spring is fitted to the wheel cylinder side of the assembly. Check that the shoes

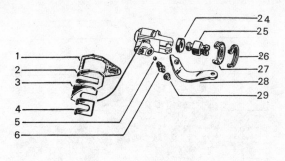
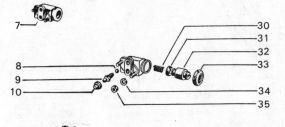
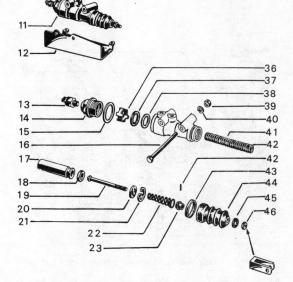

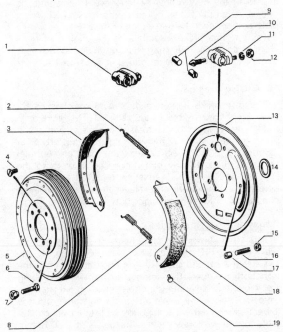

FIG 10:4 Components of a typical rear drum brake assembly

Key to Fig 10:4   1 Brake adjuster assembly
2 Adjuster side shoe return spring   3 Brake shoe
4 Screw   5 Brake drum   6 Bolt   7 Nut
8 Cylinder side shoe return spring   9 Adjuster piston
10 Adjuster wedge   11 Lockwasher   12 Nut
13 Brake backplate   14 Shim   15 Nut
16 Shoe alignment adjuster   17 Piston   18 Brake lining
19 Rivet

FIG 10:5 Components of the brake cylinders. The rear wheel cylinder is at the top of the figure, followed by the front wheel cylinder and the master cylinder

Key to Fig 10:5   1 Dust cap   2 Retaining spring
3 Securing plate   4 Spring clip   5 Ball
6 Bleeder screw   7 Wheel brake cylinder   8 Ball
9 Bleeder screw   10 Dust cap   11 Master cylinder assembly
12 Mounting bracket 13 Brake light switch 14 Closing plug
15 Seal ring   16 Mounting bolt   17 Piston
18 Piston cup   19 Pushrod   20 Stop washer   21 Circlip
22 Return spring 23 Spring seat 24 Piston cup 25 Piston
26 Retaining ring   27 Dust cover
28 Handbrake operating lever   29 Dust cap
30 Return spring 31 Piston cup 32 Piston 33 Dust cap
34 Spring washer   35 Nut   36 Spacer
37 Main piston seal 38 Washer 39 Nut 40 Spring washer
41 Return spring   42 Pin   43 Retaining ring
44 Rubber boot   45 Retaining ring   46 Locknut

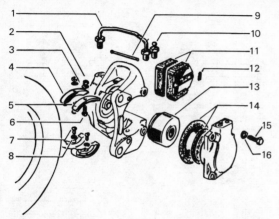

FIG 10:6 Components of the Dunlop front brake caliper

Key to Fig 10:6   1 Bridge pipe   2 Securing nut
3 Spring washer   4/5 Brake pad carriers
6/7 Mounting bolts   8 Spring washer   9 Retaining pin
10 Bleeder screw   11 Friction pads   12 Splitpin
13 Piston   14 Rubber dust seal   15 Mounting bolt
16 Washer

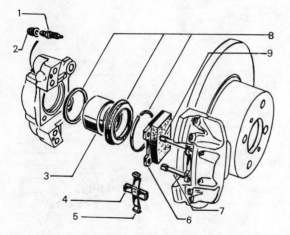

FIG 10:7   Components of the ATE front brake caliper

Key to Fig 10:7   1 Bleeder screw   2 Dust cap   3 Piston
4 Spring   5 Spring hook   6 Friction pad
7 Retaining pin   8 Piston, seals and retaining ring assembly
9 Retaining pin

are slotted into the wheel cylinder and adjuster pistons and slacken the adjuster completely before refitting the drum. On completion, adjust the brakes as described in **Section 10:2**.

Relining brake shoes:

If the linings are worn down to the rivets, renewal is necessary. It is not recommended that owners attempt to reline brake shoes themselves. It is important that the linings should be properly bedded to the shoes, ground for concentricity and correctly chamfered at their leading and trailing edges. For this reason it is best to obtain sets of replacement shoes, or have the relining carried out by a service station. **Do not allow grease, oil or brake fluid to contact brake linings**. If the linings are contaminated in any way they must be renewed as they cannot be successfully cleaned.

Servicing a wheel cylinder:

Remove the road wheel, drum and brake shoes. Disconnect the brake pipe or hose from the cylinder which is to be removed and use a plug to prevent fluid loss. Refer to **FIG 10:5** which shows the components of both the front and rear wheel cylinders.

To remove a rear wheel cylinder, detach the handbrake operating lever 28 and the dust cover 1, retaining spring 2, securing plate 3 and spring clip 4, noting the arrangement of these components to ensure correct refitting.

To remove a front wheel cylinder, remove the attaching nuts 35 and lockwashers 34.

Remove the internal components from the cylinder housing and unscrew the bleeder screw, collecting the steel ball from behind the screw. Discard the rubber cups, seals and covers and thoroughly clean the remaining parts in the correct grade of brake fluid. Inspect the piston and cylinder bore for scoring or corrosion and renew any unserviceable component.

Dip the internal parts in brake fluid and reassemble the cylinder, using the fingers to insert the new rubber cups and to fit the new rubber seals to avoid damaging the edges. Install the wheel cylinder onto the brake backing plate and connect the brake pipe or hose. Fit a new dust cover 1 to rear brake assemblies if the original cover is worn or perished. Refit the shoes, drum and road wheel, then bleed the brakes as described in **Section 10:5**.

10:4 Disc brakes

The disc brake friction pads should be checked for wear every time the brakes are serviced. The brake pads should be renewed if the total thickness of lining and backing is less than .32 inch (8 mm) for front brakes or .28 inch (7 mm) for rear brakes. New pads are .60 inch (15 mm) thick. If only one brake pad is worn to the limit, all four brake pads must be renewed at the front or rear, whichever is the case. Never change the pads over in a caliper or interchange pads between calipers.

Renewing friction pads:

FIG 10:6 shows the components of the Dunlop front brake caliper, **FIG 10:7** those of the ATE caliper.

Raise the car and support it on floor stands under the front body members, then remove the front wheels. Using a suitable drift, drive out the upper retaining pin from the caliper. Remove the retaining spring and drive out the lower retaining pin. Mark the brake pads to ensure correct refitting and withdraw them with tool A.2.0150. Before fitting new pads, clean the face of each piston and ensure that the recesses for the pads in the caliper are free from dirt or rust. Press the pistons into their bores with special pliers A.2.0147 as shown in **FIG 10:8**, noting that it may be necessary to syphon some fluid from the brake supply tank to prevent overflowing when this is done. Check the positions of the pistons in the caliper bores with the special tool available for this purpose, turning the pistons until the cut-out is in line with the inclined face of the tool as shown in **FIG 10 : 9**. The new brake pads should slide easily into the caliper. If a pad should stick, use a fine file to smooth the sides of the brake pad backing plate. The upper edge of the pad should not protrude beyond the outer edge of the brake disc. If necessary, remove excess material with a file. Use new retaining pins and springs. Insert one retaining pin and fit the spring under the pin. Press on the spring and insert the second pin, finally driving both pins fully home.

Removing and dismantling a caliper:

1 Jack up the car and remove the road wheel. Remove the friction pads as described in the previous section and disconnect the flexible hose from the caliper, using a plug to prevent fluid loss. With the caliper in a cool condition, remove the caliper attaching bolts and lift the caliper from the brake disc. If more than one caliper is removed at the same time, mark them for correct refitting.

2 Clamp the caliper assembly in a vice and remove the dust cover, using pliers as shown in **FIG 10 : 10**. Fit a piece of wood about $\frac{3}{8}$ inch (10 mm) thick into the caliper in the brake pad position to protect the pistons as they are ejected with compressed air. Remove the bleeder screw and apply a low-pressure compressed air nozzle at the bleeder screw opening to blow out the pistons.

3 Remove the retaining rings and rubber seals from the cylinder grooves, using a pointed instrument as shown in **FIG 10 : 11**. Check all parts including the bores in the caliper halves for rust or score marks. Slight rust spots can be removed from the pistons with fine steel wool, but if the piston is scored or badly rusted it must be renewed. If the caliper bores are scored the complete caliper assembly should be renewed. Always fit new seals, dust covers, retaining rings, springs and retaining pins, these parts being obtainable in the form of a repair kit.

Reassembling the caliper:

1 Thoroughly clean all internal parts with brake fluid and coat all parts with brake fluid during reassembly. Use the fingers to insert the rubber fluid seals into position to avoid damage to their edges. Slide the pistons into their bores.

2 Fit the rubber seals into the cylinder grooves and smear the inside of the dust cover with brake cylinder paste. Fit the dust cover and retainer and check that they are seated correctly. Check the positions of the pistons in the caliper bores, using the special tool as instructed previously.

3 Refit the caliper assembly to the car, tightening the mounting bolts to the specified torque. Attach the brake hose and refit the friction pad assemblies, bleeding the brakes upon completion as described in **Section 10 : 5**. Top-up the fluid supply tank.

Removing and refitting a brake disc:

Remove the road wheel and the caliper attaching bolts. Remove the caliper and wire it to the suspension to avoid straining the brake hose, then remove the hub and disc assembly. Check the disc for runout, which should not exceed .008 inch (.20 mm). The disc can be reground in order to true it but, if it should be necessary to remove

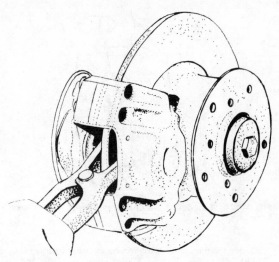

FIG 10 : 8   Pressing the pistons into the caliper bores

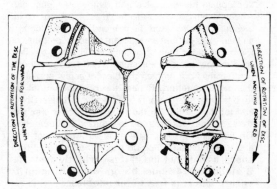

FIG 10 : 9   Checking the angle of the cutout in the pistons

more than .02 inch (.50 mm) from each side of the disc to achieve maximum runout measurement stated, the disc must be renewed.

Refit the disc, tightening the attaching bolts diagonally and evenly to the specified torque. Check the wheel bearings and repack them with grease. After refitting the hub, check the wheel bearing adjustment as described in **Chapter 8, Section 8 : 2**. Ensure that the mounting faces of the caliper and steering swivel are free from dirt and burrs then refit the caliper, tightening the attaching bolts to the specified torque.

10 : 5   Bleeding the system

This is not routine maintenance and is only necessary if air has entered the system due to parts being dismantled or because the fluid level in the master cylinder supply tank has dropped too low. The need for bleeding is indicated by a spongy feeling of the brake pedal accompanied by poor braking performance. Do not bleed the brakes with any drum or caliper removed. Always bleed the brake furthest from the master cylinder first, finishing with the brake nearest the master cylinder (refer to **Section 10 : 10** for tandem systems).

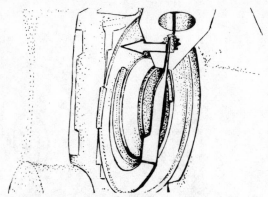

FIG 10:10 Removing the dust shield from the caliper bore

1 Check the fluid level in the master cylinder supply tank and refill if necessary, bringing the level up to the MAX mark on the tank. Clean all dirt from around the appropriate bleeder valve and remove the dust cap.

2 Attach a length of rubber or plastic tubing to the bleeder screw and lead the free end of the tubing into a clean glass jar. Get an assistant to apply pressure on the brake pedal, then open the bleeder screw to allow fluid to flow out of the system. When the brake pedal reaches the floor, tighten the bleeder screw and allow the pedal to return. Repeat the operation until the fluid flowing into the jar is free from air bubbles. Check and top-up the fluid in the supply tank to ensure that the level does not drop too low during this operation.

3 On completion, top-up the fluid to the correct level and repeat the operation on each other wheel in turn. **Discard all dirty fluid. If it is perfectly clean, let it stand for 24 hours before using it again to ensure that it is free of air bubbles.**

10:6 The master cylinder

The components of the master cylinder are shown in **FIG 10:5**. The pushrod from the brake pedal operates directly on the master cylinder piston to push it down the cylinder bore. This pressurizes the fluid which passes through the outlets into the brake lines connected to the wheel cylinders or calipers. When the piston returns fully the compensating port is opened allowing fluid from the supply tank to replace any lost in the pipes and cylinders.

Removal:

Disconnect the brake line from the connection on the master cylinder and plug the pipe to prevent the entry of dirt. Tape the master cylinder connection to prevent fluid from draining from the supply tank. Remove the two securing bolts and the clevis pin connector and lift out the master cylinder.

Dismantling:

Drain the brake fluid from the supply tank. Unscrew the clevis pin fork and its locknut and remove the retaining rings and rubber boot. Using a suitable tool, carefully remove the circlip 21 and withdraw and separate the internal parts.

Thoroughly clean the internal parts with brake fluid and inspect them for wear or damage, renewing any part found to be unserviceable. Check the surface of the piston and the bore of the cylinder and renew either component if there are signs of scoring or corrosion. Always fit new rubber cups and seals.

Reassembling:

Reassemble the master cylinder in the reverse order of dismantling, coating all internal parts with brake fluid and assembling them wet with the fluid.

Refitting:

Fit the master cylinder assembly to the car in the reverse order of removal. **There must be a minimum clearance of .04 inch (1 mm) between the piston and pushrod to prevent the rubber cup from obstructing the brake supply tank feed port.** With the brake pedal in the rest position, adjust for this minimum free play by means of the clevis fork adjusting nut. On completion, refill the supply tank with the correct grade of brake fluid and bleed the system as described in **Section 10:5**.

10:7 Vacuum servo unit

The vacuum servo unit operates in conjunction with the master cylinder and assists the pressure on the fluid applied at the brake pedal. The vacuum cylinder in the servo is connected to the engine intake manifold by a hose which incorporates a vacuum control valve. The control valve and servo air filter can be renewed if either is defective, but a faulty vacuum servo unit must be renewed as an assembly. To test the operation of the vacuum servo mechanism, switch off the engine and depress the brake pedal several times to clear all the

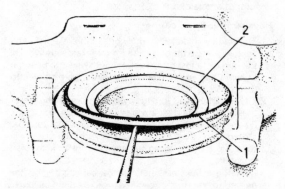

FIG 10:11 Removing the rubber seal 1 and the retaining ring 2 from the caliper bore

vacuum from the unit. Hold a steady light pressure on the brake pedal and start the engine. If the servo is working correctly, the brake pedal should move further downward without further foot pressure, due to the build up of vacuum in the unit. Failure of the servo unit does not impair the effeciency of the braking system, but greater pedal pressure will be needed to stop the car.

10:8 The handbrake

Normally, cars equipped with disc rear brakes should need no handbrake cable adjustment as the preset running clearance is maintained automatically. On cars equipped with drum rear brakes, adjustment of the rear brake shoes will automatically take up excessive handbrake free movement. If not, check the rear brake shoes and renew them if they are badly worn. If the handbrake is slack due to cable stretching or if it has been refitted after a

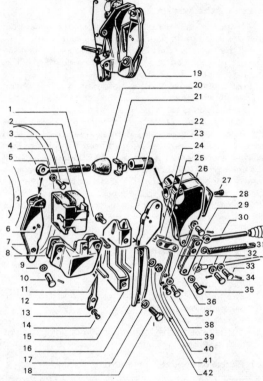

FIG 10:12 Components of the disc handbrake mechanism

Key to Fig 10:12   1 Mounting bolt   2 Pullrod
3 Brake pad   4 Mounting bolt   5 Washer   6 Pin
7 Operating lever   8 Brake pad carrier   9 Washer
10 Pivot pin   11 Guide   12 Return lever   13 Washer
14 Mounting bolt   15 Mounting frame   16 Bracket
17 Spring washer   18 Mounting bolt   19 Brake caliper
20 Dust cover   21 Spring clip   22 Bush
23 Operating lever   24/25 Operating links
26 Operating lever   27 Screw   28 Cover   29 Clevis pin
30 Pushrod   31 Return spring   32 Washer
33 Mounting bolt   34/35 Clevis pins
36 Handbrake operating lever   37 Clevis pin   38 Bolt
39 Washer   40 Return lever   41 Nut   42 Spring washer

servicing operation, act on the handbrake cable adjuster beneath the car. The cable is correctly adjusted when the rear wheels can be locked with the handbrake moved through half its total travel. On cars equipped with drum rear brakes, always check the adjustment of the rear brake shoes as described in **Section 10:2** before making a handbrake cable adjustment.

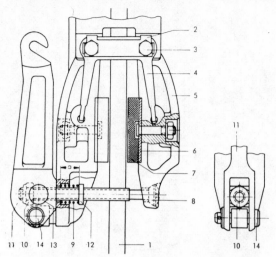

FIG 10:13 Section through a Dunlop handbrake assembly

Key to Fig 10:13   1 Brake disc   2 Lockplate
3 Mounting bolt   4 Centring spring   5 Brake pad carrier
6 Mounting bracket   7 Brake pad   8 Adjusting bolt
9 Spring   10 Self-locking nut   11 Operating lever
12 Spring seat   13 Pin   14 Pivot pin

Disc handbrake assembly:

The mechanical handbrake units are secured to the rear caliper assemblies by pivot bolts. **FIG 10:12** shows the components of a typical rear brake assembly and the layout of the handbrake operating mechanism, **FIG 10:13** a section through the Dunlop handbrake assembly. Each handbrake unit has two friction pad carriers, one on each side of the brake disc. When the handbrake is applied the friction pads are brought into contact with the brake disc by means of a pivoting operating lever, a return spring returning them to the rest position when the handbrake is released.

Renewing handbrake friction pads:

With the rear brake calipers removed, slacken the nuts in the outer face of each carrier and remove the worn pads with the aid of a hooked tool. Fit the new pads with the short side upwards, making sure that each pad is correctly located on the head of the retaining bolt. Refit the carriers to the caliper without fully tightening the pivot bolts. Operate the handbrake to allow the self-adjusting mechanism to take up any play. Finally, apply the handbrake firmly and tighten the pivot bolts, securing them with the tabwashers.

Disc/drum type:

Some later models, which have disc brakes on all four wheels, have a modified handbrake arrangement. This consists of a brake drum machined into the disc casting and includes a conventional type of expanding shoe mechanism for the handbrake, while the footbrake operates the calipers whose pads act on the disc which is in fact the rim of the drum/disc casting.

Servicing for these assemblies is similar to the procedures already described.

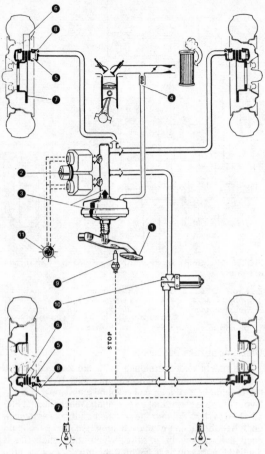

FIG 10:14   Layout of tandem brake system

Key to Fig 10:14   1 Brake pedal   2 Fluid reservoirs (with minimum level senders)   3 Vacuum servo and master cylinder   4 Vacuum port   5 Brake pistons   6 Brake pads   7 Brake discs   8 Air bleed screws   9 Stop light switch   10 Pressure regulating valve   11 Warning light for minimum level of fluid

10:9   Pressure regulator

This device is inserted in the hydraulic pressure line to the rear brake to regulate the pressure and provide a balanced braking action. It ensures that under heavy braking a greater proportion of the effort is applied to the front wheels and so prevents the rear brakes from locking the wheels under these conditions.

There is an adjusting nut on the valve, but this is sealed at the factory and should **not** be disturbed.

10:10   Tandem braking system

On later models of these cars, a dual braking system is fitted in which there are two separate hydraulic circuits as shown in **FIG 10:14**.

A tandem master cylinder is used in which there are two pistons, each with its own hydraulic fluid reservoir, of which one serves the two front brakes and the other the two rear brakes. Servo assistance is available on both circuits.

This system ensures that even in the event of a complete failure in one braking circuit a balanced brake application is still available on two wheels.

A further safety device takes the form of a warning lamp, located on the instrument panel, which will alert the driver if the level of the fluid in either reservoir falls below a minimum. On some models this lamp serves a dual function, doubling as a low engine oil pressure warning on the 1750 Berlina and a handbrake warning on 2000 Berlina and GTV versions.

Bleeding the system:

This operation is performed in a different manner from that described in **Section 10:5** and is as follows:

Fill the two reservoirs and take care to ensure that the level is not allowed to fall below three-quarters full as the fluid is used during the operation.

Push rubber pipes over the bleed nipples of a front and rear wheel on the same side of the car and lead the free ends into clean glass jars containing a supply of fluid.

Loosen the two bleed screws together and slowly press the brake pedal down and allow it to return of its own accord. At first the fluid expelled from the rubber pipes will be accompanied by air bubbles. Continue to work the brake pedal until both pipes discharge fluid completely free of bubbles then hold the pedal down, tighten the bleed screws and remove the pipes.

Repeat the procedure for the two wheels on the other side of the car.

10:11   Fault diagnosis

(a)   'Spongy' pedal

1 Leak in the system
2 Worn master cylinder
3 Leaking wheel cylinders
4 Air in the fluid system
5 Gaps between shoes and underside of linings (drum brake systems)

(b)   Excessive pedal movement

1 Check 1 and 4 in (a)
2 Excessive lining or pad wear
3 Very low fluid level in supply tank
4 Too much free movement of pedal

(c)   Brakes grab or pull to one side

1 Distorted discs or drums
2 Wet or oily pads or linings
3 Loose backplate or caliper
4 Disc loose on hub
5 Worn suspension or steering connections
6 Mixed linings of different grades
7 Uneven tyre pressures
8 Broken shoe return springs
9 Seized piston in wheel or caliper cylinder
10 Seized handbrake cable
11 Blocked flexible or rigid fluid pipe

(d)   Absence of servo assistance

1 Servo air cleaner blocked
2 Vacuum pipe blocked or broken
3 Check valve leaking
4 Servo unit inoperative due to internal fault

CHAPTER 11

THE ELECTRICAL SYSTEM

11:1 Description

All models covered by this manual are equipped with 12-volt electrical systems in which the negative terminal of the battery is earthed. The charging circuit is provided with regulating devices which may be adjusted if necessary, though it must be stressed that accurate meters are required when checking or altering their settings.

There are wiring diagrams in **Technical Data** at the end of this manual which will enable those with electrical experience to trace and correct faults.

Instructions for servicing the electrical equipment are given in this chapter, but it must be pointed out that it is not sensible to try to repair units which are seriously defective, electrically or mechanically. Such equipment should be replaced by new units which can be obtained on an exchange basis.

11:2 The battery

To maintain the performance of the battery it is essential to carry out the following operations, particularly in winter when heavy current demands must be met.

Keep the top and surrounding parts of the battery dry and clean as dampness can cause current leakage. Clean off corrosion from the metal parts of the battery mounting with diluted ammonia and paint them with anti-sulphuric paint. Clean the terminal posts and the cable clamps and smear them with petroleum jelly after remaking the connections and tightening the terminal clamps securely. High electrical resistance due to corrosion at the battery terminals can be responsible for a lack of sufficient current to operate the starter motor.

Test the condition of the cells with a hydrometer after topping up the electrolyte level with distilled water to just above the separators. **Never add neat acid. If it is necessary to prepare new electrolyte due to loss or spillage, add sulphuric acid to distilled water. It is highly dangerous to add water to acid.**

The indications from the readings of the specific gravity are as follows:

For climates below 27°C or 80°F

Cell fully charged	Specific gravity 1.270 to 1.290
Cell half discharged	Specific gravity 1.190 to 1.210
Cell discharged	Specific gravity 1.110 to 1.130

For climates above 27°C or 80°F

Cell fully charged	Specific gravity 1.210 to 1.230
Cell half discharged	Specific gravity 1.130 to 1.150
Cell discharged	Specific gravity 1.050 to 1.070

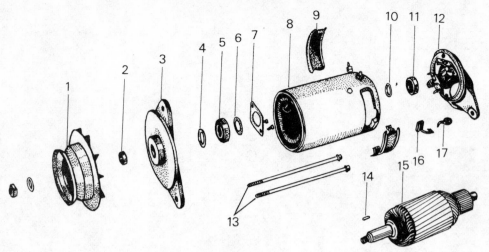

FIG 11:1   The generator components

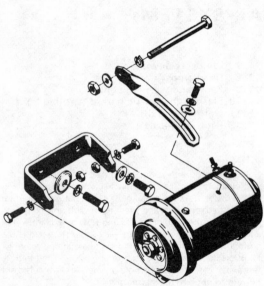

FIG 11:2   Generator mounting details

These figures assume an electrolyte temperature of 60°F or 16°C. If the temperature of the electrolyte exceeds this, add .002 to the readings for each 5°F or 3°C rise. Subtract .002 for any corresponding drop below 60°F or 16°C.

All of the cells should read approximately the same. If one differs radically from the others it may be due to an internal fault or to spillage or leakage of the electrolyte.

If the battery is in a low state of charge, take the car for a long daylight run or put the battery on a charger at 5 amps with the vent plugs removed until it gasses freely. Do not use a naked light near the battery as the gas is inflammable. If the battery is to stand unused for long periods, give a refreshing charge every month. It will be ruined if it is left uncharged.

11:3 The generator

The components of the generator are shown in **FIG 11:1**.

Testing when the generator is not charging:

1 Refer to **Chapter 4, Section 4:4** and check that a loose drive belt is not the cause of the trouble.
2 Switch off all the lights and accessories. Start the engine and connect an ammeter in series with the battery and control box by disconnecting the red lead from the B + control box terminal, then connecting the ammeter between the terminal and the red wire. Raise the engine speed and check the ammeter reading. The output should be 20 amps minimum at 2500 rev/min.
3 If the generator is in order, check the continuity of the cables to the control box. If they are in order, remove the ammeter and reconnect the cable, then test the control box as described in **Section 11:6**.

Removing the generator:

FIG 11:2 shows the generator and its mounting and adjusting bracket components. Remove the fan belt as described in **Chapter 4, Section 4:4** then disconnect the battery. Disconnect the wires from the generator. Remove the adjuster bolt and washers and the two pivot bolts, nuts and washers then lift out the generator.

Dismantling the generator:

Refer to **FIG 11:1**. Remove the brush cover bands 9. Loosen the screw securing the connecting lead to the commutator end bracket and remove the through-bolts and end bracket from the housing. Remove the pulley securing nut and withdraw the pulley from the shaft, using a suitable puller. Remove the key 14 from the shaft and pull off the drive end bracket. Remove the bearing retainer plate and press the bearing from the drive end bracket.

Servicing the brushgear:

Lift the brushes up in their holders and secure them by positioning each spring at the side of its brush. Fit the commutator end bracket over the commutator and release the brushes. Hold back each spring in turn and move the brushes by pulling gently on their flexible connectors. If a brush moves sluggishly or sticks in its holder, remove it and ease the sides against a smooth file. Refit in its original position. Renew and bed to the commutator any brush which is less than the permissible minimum of .47 inch in length. Renew any brush spring which gives a spring balance reading of less than 16 oz.

Servicing the commutator:

A commutator in good condition will be smooth and free from pitting and burned segments. Clean with a cloth and petrol and, if necessary, polish with fine glasspaper. **Do not use emerycloth.** Skim a badly worn commutator in a lathe, using a high speed and taking a light cut with a sharp tool. Remove the minimum amount necessary to clean up, then polish with fine glasspaper. Undercut the insulation between the segments to a depth of .002 inch using a special saw or a hacksaw blade ground to the thickness of the insulation.

The armature:

In the absence of armature testing facilities, the only check for faults which an owner can make is to substitute one which is known to be serviceable. Alternatively, have the armature tested for open circuits or internal earthing at a service station, fitting a new component if faults are indicated.

Field coils:

When testing with an ohmmeter, the reading should be between 3.5 and 3.85 ohms. If the reading is less than 3.5 ohms the field coils must be renewed by a service station.

Renewing bearings:

It is most unlikely that noticeable bearing wear will occur during the life of the generator. However, if bearing wear is encountered, the bearings in the commutator end bracket and drive end bracket should be renewed.

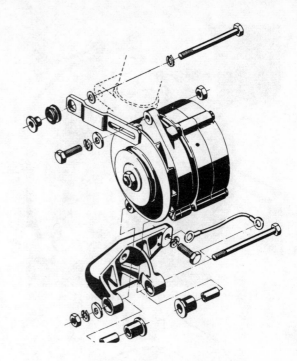

FIG 11:3   Alternator mounting details

Reassembling and refitting the generator:

This is the reverse of the dismantling procedure. If new brushes have been fitted, place a strip of fine glasspaper round the commutator and grind them in until they make good contact on their bearing faces. Reconnect the lead to the commutator end bracket and refit the brush cover bands. Adjust the fan belt tension as described in **Chapter 4, Section 4:4.**

11:4 The alternator

FIG 11:3 shows the mounting and adjustment bracket components of a typical Bosch alternator installation.

FIG 11:4   The alternator components

Key to Fig 11:4   1 Pulley   2 Cooling fan   3 Spacer   4 Drive end bracket   5 Bearing   6 Retaining plate   7 Spacer   8 Securing ring   9 Rotor   10 Slip rings   11 Stator   12 Brush holder   13 Bearing   14 Shim   15 Negative diodes   16 Rear end bracket   17 Field diodes   18 Positive diodes

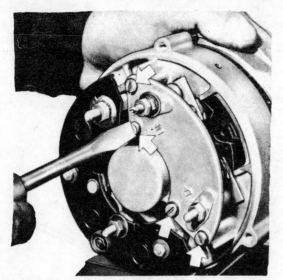

FIG 11:5 Removing the diode cover and brush holder

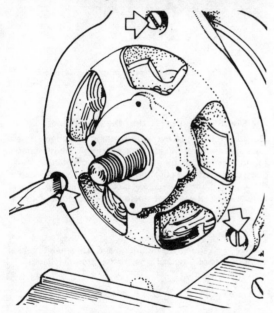

FIG 11:6 Removing the drive end bracket

Testing when the alternator is not charging:

Refer to the previous section for testing a generator and carry out instructions 1, 2 and 3. The ammeter reading when testing an alternator should be 30 amps minimum at 2500 rev/min.

Removing the alternator:

Remove the fan belt as described in **Chapter 4, Section 4:4** then disconnect the battery. Disconnect the wires from the alternator. Remove the securing bolts and lift out the alternator.

Dismantling the alternator:

Refer to **FIG 11:4.** Unscrew the retaining nut and remove the pulley and fan from the rotor shaft. Remove the diode cover and brush holder as shown in **FIG 11:5.** Mark the drive end bracket, stator and rear end bracket to ensure correct reassembly, then remove the drive end bracket as shown in **FIG 11:6** together with the rotor assembly. Use a puller to remove the drive end bracket from the rotor shaft as shown in **FIG 11:7.**

From the rear of the alternator dismantle the diode holders into the order shown in **FIG 11:8.** Unscrew the bearing retainer from the drive end bracket as shown in **FIG 11:9** and remove the ballbearing from the bracket. Use a suitable puller to remove the rear bearing from the rotor shaft.

Servicing the alternator:

Brushgear:

Check the brushes and renew them if they are worn to a length of $\frac{3}{8}$ inch or less. Unsolder the connecting wire and remove the old brush. When soldering the connecting wire to attach a new brush, hold the wire to the work with a pair of flat-nosed pliers to prevent the solder from flowing down the wire strands, otherwise the wire will become rigid and the brush unserviceable. Check that the brushes move freely in their holders. If a brush binds or sticks, remove it and ease the sides against a smooth file.

Slip rings:

The faces of the slip rings must be in a clean and polished condition. Clean them with fine sandpaper and polish them. To avoid causing flat surfaces on the slip rings this operation is best carried out while spinning the rotor assembly in a lathe.

Rotor:

Test the rotor windings and slip rings electrically, using a test lamp or ohmmeter as shown in **FIG 11:10.** A test

FIG 11:7 Removing the drive end bracket from the rotor shaft

lamp should not light up; an ohmmeter should indicate near infinite resistance. Test the rotor windings for short-circuits by connecting the ohmmeter between the two slip rings as shown in **FIG 11:11**. The reading obtained should be between 4.0 and 4.4 ohms. If any test is failed, the rotor and slip rings assembly is faulty and must be renewed.

Stator:

Test the stator windings for earthing by connecting a test lamp or an ohmmeter in the manner shown in **FIG 11:12**. A test lamp should not light up; an ohmmeter should indicate near infinite resistance. Check the stator windings for shortcircuits, using a low-reading ohmmeter as shown in **FIG 11:13**. Check two phases at a time, connecting the ohmmeter between the wire ends alternately. The readings should be between .26 and .29 ohms. If any test is failed, the stator assembly is faulty and must be renewed.

Diodes:

If the alternator current output is low, one or more of the diodes may be defective. **FIG 11:14** shows the diode configuration in the alternator charging circuit, while **FIG 11:15** shows the current flow through diodes of both positive and negative types. Carefully disconnect each diode before testing it, otherwise it will not be possible to determine which diode, if any, is at fault. Use a 12-volt test lamp and current supply. Connect the test lamp between the diode connection and housing, then reverse the connections. The test lamp should light brightly in one direction, but should not light at all in the other direction. Diodes in each set of three should pass and block current in the same direction as others in the set. Any diode that fails the tests should be renewed by a service station, using special press equipment.

Reassembling and refitting the alternator:

This is a reversal of the removal procedure, noting the following points. Reconnect any diodes that were disconnected during servicing, using a very hot soldering iron and working quickly to avoid damaging the diodes, which are very sensitive to heat. Lubricate both alternator bearings with high melting point grease. On completion, adjust the fan belt tension as described in **Chapter 4, Section 4:4**.

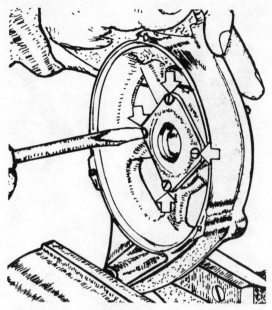

FIG 11:9 Removing the bearing retainer from the drive end bracket

FIG 11:10 Testing the rotor windings and slip rings

11:5 The starter

The Bosch starter is a brush type series wound motor equipped with an overrunning clutch and operated by a solenoid. The armature shaft is supported in sintered bronze bushes which are factory packed with lubricant and require no servicing between overhauls. **FIG 11:16** shows the starter components. When the starter is operated from the switch, the engagement lever moves the pinion into mesh with the flywheel ring gear. When the pinion meshes with the ring gear teeth, the solenoid

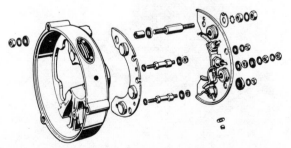

FIG 11:8 The diode support assemblies

FIG 11:11   Testing the rotor for shortcircuits

Tests for a starter which does not operate

Check that the battery is in good condition and fully charged and that its connections are clean and tight. Switch on the headlights and operate the starter switch. Current is reaching the starter if the lights go dim, in which case it will be necessary to remove the starter for servicing. If the lights do not go dim, check the switch and the starter cables. Check the brushes by the method described later, it not being necessary to remove the starter to do this. If the switch, cables and brushes are in order, the starter must be removed and serviced.

Removing the starter:

Disconnect the battery, the main starter lead and the control wire. Remove the starter mounting bolts and lift out the starter.

Servicing the brushgear:

Remove the brush cover from the starter and detach the brushgear, marking the position of the brushes for correct reassembly. Renew any brush which is worn to less than $\frac{1}{2}$ inch in length. If a brush binds or sticks in its holder, remove it and ease the sides against a smooth file. When fitting new brushes, hold the connecting wire close to the work with a pair of flat-nosed pliers to prevent solder from flowing down the wire strands, otherwise the wire will become rigid and the brush unserviceable.

Dismantling the starter:

Remove the brushgear as previously described. Remove the screws attaching the small cover at the end of the shaft and detach the cover. Remove the lockwasher and shim from the shaft and remove the two through-bolts. Detach the commutator end bracket then remove the brush holder plate, collecting the shims between the plate and the commutator.

FIG 11:12   Testing the stator windings for earthing

contact disc closes the circuit and the starter motor operates to turn the engine over. When the engine starts, the speed of the flywheel causes the pinion to overrun the starter clutch and armature. The pinion continues to be engaged in the ring gear teeth until the engagement lever is released, when it returns under spring action.

FIG 11:13   Testing the stator windings for shortcircuits

Detach the starter solenoid by removing the two screws shown in **FIG 11:17**. Remove the rubber and metal plate from the drive end bracket as shown in **FIG 11:18**. Remove the engagement lever pivot pin, engagement lever and the armature from the drive end bracket. Drive back the retaining ring on the armature shaft and remove the circlip, then pull off the retaining ring, overrunning clutch and pinion assembly.

Servicing the starter:

The commutator:

Clean the commutator with a cloth and petrol and, if necessary, polish with fine glasspaper. **Do not use emerycloth.** Skim a badly worn commutator in a lathe, using a high speed and taking a light cut with a sharp tool, noting that the minimum diameter for starter motor commutators is 1.25 inches. If cleaning up would remove enough metal to reduce the diameter below this figure the armature must be renewed. Undercut the insulation between the segments to a depth of .002 inch using a special saw or a hacksaw blade ground to the thickness of the insulation.

The armature:

A damaged armature should always be renewed. No attempt should be made to straighten a bent shaft or to machine the core.

Testing the field coils:

Test the continuity with a 12-volt test lamp and current supply between the terminal post and each field brush in turn. Test for breakdown of the insulation by connecting a test lamp between the terminal post and the starter body. If the lamp lights, defective insulation is indicated. The renewal of field coils should be entrusted to a service station.

Starter bearings:

Press out the old bearing bushes if they are worn and renew them as follows. Allow the new bushes to stand fully immersed in engine oil for at least 30 minutes before pressing them into the starter brackets. Press them into position with a shouldered mandrel having a polished pilot of the same diameter as the armature shaft and slightly longer than the bushes.

Pinion and clutch assembly:

Do not clean the overrunning clutch with solvents as this would wash the grease from inside the clutch. Check the components for wear or damage and renew any found unserviceable. Coat the armature shaft splines and the contact areas for the engagement lever with high melting point grease.

Reassembling and refitting the starter:

These operations are the reverse of the dismantling and removal instructions.

11:6 The control box

The control box on cars equipped with alternators contains only a voltage regulator, the use of diodes in the alternator making a cut-out relay unnecessary. The alternator charging circuit is shown in **FIG 11:14**.

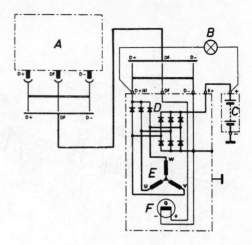

A = Regulator   D = Diodes

B = Charging Indicator   E = Stator

C = Battery   F = Rotor

FIG 11:14   The alternator charging circuit

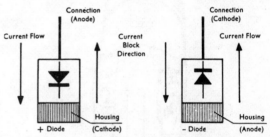

FIG 11:15   Current flow through positive and negative diodes

On cars equipped with generators the control box contains a voltage regulator and a cut-out relay, this type of circuit being shown in **FIG 11:19**.

Checking the charging circuit:

Do not disturb the control box settings until the generator or alternator has been checked as described in **Section 11:3** or **11:4**.

It must be stressed that the use of first grade electrical meters is essential to check and make any necessary adjustments to the control box. All checks and adjustments must be made as quickly as possible to avoid errors due to heating up of the control box operating coils. If the control box fails to respond correctly to any adjustment it should be examined at a service station.

Adjusting the voltage regulator:

1 Remove the red battery lead from the control box B + terminal. Connect the voltmeter positive lead to the B + terminal and the negative lead to earth on the base of the control box.

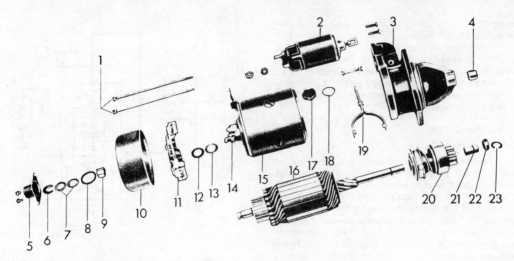

FIG 11:16   The starter components

Key to Fig 11:16   1 Through-bolts   2 Solenoid   3 Drive end bracket   4 Bush   5 End cap   6 Retainer
7 Shims   8 Rubber seal   9 Bush   10 Commutator end bracket   11 Negative brush plate   12 Fibre washer
13 Washer   14 Positive brushes on field coils   15 Starter motor housing   16 Armature   17 Rubber washer
18 Washer   19 Engagement lever   20 Pinion and clutch   21 Bush   22 Thrust washer   23 Retainer

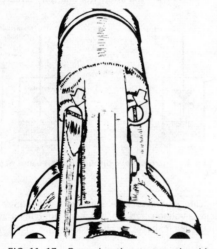

FIG 11:17   Removing the starter solenoid

2 Start the engine and slowly increase its speed while observing the voltmeter. The reading should be between 13.5 and 14.5 volts. If the reading is not within the specified range, remove the control box cover and adjust the voltage regulator armature spring to obtain a reading between the figures quoted. If the reading fluctuates, the contacts are dirty and must be cleaned as described later.

3 Replace the control box cover and recheck the setting.

Adjusting the cut-out relay (generator systems only):

1 Connect the voltmeter positive lead to the control box terminal 61 and the negative lead to earth. Connect an

ammeter in series with the B + terminal and disconnect the red wire.

2 Start the engine and increase the speed while observing the voltmeter. The voltage will increase until the cut-out relay points close, then drop slightly as the circuit is completed to the battery. The highest voltage reading just before it drops off is the closing voltage. This voltage should be between 12.3 and 13.4 volts. If the voltage as tested is not between these limits, remove the control box cover and adjust the closing voltage by bending the cut-out relay spring support. Increase the tension on the spring to increase the closing voltage, decrease tension to decrease the voltage.

3 Replace the control box cover and recheck the setting.

Cleaning contact points:

Clean the contact points in the voltage regulator and cut-out relay with fine glasspaper. Clean off all dust with methylated spirits.

11:7 Windscreen wipers

The wiper assembly consists of a permanent magnet type motor with a reduction gearbox driving the wiper arms through a connecting linkage. Apart from renewal of worn wiperblades the wiper assembly needs no routine maintenance.

Checking the wiper operation:

If the motor is completely inoperative, check the fuse and the connections at the fuse block and wiper switch. Disconnect the positive lead from the wiper motor terminal, turn on the ignition and wiper switches and use a voltmeter to check the voltage available to the motor, which should be 12-volts if the battery is fully charged. A further check can be made by connecting a temporary lead between the battery and the positive terminal of the

FIG 11:18 Removing the rubber and metal plate from the drive end bracket

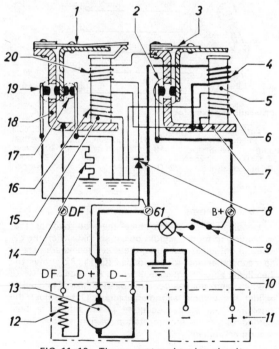

FIG 11:19 The generator charging circuit

Key to Fig 11:19

2 Cut-out relay points   1 Voltage regulator spring
                         3 Cut-out relay spring
4 Cut-out relay current coil   5 Iron core of cut-out relay
6 Cut-out relay voltage coil   7 Cut-out relay armature support
8 Variode   9 Ignition switch   10 Charging indicator lamp
11 Battery   12 Field coils   13 Generator armature
14 Resistor   15 Iron core of regulator
16 Regulator voltage coil   17 Regulator lower points
18 Regulator armature support   19 Regulator upper points
20 Regulator control coil

The following images were detected on the right column:

FIG 11:20 Components of a Bosch wiper motor

Key to Fig 11:20
                              1 Attaching screws
2 Transmission cover   3 Nut   4 Play pin (threaded end)
5 Gasket   6 Ball   7 Driven gear   8 Washer
9 Play pin (threaded end)   10 Sleeve   11 Mounting plate
12 Gasket   13 Toothed washers   14 Attaching screws
15 Transmission housing   16 Negative brush
17 Attaching screw   18 Retaining plate   19 Positive brush
20 Wire   21 Thrust spring   22 Rubber mounts
23 Armature   24 Attaching screws   25 Lockwasher
26 Angle brackets   27 Motor housing   28 Magnet ring
29 Magnet threaded pin locators   30 North pole paint
marking on this side

wiper motor. If the motor then runs the fault is in the wiring circuit or switch. If not, the motor must be removed for service.

If the wiper operation is sluggish, detach the linkage crank arm from the motor and operate the wipers by hand to check for binds in the linkage.

Removing the motor:

Detach the crank arm from the motor drive shaft, then disconnect the electrical connections and the wiper motor attaching nuts. Refit in the reverse order, making sure that the wiring is reconnected correctly.

Servicing the motor:

FIG 11:20 shows the components of the Bosch wiper motor, **FIG 11:21** the components of the Marelli wiper motor. Remove the transmission housing together with the armature from the motor housing and check that the brushes are free and that the brush springs function adequately. Renew the brushes if they are less than .24 inch in length. To remove a negative brush, remove the retaining screw from the commutator end frame. To remove a positive brush, the lead must be cut off at the brush holder. New positive brushes must be soldered into position, making sure that the solder does not run down the flexible lead as this would stiffen the lead and make the brush unserviceable. Clean the commutator with a cloth and petrol and polish with fine glasspaper. Lightly oil the armature shaft and lubricate the transmission with the correct grade of grease.

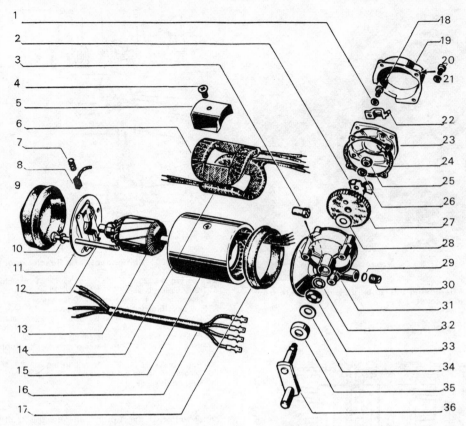

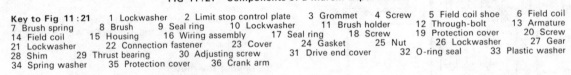

FIG 11:21   Components of a Marelli wiper motor

Key to Fig 11:21   1 Lockwasher   2 Limit stop control plate   3 Grommet   4 Screw   5 Field coil shoe   6 Field coil
7 Brush spring   8 Brush   9 Seal ring   10 Lockwasher   11 Brush holder   12 Through-bolt   13 Armature
14 Field coil   15 Housing   16 Wiring assembly   17 Seal ring   18 Screw   19 Protection cover   20 Screw
21 Lockwasher   22 Connection fastener   23 Cover   24 Gasket   25 Nut   26 Lockwasher   27 Gear
28 Shim   29 Thrust bearing   30 Adjusting screw   31 Drive end cover   32 O-ring seal   33 Plastic washer
34 Spring washer   35 Protection cover   36 Crank arm

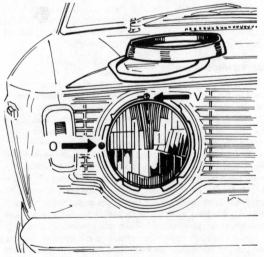

FIG 11:22   The headlamp beam setting screws

11:8 Headlamps

Headlamps, of which there may be two or four according to model, should be set so that, when the car is in an unloaded condition, the main beams are parallel to each other and to the road. **FIG 11:22** shows the headlamp adjustment screws which are accessible when the headlamp rim has been removed. Screw V is used to adjust the vertical alignment, screw O to adjust the horizontal alignment. Accurate beam setting is best carried out by a service station having special beam setting equipment.

11:9 Panel and warning lights

The removal of the instrument panel will give access for the replacement of instrument and warning lights. When working on electrical units in this manner, the battery should be disconnected to avoid the occurence of accidental shortcircuits.

11:10 Flasher and traffic hazard warning lights

Flasher unit:

The flasher unit, in which a switch is operated by alternate heating and cooling of an actuating wire, is housed in a small cylindrical container behind the dashboard. A small relay to flash the pilot light is incorporated.

In case of trouble check the bulbs and main fuses. If one bulb is defective, the other bulb and the pilot light will flash at twice the normal speed, which will indicate this fault. If the flasher unit is defective it must be renewed. Mark the connections before removing the old unit to ensure that the new unit is correctly wired.

Traffic hazard warning system:

This system, when fitted, operates in conjunction with flashing direction indicator lights. When the hazard warning light switch on the instrument panel is turned on, all four flasher lights operate simultaneously through the flasher unit. The system will operate with the ignition switched off so that, if necessary, the car can be locked up and the lights left flashing in the event of a breakdown. As the system is meant as a warning to other traffic of a stationary vehicle, the hazard warning should not be switched on when the car is moving.

11:11 Lighting circuits

Lamps give insufficient light:

Refer to **Section 11:2** and check the condition of the battery. Recharge if necessary. Check the setting of the headlights as described in **Section 11:8** and renew any bulbs that have darkened with age.

Bulbs burn out frequently:

Refer to **Section 11:6** and check the control box settings.

Lamps light when switched on but gradually fade:

Refer to **Section 11:2** and check the battery as it is not capable of supplying current for any length of time.

Lamp brilliance varies with the speed of the car:

Check the condition of the battery and its connections. Make sure they are tight and renew any faulty cables.

11:12 Fault diagnosis

(a) Battery discharged

1 Terminal connections loose or dirty
2 Shorts in lighting circuit
3 Generator or alternator not charging
4 Control box faulty
5 Battery internally defective

(b) Insufficient charging rate

1 Check 1 and 4 in (a)
2 Drive belt slipping

(c) Battery will not hold charge

1 Low electrolyte level
2 Battery plates sulphated
3 Electrolyte leakage from cracked case
4 Battery plate separators defective

(d) Battery overcharged

1 Control box needs adjusting

(e) Generator or alternator output low or nil

1 Belt broken or slipping
2 Control box out of adjustment
3 Worn bearings, loose polepieces
4 Commutator worn, burned or shorted
5 Armature shaft worn or bent
6 Insulation proud between segments
7 Brushes sticking, springs weak or broken
8 Field coil windings broken, shorted or burned
9 Alternator diode(s) defective

(f) Starter motor lacks power or will not turn

1 Battery discharged
2 Starter pinion jammed in flywheel ring gear
3 Starter switch or solenoid faulty
4 Brushes worn or sticking, leads detached or shorting
5 Commutator dirty or worn
6 Starter shaft bent
7 Engine abnormally stiff, perhaps due to rebore

(g) Starter runs but does not turn engine

1 Pinion engagement mechanism faulty
2 Broken teeth on pinion or flywheel gears

(h) Noisy starter pinion when engine is running

1 Pinion return mechanism faulty

(j) Starter motor inoperative

1 Check 1 and 4 in (f)
2 Armature or field coils faulty

(k) Starter motor rough or noisy

1 Mounting bolts loose
2 Damaged pinion or flywheel teeth
3 Pinion engagement mechanism faulty

(l) Lamps inoperative or erratic

1 Battery low, bulbs burned out
2 Faulty earthing or lamps or battery
3 Lighting switch faulty, loose or broken connections

(m) Wiper motor sluggish, taking high current

1 Faulty armature
2 Commutator dirty or shorting
3 Brushes worn or sticking, springs weak or broken
4 Lack of lubrication
5 Linkage worn or binding
6 Wiper motor fixing bolts loose
7 Motor transmission binding, no armature shaft end float

(n) Wiper motor runs but does not drive arms

1 Wiper linkage faulty
2 Transmission components worn

(o) Fuel, temperature or pressure gauges do not work

1 Check wiring for continuity
2 Check instruments and transmitters for continuity

NOTES

CHAPTER 12

THE BODYWORK

12:1 Bodywork finish

Large scale repairs to body panels are best left to expert panel beaters. Even small dents can be tricky, as too much hammering will stretch the metal and make things worse instead of better. Filling minor dents and scratches is probably the best method of restoring the surface. The touching-up of paintwork is well within the capabilities of most owners, particularly as self-spraying cans of paint in the correct colours are now readily available. A paint may change colour with age and it is better to spray a whole wing or panel rather than touch-up a small area.

Before spraying, remove all traces of wax polish with white spirit. More drastic treatment is required if silicone polishes have been applied. Use a primer surfacer or paste stopper according to the amount of filling required and, when it is dry, rub it down with 'Wet or Dry' paper, finishing with 400 grade until the surface is smooth and flush with the surrounding area. Spend time on getting the best finish possible at this stage, as it will control the final effect. Apply the retouching paint, keeping it wet in the centre and light and dry round the edges. After a few hours of drying, use a cutting compound to remove the dry spray at the edges of the work and to blend the new finish to the old. Finally, apply a good liquid polish and buff to a shine.

12:2 Removing door trim

A typical arrangment of door trim panels, fixing screws and cover mouldings can be seen in **FIG 12:1**, the components shown being those for the Giulia TI 1600 model. The side window and ventilator regulator handles or knobs must be removed, also the door release handle and any mouldings that retain the trim panels to the door. Remove the trim panel securing screws and detach the panel, collecting the cup washers from the panel screw holes. Refitting is the reverse of the removal procedure.

12:3 Door hinges and lock mechanisms

Hinges:

The removal and refitting of door hinges should be entrusted to an Alfa-Romeo main dealer, as the operation requires the door to be carefully aligned and the hinge welded into position. However, a door can be removed if required by unscrewing the upper and lower hinge pins. These are items 5 and 6 in **FIG 12:2**.

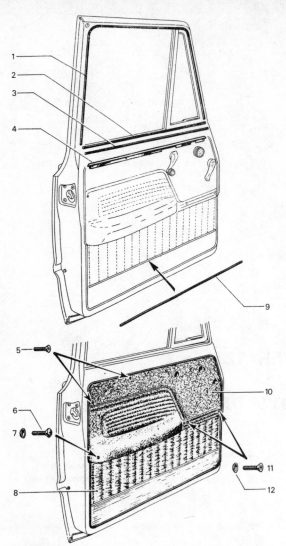

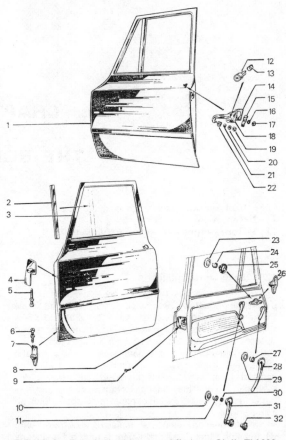

Removal:

Remove the door trim panel as described in **Section 12 : 2**. Refer to **FIG 12 : 3** and detach the window support bracket 23, then slide the door glass up and prop it in position. Remove the securing screws and lift out the mechanism.

Refitting:

Refitting is a reversal of the removal procedure.

Electric regulator mechanism:

FIG 12 : 4 shows a cable and pulley type of electric window winding mechanism as installed in Sprint and Spider models. **FIG 12 : 5** shows the installation of a gear and crank linkage type of mechanism on a Giulia GTC

FIG 12:1   Removing door trim panels. Giulia TI 1600 components shown

Key to Fig 12:1   1 Upper moulding   2 Weatherstrip
3 Sill moulding   4 Upper trim moulding   5/6 Screws
7 Cup washer   8 Trim panel   9 Lower panel moulding
10 Trim panel   11 Screw   12 Cup washer

Door locks:

Removal:

Remove the trim panel as described in **Section 12 : 2** and disconnect the door release lever remote control linkage from the door lock mechanism. Remove the outer door handle and the door lock assembly as shown in **FIG 12 : 2**. Refit in the reverse order, checking the operation of the lock before shutting the door.

12 : 4   Window winding mechanism

Manual regulator mechanism:

The window regulator handle is shown in **FIG 12 : 2** and a typical manual window winding mechanism in **FIG 12 : 3**.

FIG 12:2   Door locks, hinges and fittings. Giulia TI 1600 components shown

Key to Fig 12:2   1 Door   2 Glass channel   3 Door panel
4 Upper door hinge   5 Upper hinge pin
6 Lower hinge pin   7 Lower door hinge   8 Lockplate
9 Screw   10 Escutcheon   11 Spring   12 Door lock
13 Spring   14 Escutcheon   15 Handle attaching plate
16 Washer   17 Nut   18 Outer door handle   19 Nut
20 Washer   21 Spring washer   22 Escutcheon
23 Escutcheon   24 Spring   25 Knob   26 Wing   27 Spring
28 Inner door lever handle   29 Escutcheon   30 Bush
31 Window regulator handle   32 Knob

model. In the event of failure, check the main fuses, operating switches and wiring. If the fault lies in the motor or linkage, the remedial work should be entrusted to an Alfa-Romeo service station. If the unit is defective electrically, the window can be raised or lowered manually by, in the case of crank linkage mechanisms, removing the trim panel and carefully moving the linkage to the required position or, in the case of cable and pulley mechanisms, removing the trim panel and operating the emergency regulator handle shown as item 18 in **FIG 12:4**.

12:5 Bonnet and luggage compartment locks

FIG 12:6 shows a typical bonnet lock and cable release mechanism and a typical luggage compartment lock and cable release assembly is shown in **FIG 12:7**. The cable should have a small amount of free play when the lid it serves is closed, and the linkage and cable should be lubricated when necessary to ensure smooth operation.

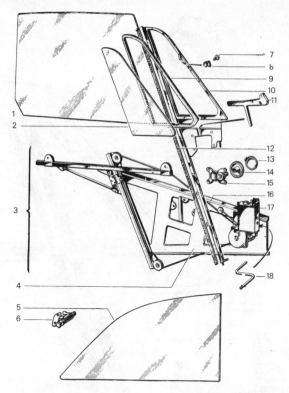

FIG 12:4 Door glasses and window regulating mechanisms, Sprint and Spider models

Key to Fig 12:4 1 Side window glass
2 Ventilator glass 3 Regulator motor assembly
4 Regulator mounting plate 5 Rear side window glass
6 Rear window catch 7 Screw 8 Hinge
9 Weatherstrip 10 Ventilator frame 11 Swivel bracket
12 Window guide channel 13 Plastic cover
14 Ventilator control knob 15 Ventilator control mechanism
16 Window regulator cable 17 Regulator motor unit
18 Emergency regulator handle for manual operation

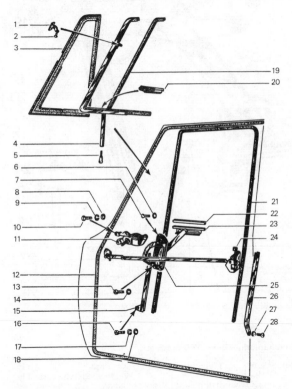

FIG 12:3 Window regulator mechanism and weatherstrip. Giulia TI 1600 components shown

Key to Fig 12:3 1 Ventilator bracket 2 Rivet
3 Ventilator weatherstrip 4 Ventilator frame
5 Attaching screw 6 Washer 7 Screw 8 Washer
9 Spring washer 10 Screw 11 Ventilator regulator assembly
12 Weatherstrip 13 Screw 14 Washer
15 Window guide channel 16 Screw 17 Spring washer
18 Washer 19 Weatherstrip 20 Gutter
21 Velvet window guide channel 22 Window support channel
23 Window support bracket 24 Inner door lock
25 Window regulator mechanism 26 Guide channel
27 Lockwasher 28 Screw

If servicing of a lock assembly or operating mechanism is required, the component in question should be removed and dismantled into the order shown in the appropriate figure and worn or damaged parts renewed as necessary. Do not shut the bonnet or luggage compartment lids when their operating cables are removed or disconnected.

12:6 Fitting windscreen and backlight glasses

To remove the original glass, lift the wiper arms clear and remove the interior mirror then remove the escutcheons and metal trim moulding for windscreen removal, remove the escutcheons and metal trim moulding for backlight removal.

Loosen the rubber channel from the body with the aid of a flat-bladed tool. Starting at one corner, gradually push the glass out until it is free.

Before fitting a new glass, clean the windshield or backlight aperture flange of all old sealing compound and make sure that there are no particles of broken glass in the rubber channels. Fit the rubber to the glass and then

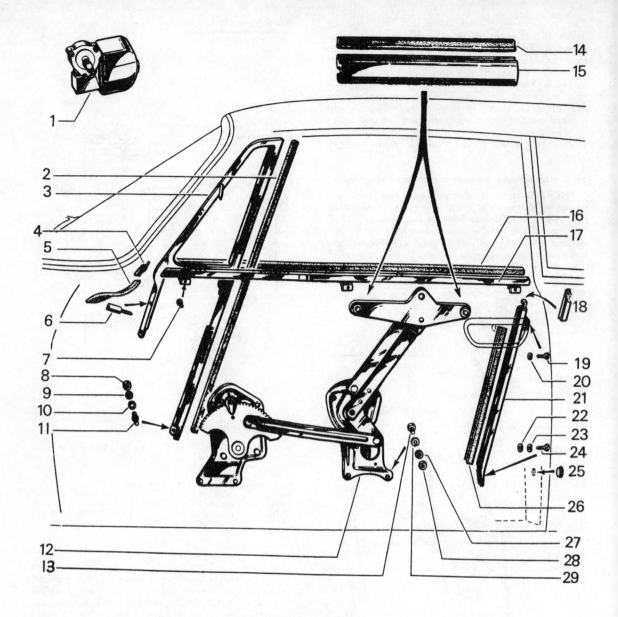

FIG 12:5 Window regulating mechanism, Giulia GTC models

Key to Fig 12:5   1 Window regulator motor unit   2 Weatherstrip   3 Ventilator frame   4 Gasket   5 Gasket
6 Screw   7 Drive screw   8 Nut   9 Lockwasher   10 Washer   11 Pin   12 Window regulator assembly
13 Screw   14 Weatherstrip   15 Window support channel   16 Velvet weatherstrip   17 Door moulding   18 Channel cap
19 Screw   20 Lockwasher   21 Sliding channel   22 Washer   23 Lockwasher   24 Screw   25 Plug   26 Weatherstrip
27 Washer   28 Nut   29 Lockwasher

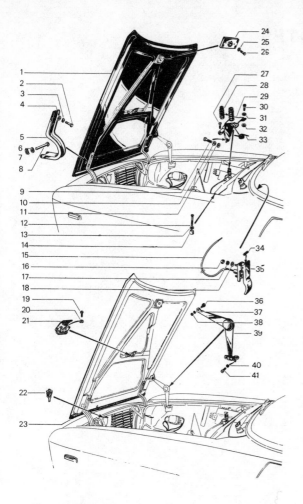

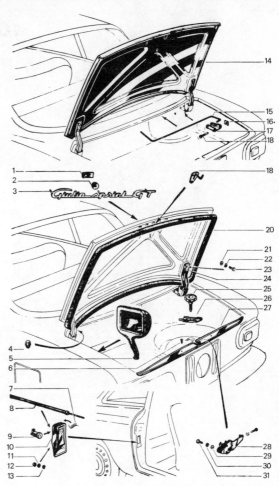

FIG 12:6 Bonnet hinges and locking and release mechanisms, Giulia GTC components shown

Key to Fig 12:6   1 Bonnet   2 Screw   3 Lockwasher
4 Washer   5 Bonnet hinge   6 Washer   7 Spring
8 Hinge pin   9 Screw   10 Lockwasher   11 Washer
12 Screw   13 Washer   14 Buffer   15 Bonnet release cable
16 Nut   17 Lockwasher   18 Washer   19 Screw
20 Lockwasher   21 Bulb holder   22 Light switch
23 Weatherstrip   24 Lock striker plate   25 Washer
26 Screw   27 Screw   28 Lock spring
29 Bonnet lock assembly   30 Screw   31 Washer
32 Lock spacer   33 Bonnet release spring
34 Release handle spring   35 Bonnet release handle assembly
36 Screw   37 Washer   38 Nut   39 Bonnet stay
40 Washer   41 Screw

FIG 12:7 Luggage compartment lid, hinges, lock and release mechanism. Spider 1600 components shown

Key to Fig 12:7   1 Securing plate   2 Seal   3 Emblem
4 Buffer   5 Tank filler funnel   6 Screw
7 Release lever return spring   8 Release cable
9 Release lever lock   10 Release lever assembly
11 Washer   12 Nut   13 Lockwasher
14 Luggage compartment lid   15 Torsion bar
16 Hinge pin spring   17 Hinge link   18 Hinge pin
19 Lid fastening hook   20 Weatherstrip   21 Washer
22 Lockwasher   23 Screw   24 Hinge
25 Spare wheel attaching screw   26 Plate
27 Carpet fixing plate   28 Lid catch plate   29 Washer
30 Lockwasher   31 Screw

fit a length of strong blind cord around the rubber channel into which the flange of the aperture fits. Cross the ends of the cord at the lower centre of the glass. Lubricate the rubber channel flange with a soap-and-water solution to facilitate fitting.

Place the glass and rubber channel onto the flange at the bottom of the aperture and centre it. Apply steady hand pressure to the glass while an assistant pulls out the

cord to lip the rubber channel over the flange in the aperture. Work equally on each side of the glass. **Do not fit one end then try to fit the other.** Use a pressure gun to inject sealing compound between the glass and the rubber and between the rubber and the flange. Remove excess compound with a rag and white spirit. Do not use thinners as this will damage the paintwork. Refit the metal trim moulding.

NOTES

APPENDIX

TECHNICAL DATA

Engine   Fuel system   Ignition system   Cooling system
Clutch   Transmission   Steering   Brakes
Electrical equipment   Capacities   Torque wrench settings
Wiring diagrams

HINTS ON MAINTENANCE AND OVERHAUL

GLOSSARY OF TERMS

INDEX

Inches		Decimals	Milli-metres	Inches to Millimetres		Millimetres to Inches	
				Inches	mm	mm	Inches
	1/64	.015625	.3969	.001	.0254	.01	.00039
	1/32	.03125	.7937	.002	.0508	.02	.00079
	3/64	.046875	1.1906	.003	.0762	.03	.00118
1/16		.0625	1.5875	.004	.1016	.04	.00157
	5/64	.078125	1.9844	.005	.1270	.05	.00197
3/32		.09375	2.3812	.006	.1524	.06	.00236
	7/64	.109375	2.7781	.007	.1778	.07	.00276
1/8		.125	3.1750	.008	.2032	.08	.00315
	9/64	.140625	3.5719	.009	.2286	.09	.00354
5/32		.15625	3.9687	.01	.254	.1	.00394
	11/64	.171875	4.3656	.02	.508	.2	.00787
3/16		.1875	4.7625	.03	.762	.3	.01181
	13/64	.203125	5·1594	.04	1.016	.4	.01575
7/32		.21875	5.5562	.05	1.270	.5	.01969
	15/64	.234375	5.9531	.06	1.524	.6	.02362
1/4		.25	6.3500	.07	1.778	.7	.02756
	17/64	.265625	6.7469	.08	2.032	.8	.03150
9/32		.28125	7.1437	.09	2.286	.9	.03543
	19/64	.296875	7.5406	.1	2.54	1	.03937
5/16		.3125	7.9375	.2	5.08	2	.07874
	21/64	.328125	8.3344	.3	7.62	3	.11811
11/32		.34375	8.7312	.4	10.16	4	.15748
	23/64	.359375	9.1281	.5	12.70	5	.19685
3/8		.375	9.5250	.6	15.24	6	.23622
	25/64	.390625	9.9219	.7	17.78	7	.27559
13/32		.40625	10.3187	.8	20.32	8	.31496
	27/64	.421875	10.7156	.9	22.86	9	.35433
7/16		.4375	11.1125	1	25.4	10	.39370
	29/64	.453125	11.5094	2	50.8	11	.43307
15/32		.46875	11.9062	3	76.2	12	.47244
	31/64	.484375	12.3031	4	101.6	13	.51181
1/2		.5	12.7000	5	127.0	14	.55118
	33/64	.515625	13.0969	6	152.4	15	.59055
17/32		.53125	13.4937	7	177.8	16	.62992
	35/64	.546875	13.8906	8	203.2	17	.66929
9/16		.5625	14.2875	9	228.6	18	.70866
	37/64	.578125	14.6844	10	254.0	19	.74803
19/32		.59375	15.0812	11	279.4	20	.78740
	39/64	.609375	15.4781	12	304.8	21	.82677
5/8		.625	15.8750	13	330.2	22	.86614
	41/64	.640625	16.2719	14	355.6	23	.90551
21/32		.65625	16.6687	15	381.0	24	.94488
	43/64	.671875	17.0656	16	406.4	25	.98425
11/16		.6875	17.4625	17	431.8	26	1.02362
	45/64	.703125	17.8594	18	457.2	27	1.06299
23/32		.71875	18.2562	19	482.6	28	1.10236
	47/64	.734375	18.6531	20	508.0	29	1.14173
3/4		.75	19.0500	21	533.4	30	1.18110
	49/64	.765625	19.4469	22	558.8	31	1.22047
25/32		.78125	19.8437	23	584.2	32	1.25984
	51/64	.796875	20.2406	24	609.6	33	1.29921
13/16		.8125	20.6375	25	635.0	34	1.33858
	53/64	.828125	21.0344	26	660.4	35	1.37795
27/32		.84375	21.4312	27	685.8	36	1.41732
	55/64	.859375	21.8281	28	711.2	37	1.4567
7/8		.875	22.2250	29	736.6	38	1.4961
	57/64	.890625	22.6219	30	762.0	39	1.5354
29/32		.90625	23.0187	31	787.4	40	1.5748
	59/64	.921875	23.4156	32	812.8	41	1.6142
15/16		.9375	23.8125	33	838.2	42	1.6535
	61/64	.953125	24.2094	34	863.6	43	1.6929
31/32		.96875	24.6062	35	889.0	44	1.7323
	63/64	.984375	25.0031	36	914.4	45	1.7717

UNITS	Pints to Litres	Gallons to Litres	Litres to Pints	Litres to Gallons	Miles to Kilometres	Kilometres to Miles	Lbs. per sq. In. to Kg. per sq. Cm.	Kg. per sq. Cm. to Lbs. per sq. In.
1	.57	4.55	1.76	.22	1.61	.62	.07	14.22
2	1.14	9.09	3.52	.44	3.22	1.24	.14	28.50
3	1.70	13.64	5.28	.66	4.83	1.86	.21	42.67
4	2.27	18.18	7.04	.88	6.44	2.49	.28	56.89
5	2.84	22.73	8.80	1.10	8.05	3.11	.35	71.12
6	3.41	27.28	10.56	1.32	9.66	3.73	.42	85.34
7	3.98	31.82	12.32	1.54	11.27	4.35	.49	99.56
8	4.55	36.37	14.08	1.76	12.88	4.97	.56	113.79
9		40.91	15.84	1.98	14.48	5.59	.63	128.00
10		45.46	17.60	2.20	16.09	6.21	.70	142.23
20				4.40	32.19	12.43	1.41	284.47
30				6.60	48.28	18.64	2.11	426.70
40				8.80	64.37	24.85		
50					80.47	31.07		
60					96.56	37.28		
70					112.65	43.50		
80					128.75	49.71		
90					144.84	55.92		
100					160.93	62.14		

UNITS	Lb ft to kgm	Kgm to lb ft	UNITS	Lb ft to Kgm	Kgm to lb ft
1	.138	7.233	7	.967	50.631
2	.276	14.466	8	1.106	57.864
3	.414	21.699	9	1.244	65.097
4	.553	28.932	10	1.382	72.330
5	.691	36.165	20	2.765	144.660
6	.829	43.398	30	4.147	216.990

TECHNICAL DATA

Dimensions are in inches and (millimetres) unless otherwise stated

ENGINE

Bore and stroke:

1300	...	...	...	...	...	2.91 × 2.95 (74 × 75)
1600	...	...	...	...	...	3.07 × 3.32 (78 × 82)
1750	...	...	...	...	...	3.15 × 3.48 (80 × 88.5)
2000	...	...	...	...	...	3.30 × 3.48 (84 × 88.5)

Capacity:

1300	...	...	...	...	...	79 cu in (1290 cc)
1600	...	...	...	...	...	96 cu in (1570 cc)
1750	...	...	...	...	...	109 cu in (1779 cc)
2000	...	...	...	...	...	120 cu in (1962 cc)

Cylinder liners:

Bore diameter:

	1300	*1600*
Blue	2.9128 to 2.9131 (73.985 to 73.994)	3.0703 to 3.0706 (77.985 to 77.994)
Pink	2.9132 to 2.9135 (73.995 to 74.004)	3.0707 to 3.0710 (77.995 to 78.004)
Green	2.9136 to 2.9139 (74.005 to 74.014)	3.0711 to 3.0714 (78.005 to 78.014)
	1750	*2000*
Blue	3.1490 to 3.1494 (79.985 to 79.994)	3.3065 to 3.3069 (83.985 to 83.994)
Pink	3.1494 to 3.1498 (79.995 to 80.004)	3.3069 to 3.3072 (83.995 to 84.004)
Green	3.1498 to 3.1502 (80.005 to 80.014)	3.3073 to 3.3076 (84.005 to 84.014)

Clearance between liner and pistons:

	1300	*1600*
Borgo pistons	.0018 to .0025 (.045 to .064)	.0022 to .0029 (.055 to .074)
Mahle and KS pistons	.002 to .0027 (.050 to .069)	.0012 to .0019 (.030 to .049)
	1750	*2000*
Borgo pistons	.0012 to .0019 (.030 to .049)	.0016 to .0023 (.040 to .059)

All types

Wear limit	.0059 (.150)

Ovality and taper limits:

New liner	.0004 (.01)
Used liner	.002 (.05)
Liner height above block	.0004 to .0024 (.01 to .06)

Pistons, diameters:

	1300	*1600*
Borgo, class A, blue	2.9106 to 2.9110 (73.930 to 73.940)	3.0677 to 3.0681 (77.920 to 77.930)
class B, pink	2.9110 to 2.9114 (73.940 to 73.950)	3.0681 to 3.0685 (77.931 to 77.940)
class C, green	2.9114 to 2.9118 (73.950 to 73.960)	3.0685 to 3.0689 (77.940 to 77.950)
Mahle and KS, class A, blue	2.9104 to 2.9108 (73.925 to 73.935)	3.0687 to 3.0691 (77.945 to 77.955)
class B, pink	2.9108 to 2.9112 (73.935 to 73.945)	3.0691 to 3.0695 (77.956 to 77.965)
class C, green	2.9112 to 2.9116 (73.945 to 73.955)	3.0695 to 3.0699 (77.966 to 77.925)

Borgo new construction piston,
class A, blue	...	...	...	...	2.9112 to 2.9116 (73.945 to 73.955)

class A, blue ... ... 2.9112 to 2.9116
(73.945 to 73.955)

class B, pink ... ... 2.9116 to 2.9120
(73.955 to 73.965)

class C, green ... ... 2.9120 to 2.9124
(73.965 to 73.975)

	1750	*2000*
Borgo, class A, blue	3.1474 to 3.1478 (79.945 to 79,955)	3.3045 to 3.3049 (83.935 to 83.945)
class B, pink	3.1478 to 3.1482 (79.955 to 79.965)	3.3049 to 3.3053 (83.945 to 83.955)
class C, green	3.1482 to 3.1486 (79.966 to 79.975)	3.3053 to 3.3057 (83.955 to 83.965)

Piston ring to groove clearance:

	1300	*1600*
Chrome compression	.0013 to .0027 (.032 to .069)	.0018 to .0029 (.045 to .072)
Plain compression	.0013 to .0027 (.032 to .069)	.0014 to .0024 (.035 to .062)
Oil control	.0014 to .0029 (.036 to .073)	.0010 to .0020 (.025 to .052)

Borgo new construction piston:

Compression	.0018 to .0019 (.045 to .047)	
Oil scraper	.0014 to .0026 (.035 to .067)	
Oil control	.0010 to .0022 (.025 to .057)	

	1750	*2000*
Chrome compression	.0014 to .0026 (.035 to .067)	
Plain compression	.0014 to .0026 (.035 to .067)	as 1750
Oil control	.0010 to .0022 (.025 to .057)	

Fitted gap in cylinder:

	1300	*1600*
All rings	.0098 to .0157 (.250 to .400)	.0118 to .0177 (.300 to .450)

Borgo new construction piston:

All rings	.0079 to .0140 (.200 to .350)	

	1750	*2000*
Compression	.0118 to .0177 (.300 to .450)	as 1750
Oil control	.0098 to .0157 (.250 to .400)	

Gudgeon pin, diameter:

	1300	*1600*
Black mark	.7872 to .7873 (19.994 to 19.997)	.8659 to .8660 (21.994 to 21.997)
White mark	.7873 to .7874 (19.997 to 20.000)	.8660 to .8661 (21.998 to 22.000)

	1750	*2000*
Black mark	.8659 to .8660 (21.994 to 21.997)	as 1750
White mark	.8660 to .8661 (21.997 to 22.000)	

					1300	1600
Bore in piston, Borgo:						
Black mark	...	...	...	...	.7874 to .7875 (20.000 to 20.002)	.8661 to .8662 (22.000 to 22.002)
White mark	...	...	...	...	.7875 to .7876 (20.003 to 20.005)	.8662 to .8663 (22.003 to 22.005)
Mahle, black mark	...	...	...	...	.7872 to .7874 (19.996 to 19.999)	.8660 to .8661 (21.996 to 21.999)
white mark	...	...	...	...	.7874 to .7875 (19.999 to 20.002)	.8661 to .8662 (21.999 to 22.002)
					1750	*2000*
Borgo, black mark	...	...	...	...	.8661 to .8662 (22.000 to 22.002)	} as 1750
white mark	...	...	...	...	.9056 to .9057 (23.003 to 23.005)	

					All models
Pin to bore clearance, connecting rod					
black mark	...	...	...	...	.0003 to .0008 (.008 to .021)
white mark	...	...	...	...	.0002 to .0007 (.005 to .017)
Pin to bore clearance, piston:					*All models*
Borgo, black mark	...	...	...	...	.00012 to .00032 (.003 to .008)
white mark	...	...	...	...	.00012 to .00028 (.003 to .007)
Mahle, black	...	...	...	...	.00004 to .00032 (.001 to .008)
white	...	...	...	...	$0 \pm .00016$ ($0 \pm .004$)

Crankshaft, diameters:

					All models except 2000	
Main journal, standard	...	...	...	...	2.3606 to 2.3611 (59.960 to 59.973)	
1st US	...	...	...	...	2.3506 to 2.3511 (59.706 to 59.719)	
2nd US	...	...	...	...	2.3406 to 2.3411 (59.452 to 59.465)	
					2000	
Standard, pink	...	...	...	...	2.3607 to 2.3611 (59.961 to 59.971)	
Blue	...	...	...	...	2.3603 to 2.3607 (59.951 to 59.961)	
					1300	*Except 2000*
Crankpin, standard	...	...	...	1.7702 to 1.7707 (44.964 to 44.975)	1.9680 to 1.9685 (49.987 to 50.000)
1st US	...	...	...	...	1.7602 to 1.7607 (44.709 to 44.721)	1.9580 to 1.9585 (49.733 to 49.746)
2nd US	...	...	...	...	1.7502 to 1.7507 (44.455 to 44.467)	1.9480 to 1.9485 (49.479 to 49.492)
					2000	
Standard, pink	...	...	...	...	1.9680 to 1.9684 (49.988 to 49.998)	
Blue	...	...	...	...	1.9676 to 1.9680 (49.978 to 49.988)	
End float, except 2000	...	...	...	.0030 to .0104 (.076 to .264)	
2000	...	...	...	...	.0031 to .0104 (.080 to .264)	

Thrust washers, except 2000:
Standard ...	...	...	...	...	.0910 to .0930 (2.311 to 2.362)
1st OS ...	...	...	...	...	.0934 to .0955 (2.373 to 2.425)
2nd OS ...	...	...	...	...	.0960 to .0983 (2.438 to 2.498)
2000 ...	...	...	...	...	.0909 to .0929 (2.310 to 2.360)

Bearing clearances: *All models except 2000*

Main ...	...	...	...	...	.0006 to .0023 (.014 to .058)
Big-end ...	...	...	...	...	.0010 to .0025 (.025 to .064)

2000

Main, class A, pink, SFCM ...	...	...	...	.0010 to .0026 (.026 to .067)
Clevite ...	...	...	...	...	.0006 to .0023 (.016 to .057)
Class B, blue, SFCM	...	...	...	...	.0010 to .0025 (.024 to .065)
Clevite ...	...	...	...	...	.0006 to .0022 (.014 to .055)
Big-end, class A, pink	...	...	...	.0009 to .0023 (.023 to .058)
Class B, blue	...	...	...	...	.0008 to .0022 (.021 to .056)

Connecting rods:

	1300	*1600*
Length between centres	5.2344 to 5.2380 (132.955 to 133.045)	5.8250 to 5.8285 (147.955 to 148.045)
Big-end bore diameter	1.9157 to 1.9162 (48.658 to 48.671)	2.1140 to 2.1145 (53.695 to 53.708)
Small-end bush ID	.7876 to .7880 (20.005 to 20.015)	.8663 to .8667 (22.005 to 22.015)
End float	.0079 to .0118 (.20 to .30)	.0079 to .0118 (.20 to .30)

	1750	*2000*
Length between centres	6.1791 to 6.1831 (156.950 to 157.050)	
Big-end bore diameter	2.1140 to 2.1145 (53.695 to 53.708)	as 1750
Small-end bush ID	.8663 to .8667 (22.005 to 22.015)	
End float	.0079 to .0118 (.20 to .30)	

Valves:

	Head diameter	*Stem diameter*	*Length*
1300 GT Junior and 1300 Giulia TI:			
Inlet, LIVIA H	1.4567 to 1.4625 (37.00 to 37.15)	.3528 to .3538 (8.962 to 8.987)	4.2913 to 4.3031 (109.0 to 109.30)
Exhaust, LIVIA C	1.3386 to 1.3445 (34.00 to 34.15)	.3518 to .3528 (8.935 to 8.960)	4.2756 to 4.2874 (108.6 to 108.90)
1600 Giulia TI and Super:			
Inlet, LIVIA H	1.6142 to 1.6201 (41.00 to 41.15)	.3528 to .3538 (8.962 to 8.987)	4.2087 to 4.2189 (106.9 to 107.16)
Exhaust, LIVIA C	1.4567 to 1.4625 (37.00 to 37.15)	.3518 to .3528 (8.935 to 8.960)	4.1799 to 4.1902 (106.17 to 106.43)

Exhaust, ATE	1.4567 to 1.4646 (37.00 to 37.20)	.3518 to .3528 (8.935 to 8.960)	4.1752 to 4.1791 (106.05 to 106.15)

1600 GT Junior, Spider Veloce, Sprint GTV and SS: ... ...

Inlet, LIVIA H	1.6142 to 1.6201 (41.00 to 41.15)	.3528 to .3538 (8.962 to 8.987)	4.2087 to 4.2189) (106.9 to 107.15)
Inlet, ATE	1.6142 to 1.6220 (41.00 to 41.20)	.3528 to .3538 (8.962 to 8.987)	4.2047 (106.8)
Inlet, GARONNE	1.6142 to 1.6201 (41.00 to 41.15)	.3528 to .3538 (8.962 to 8.987)	4.2126 (107.0)
Exhaust, ATE	1.4567 to 1.4646 (37.00 to 37.20)	.3518 to .3528 (8.935 to 8.960)	4.1752 to 4.1791 (106.05 to 106.15)
Exhaust, LIVIA C	1.4567 to 1.4625 (37.00 to 37.15)	.3518 to .3528 (8.935 to 8.960)	4.1850 (106.3)

1600 Giulia Sprint GT and Sprint GTC:

Inlet, LIVIA H	1.6142 to 1.6201 (41.00 to 41.15)	.3528 to .3538 (8.960 to 8.987)	4.1980 to 4.2138 (106.63 to 107.03)
Inlet, LIVIA H	1.7657 to 1.7717 (44.85 to 45.00)	.3329 to .3339 (8.455 to 8.480)	4.1917 to 4.2020 (106.47 to 106.73)
Exhaust, LIVIA C	1.4567 to 1.4625 (37.00 to 37.15)	.3518 to .3528 (8.935 to 8.960)	4.1799 to 4.1902 (106.17 to 106.43)
Exhaust, ATE	1.4567 to 1.4646 (37.00 to 37.20)	.3518 to .3528 (8.935 to 8.960)	4.1752 to 4.1791 (106.05 to 106.15)

1750:

Inlet, LIVIA H	1.6142 to 1.6201 (41.00 to 41.15)	.3531 to .3539 (8.97 to 8.99)	4.2087 to 4.2189 (106.9 to 107.15)
Inlet, ATE	1.6142 to 1.6220 (41.00 to 41.20)	.3531 to .3539 (8.97 to 8.99)	4.2047 (106.8)
Inlet, GARRONE	1.6142 to 1.6201 (41.00 to 41.15)	.3531 to .3539 (8.97 to 8.99)	4.2126 (107.0)
Exhaust, LIVIA C (sodium cooled)	1.4567 to 1.4625 (37.00 to 37.15)	.3516 to .3528 (8.93 to 8.96)	4.1850 (106.3)

2000:

Inlet, LIVIA H and ATE ...	1.7323 to 1.7382 (44.00 to 44.15)	.3532 to .3538 (8.972 to 8.987)	4.1323 (104.96)
Exhaust, LIVIA C (sodium cooled)	1.5748 to 1.5807 (40.00 to 40.15)	.3518 to .3528 (8.935 to 8.960)	4.1154 to 4.1339 (104.53 to 105.0)
Exhaust, ATE (sodium cooled)	1.5748 to 1.5807 (40.00 to 40.15)	.3518 to .3528 (8.935 to 8.960)	4.1224 to 4.1323 (104.71 to 104.96)

Valve guides:

Outer diameter	.5525 to .5529 (14.033 to 14.044)
Inner diameter	.3543 to .3549 (9.00 to 9.015)

Height protruding from head (except 2000):

Inlet	.5433 to .5512 (13.80 to 14.00)
Exhaust	.6614 to .6693 (16.80 to 17.00)
2000, inlet	.5236 to .5315 (13.30 to 13.50)
exhaust	.6417 to .6496 (16.30 to 16.50)

Valve stem clearance, inlet	...	...	...	.0005 to .0017	
				(.013 to .043)	
exhaust		...	...	.0016 to .0031	
				(.040 to .080)	

Valve seat inserts: *1300*   *1600 and 1750*

Diameter, standard, inlet	...	...	...	1.5170 to 1.5180	1.6770 to 1.6791
				(38.532 to 38.557)	(42.597 to 42.648)
exhaust		...	...	1.3920 to 1.3930	1.5196 to 1.5216
				(35.357 to 35.381)	(38.597 to 38.648)
oversize, inlet	...	...	...	1.5288 to 1.5298	1.6889 to 1.6909
				(38.832 to 38.857)	(42.897 to 42.948)
exhaust		...	...	1.4038 to 1.4048	1.5314 to 1.5334
				(35.657 to 35.682)	(38.897 to 38.948)

2000

Diameter, standard, inlet	...	...	...	1.7742 to 1.7756
				(45.065 to 45.10)
exhaust		...	...	1.6167 to 1.6181
				(41.065 to 41.10)
oversize, inlet	...	...	...	1.7860 to 1.7874
				(45.365 to 45.40)
exhaust		...	...	1.6285 to 1.6299
				(41.365 to 41.40)

Valve springs:

Free length, inner spring	...	...	...	Red 1.8622	Green 1.8307
				(47.3)	(46.5)
outer spring (except 2000)			...	Red 2.0787	Green 2.0197
				(52.8)	(51.3)
2000, outer	...	...	...	1.9528	
				(49.6)	
Fitted length, inner spring	...	...	...	1.0236	
				(26.0)	
outer spring	...	...	...	1.0827	
				(27.5)	

Valve tappets:

Diameter, standard	...	...	...	1.3769 to 1.3775
				(34.973 to 34.989)
oversize	...	...	...	1.3848 to 1.3854
				(35.173 to 35.189)
Bore diameter, standard	...	...	...	1.3780 to 1.3789
				(35.000 to 35.025)
oversize	...	...	...	1.3858 to 1.3868
				(35.200 to 35.225)

Camshafts:

Journal diameter	...	...	...	1.0614 to 1.0622
				(26.959 to 26.980)
Bearing clearance	...	...	...	.0008 to .0029
				(.020 to .074)
End float	...	...	...	.0026 to .0072
				(.065 to .182)

Timing chain tensioner:

Spring free length	...	...	...	3.9 (99.0)
Minimum test length	...	...	...	2.3 (58.5) under load of 50 lb (22 kg)

FUEL SYSTEM

Dellorto carburetters:	*GT Junior 1.3*	*1750*	*2000*
Type	DHLA 40	DHLA 40	DHLA 40
Choke tube	28	32	32
Main jet	110	135	135
Air correction jet	200	200	200

Slow running jet ...	48	50	50
Pump jet	—	40	33
Choke jet	70	70	70
Float needle ...	1.5	1.5	1.5
Float weight ...	10 gr	10 gr	10 gr

Dellorto carburetters:

	Super 1600	*GT Junior 1.6*
Type	DHLA 40	DHLA 40
Choke tube	30	30
Main jet	120	120
Air correction jet	200	200
Slow-running jet	48	48
Pump jet	33	33
Float needle	1.5	1.5
Float weight	10 gr	10 gr

Weber carburetters:

	GTV, SS 1600	*GT, GTC 1600*	*Super 1600*	*Spider 1600*
Type	40 DCOE	40 DCOE 4	40 DCOE 24	40 DCOE 27
Choke tube	30 mm	30 mm	27 mm	30 mm
Main jet	115 or 120	127/3	110	120
Air correction jet	180	220	180	180
Slow-running jet	55 F 11	50	50	50 F 11
Starter jet... ...	65 FS	65 F5	65 F5	65 F5
Slow-running air jet ...	120	120	120	120
Accelerator pump jet ...	35	35	35	35
Float needle valve ...	150	150	150	150
Float weight	23 gr.	23 gr.	26 gr.	26 gr.

Weber carburetters:

	Super 1600	*GT Junior 1.6*	*Early 1750*	*Later 1750*
Type	40 DCOE 27	40 DCOE 27, 44, 45	40 DCOE 32	40 DCOE 32
Choke tube	30 mm	30 mm	32 mm	32 mm
Main jet	117	117	125	130
Air correction jet	180	180	200	200
Slow-running jet	50 F 14	50 F 14	50 F 14	50 F 8
Starter jet...	—	—	65 F 5	65 F 5
Slow-running air jet ...	120	120	—	—
Accelerator pump jet ...	35	35	35	35
Float needle valve ...	150	150	150	150
Float weight	26 gr	26 gr	26 gr	25 gr

Solex carburetters:

	TI, Super, GT 1600	*Super, GTV, Spider 1600*	*Super 1600, GT Junior 1.6*
Type	C 40 DDH	C 40 DDH	C 40 DDH
Choke tube	30	30	30 mm
Main jet	125	125	130
Air correction jet	130	140	140
Slow-running jet	50	45	47
Starter fuel jet	140	140	—
Injector tube	35	35	35

Solex carburetters:

	1750	*GTV 1750*	*2000*
Type	C 40 DDH	C 40 DDH	C 40 DDH
Choke tube	32	32	32
Main jet	135	140	140
Air correction jet	180	150	150
Slow running jet	47.5	50	47
Starter fuel jet	140	140	140
Injector tube	35	35	35

Solex carburetters:		GT, Spider		TI	
Type		C 32 PAIA 5		C 32 PAIA 7	
Barrels		*1st*	*2nd*	*1st*	*2nd*
Choke tube		23	23	23	23
Main jet		125	135	125	130
Air correction jet		220	200	190	190
Slow-running jet		45	70	45	70
Emulsion tube		17	17	73	73
Starter fuel jet		120		120	

Solex carburetters:		GT	Super
Type		C 40 PHH/2	C 40 PHH/2
Choke tube		30	28
Main jet		135	125
Air correction jet		135	125
Slow-running jet		50	50
Emulsion tube		19	19
Starter fuel jet		100	100

Solex carburetters:		GT Junior 1.3	GT Junior 1.6
Type		C 30 ADDHE	C 40 ADDHE
Choke tube		28	30
Main jet		135	150
Air correction jet		210	140
Slow-running jet		60	57
Slow-running air jet		175	175
Accelerator pump jet		60	60
Float needle valve		1.6	1.6

IGNITION SYSTEM

Distributor

Type	Bosch or Marelli
Contact points gap:	
Bosch	.014 to .016 inch (.35 to .40 mm)
Marelli	.016 to .019 inch (.40 to .50 mm)
Dual ignition systems	.012 to .016 inch (.30 to .40 mm)
Dwell angle	60 ± 3 deg.

COOLING SYSTEM

Thermostat:

Opening temperature	82° to 87°C

CLUTCH

Mechanically operated:

Thrust springs, free length	1.6929 to 1.8110 (43 to 46)
fitted length	1.1417 (29)
fitted load	99 to 108 lb (45 to 49 kg)
Release bearing clearance	.0787 (2)
Minimum driven plate thickness	.2362 (6)

Hydraulically operated:

Clutch pedal free travel	1.1811 to 1.2598 (30 to 32) (1970 models on-automatically adjusted)
Relase bearing clearance	.0787 (2)
Hydraulic fluid specification	SAE 70 R3

TRANSMISSION

Gearbox

Number of forward speeds	Five
Synchromesh	All five forward gears
Gear ratios:	
First	3.304:1
Second	1.988:1
Third	1.355:1
Fourth	1.000:1
Fifth	.791:1 (.86:1 GT Junior 1.3)
Reverse	3.010:1

Differential ratio

Giulia TI, standard	41:8
Giulia TI, optional alternatives	41:9, 41:10
Giulia TI Super, standard	41:8
Giulia TI Super, optional alternatives	41:9, 43:9, 41:10, 41:11
Giulia Super, Giulia Sprint GT, Giulia Sprint GT Veloce, Giulia GTC, Spider 1600, GT Junior 1.3, 1.6	41:9
1750 and 2000 Berline	43:10
2000 Spider and GT Veloce	41:10

STEERING

Geometry:

Castor angle	$1\frac{1}{2}$ deg. $\pm \frac{1}{2}$ deg.
Camber angle	0 deg. 50′ ± 30′,
	0 deg. 20′ ± 30′ (GT Junior 1.6, 1750, 2000)
Toe-in, each wheel	.06 inch

BRAKES

Type:

Early saloons	Drum, three shoe front, two shoe rear
Intermediate models	Disc front, drum rear
All later models	Disc front and rear
Front disc diameter:	
Dunlop	10.5 (266)
ATE	10.7 (272)
Rear disc diameter:	
Dunlop	9.7 (246)
ATE	10.5 (267)
Pad wear limit:	
Front	.32 (8)
Rear	.28 (7)

ELECTRICAL EQUIPMENT

Battery

Voltage	12 v
Earth polarity	Negative
Generator, type	Bosch EG (R) 14V25A29 or Marelli DN 62EP
Alternator, type	Bosch RSVA 14V 25A or Bosch K1 (RL) 14V 35A 20 or Bosch K1 14V 45A 22 or Motorola A14 45/55

Starter motor, type	Bosch EF (R) 12 VO 7Ps or Marelli MT 54B
Windscreen wiper motor, type 1st series	Bosch WS 13/11 S 1A
2nd series Berline	Bosch WS 4902 AR 5A (0)
Coupé...	Bosch WS 4903 AR 2 A (0)
Veloce...	Bosch WS 4904 AR 2 A (0)
Control box, type	Bosch RSVA 14V 25 A or Bosch AD 1/14 V or Motorola 724.16602

CAPACITIES

Engine sump	
1600	11.2 pints
1750 and 2000	11.6 pints
Gearbox, synchromesh	3.2 pints
Rear axle	2.5 pints
Cooling system	
1600	13 pints
1750 and 2000	16.8 pints
Steering box	.7 pint
Fuel tank	11.7 gallons

TORQUE WRENCH SETTINGS

Engine	Lb ft
Cylinder head nuts (cold) oiled:	
1750	52 to 53.5
2000	57 to 58.5
Others	44.8 to 46.3
Cylinder head nuts (hot) oiled:	
1750	55 to 55.7
2000	60.7 to 61.5
Others	47.7 to 48.5
Spark plugs oiled...	18 to 25
Camshaft cap nuts, oiled	14.5 to 16.3
Big-end cap nuts oiled:	
GT Junior 1300	24.5 to 26
Others	36.2 to 38.3
Main bearing cap nuts, oiled:	
GT Junior 1300	23 to 25.3
Others	34 to 36.2
Main bearing cap palnuts, oiled	8 to 9.4
Transducer on manifold, oiled:	
GT Junior	25.3 to 30
Crankshaft pulley, oiled:	
GT Junior	137.4 to 145
2000	70 to 72.3
Flywheel bolts, oiled:	
2000	79.5 to 94
Others	30.4 to 32.5
Sump drain plug	50.6 to 57.8
Clutch to flywheel:	
GT Junior, 1750	9.2 to 11.9
Others	14.8 to 18.2
Oil filter plug, 1750	25.3 to 30
Thermostat on manifold, 2000	25.3 to 29

Gearbox

Drive flange nut:

GT Junior, 1750	79.5 to 86.8
2000	68.7 to 77.4
Others	86 to 86.8

Layshaft nut:

GT Junior, 1750	32.5 to 39.8
2000	68.7 to 77.4
Others	43.4 to 57.8
Gearbox case halves	13

Drive flange to propeller shaft:

GT Junior, 1750, 2000	39.8 to 41.2
Others	32.5 to 40
Inner selector lever	23.5 to 26.4
Filler/drain plugs, 2000	34.4 to 37.9

Rear axle

Propeller shaft front flange nut:

GT Junior	65 to 79.5
2000	72.3 to 101

Propeller shaft section bolts:

GT Junior	23 to 25.3
2000	27.5 to 29

Crownwheel screws:

2000	43.4 to 47.7
Others	32.5 to 36
Pinion shaft ring nut	57.8 to 101

Radius rods to body:

GT Junior, 1750, 2000	58.6 to 72.3
Others	72 to 83

Radius rods to axle:

GT Junior, 1750, 2000	79.5 to 98.7
Others	83 to 94

Reaction trunnion to body:

GT Junior, 1750, 2000	31.8 to 39.4
Others	34.8 to 39.7

Reaction trunnion to axle:

GT Junior, 1750, 2000	73.8 to 91
Others	79.6 to 108.5
Stabiliser rod to axle	23.8 to 25.3

Wheel nuts, rear:

GT Junior, 1750, 2000	43.4 to 57.8
Others	25.3 to 28.9

Pinion yoke to propeller shaft:

GT Junior, 1750	23 to 25.3
2000	27.5 to 28.9
Others	25.3 to 28.9
Rebound strap	3.6
Axle tubes to carrier	14.5 to 17.4
Dampers to body	17.4 to 21.3
Differential filler/drain plugs, 2000	10.8 to 13

Front suspension and steering

Steering wheel nut	36 to 39.8
Burman steering box cover	16.6 to 18

Steering box to body:

GT Junior, 1750, 2000	37 to 39.4
Others	34.7 to 40

	Lb ft
Crank bracket and steering lock to body	31.8 to 39.4
Steering linkage ball joints	34.7 to 39.8
Drop arm	90.4 to 101.2
Upper wishbone front arm to body:	
GT Junior, 1750, 2000	15.9 to 19.9
Others	16.6 to 20.2
Upper wishbone front arm to rear arm	27.5 to 33.9
Upper wishbone rear arm to body:	
GT Junior, 1750, 2000	79.5 to 98.7
Others	83.1 to 94
Lower wishbone shaft to crossmember	40.5 to 42.7
Steering arm to swivel:	
GT Junior, 1750, 2000	28.9 to 32.5
Others	34.7 to 40
Upper wishbone rear arm to swivel	54.2 to 61.5
Lower ball joint to wishbone:	
GT Junior, 1750, 2000	59.3 to 66.5
Others	54.2 to 61.5
Lower ball joint to swivel	54.2 to 61.5
Wheels/discs, front:	
GT Junior, 1750, 2000	43.4 to 57.8
Others (wheels)	54.2 to 61.5
Steering column to bracket, GT Junior, 2000 ...	11.7 to 13.8
Damper to lower arm	54.2 to 61.5
Brakes	
Servo to bracket	8.7 to 10.8
Caliper bracket to housing (rear)	34.7 to 39.8
Caliper to carrier (rear):	
GT Junior, 1750, 2000	39.7 to 47
Others	54.2 to 61.5
Caliper to swivel:	
GT Junior, 1750, 2000	54.2 to 61.5
Others	34.7 to 40
Splash shields	5.8 to 7.2
Bleed screw (ATE)	1.5 to 2.5
Caliper joining bolts	21 to 24.6
Inlet to caliper:	
With gasket	5.8 to 7.9
Without gasket	7.2 to 10.8

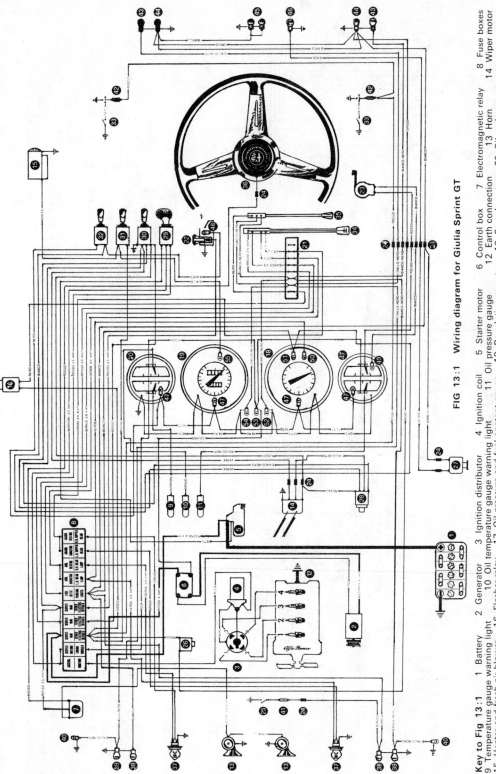

FIG 13:1 Wiring diagram for Giulia Sprint GT

Key to Fig 13:1 1 Battery 2 Generator 3 Ignition distributor 4 Ignition coil 5 Starter motor 6 Control box 7 Electromagnetic relay 8 Fuse boxes
9 Temperature gauge warning light 10 Oil temperature gauge warning light 11 Oil pressure gauge 12 Earth connection 13 Horn 14 Wiper motor
15 Heater and fresh air blower 16 Flasher relay 17 Oil pressure and fuel content gauge 18 Revolution counter 19 Speedometer 20 Oil and water temperature gauge
21 Junction box 22 Cigar lighter control light 23 Fuel gauge tank unit 24 Cable connector 25 Engine compartment lamp switch 26 Brake light switch 27 Reversing
light switch 28 Foot switch for screen washer 29 Ignition switch 30 Windscreen wiper switch 31 Heater and fresh air blower switch 32 Instrument light switch
33 Roof light switch 34 Light switch 35 Flasher switch 36 Horn

Bulbs 37 Headlamp driving and dipped beam 45/50 watts 38 Front pilot lamps 5 watts 39 Front flasher lamp 20 watts 40 Side flasher lamp 3 watts
41 Engine compartment light (festoon) 5 watts 42 Roof light (festoon) 5 watts 43 Rear flasher lamp 20 watts 44 Tail/brake lights 5/20 watts
45 Number plate lamp 5 watts 46 Reversing lamp 20 watts 47 Instrument lights 3 watts 48 Cigar lighter 3 watts 49 Fuel contents warning light 3 watts
50 Headlamp driving beam warning light 3 watts 51 Pilot lamp warning light 3 watts 52 Direction indicator warning light 3 watts 53 Ignition warning light 3 watts
54 Direction indicator warning light 3 watts 55 Heater blower warning light 3 watts

Key to cable colour code Verde=Green Bianco=White Rosso=Red Nero=Black Grigio=Grey Rosa=Pink Marrone=Brown Giallo=Yellow
Giallo-nero=Yellow-black Bianco-nero=White-black

ARG1600

145

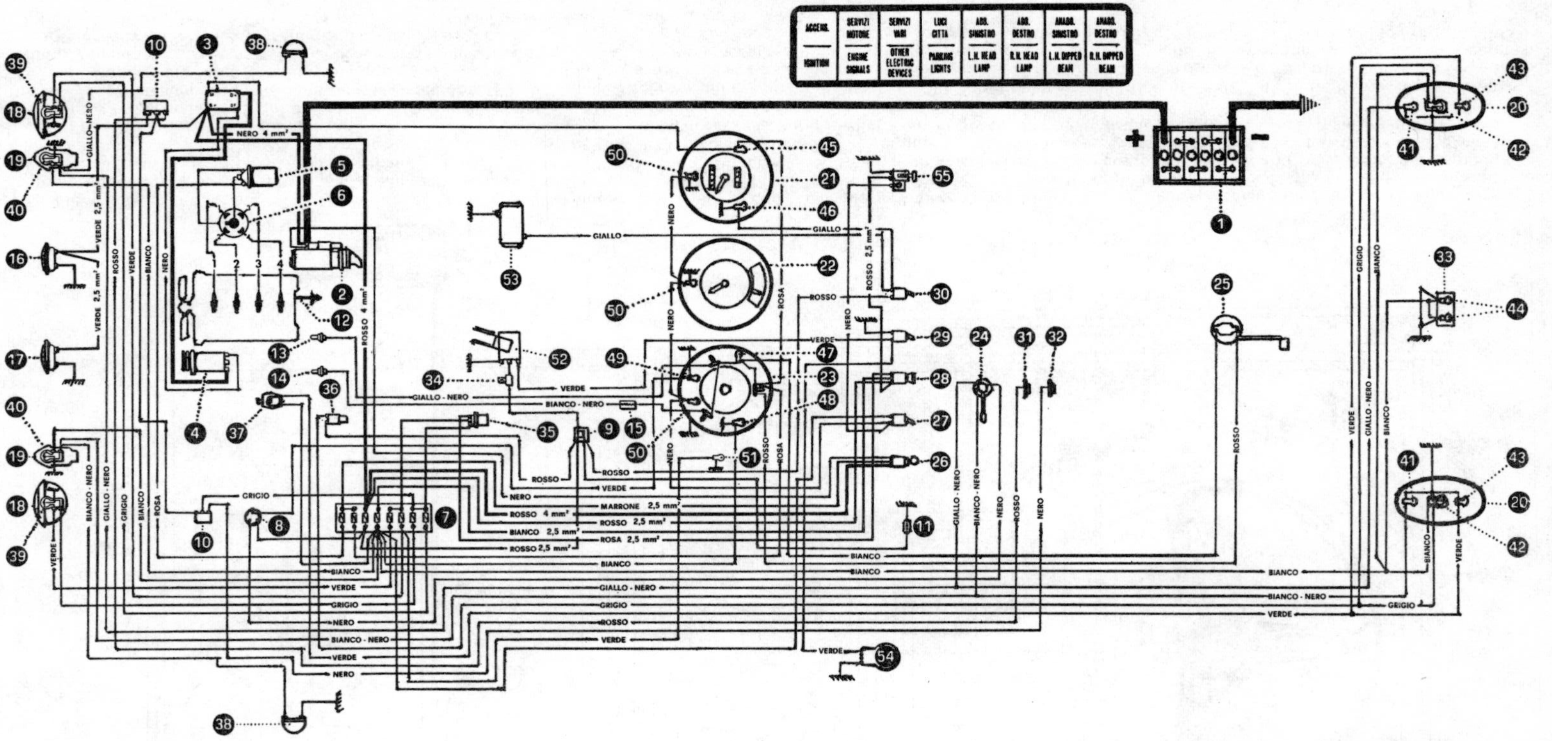

FIG 13:2 Wiring diagram for Giulia Spider and Giulia Spider Veloce

Key to Fig 13:2 1 Battery 2 Starter motor 3 Control box 4 Generator 5 Ignition coil 6 Ignition distributor 7 Fuse boxes 8 Flasher relay 9 Connection 10 Electromagnetic relay 11 Map reading light 12 Earth connection 13 Water temperature sender unit 14 Oil temperature sender unit 15 Resistor for oil circuit 16 Horn 17 Horn 18 Headlamps 19 Front pilot lamps 20 Rear lamps 21 Speedometer 22 Revolution counter and oil pressure gauge 23 Oil and water temperature gauge with fuel contents gauge 24 Direction indicator switch 25 Fuel gauge tank unit 26 Ignition and starter switch 27 Instrument light switch 28 Light switch 29 Windscreen wiper switch 30 Heater blower switch 31 Horn push switch 32 Headlamp flasher switch 33 Number plate lights 34 Thermo switch 35 Dipswitch 36 Brake light switch 37 Reversing light switch 38 Side flasher lamps 52 Windscreen wiper motor 53 Heater blower motor 54 Foot switch for screen washer 55 Cigar lighter

Bulbs 39 Headlamp driving and dipped beam 45/40 watts 40 Front pilot lamps and flasher lamps 5/20 watts 41 Rear flasher lamps 20 watts 42 Tail/brake lights 5/20 watts 43 Reversing light 20 watts 44 Number plate lights 5 watts 45 Ignition warning light 3 watts 46 Heater blower warning light 3 watts 47 Fuel contents warning light 3 watts 48 Pilot warning light 3 watts 49 Direction indicator warning light 3 watts 50 Instrument lights 3 watts 51 Driving beam warning light 3 watts

Key to cable colour code Verde= Green Bianco= White Nero= Black Rosso= Red Grigio= Grey Rosa= Pink Marrone= Brown Giallo= Yellow Giallo-nero= Yellow-black Bianco-nero= White-black

146

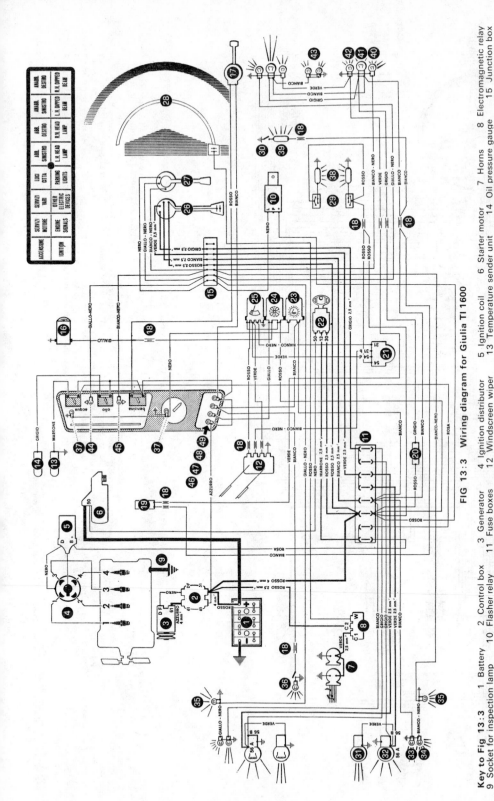

FIG 13:3   Wiring diagram for Giulia TI 1600

Key to Fig 13:3   1 Battery   2 Control box   3 Generator   4 Ignition distributor   5 Ignition coil   6 Starter motor   7 Horns   8 Electromagnetic relay
9 Socket for inspection lamp   10 Flasher relay   11 Fuse boxes   12 Windscreen wiper   13 Temperature sender unit   14 Oil pressure gauge   15 Junction box
16 Heater blower   17 Fuel gauge tank unit   18 Cable connectors   19 Reversing light switch   20 Brake light switch   21 Foot switch for screen washer   22 Ignition
and starter switch   23 Instrument light switch   24 Heater blower switch   25 Windscreen wiper switch   26 Light switch   27 Flasher lamp switch   28 Horn push
switch   29 Three-way switch for interior light   30 Luggage compartment switch
Bulbs   31 Headlamp driving beam 45/40 watts   32 Headlamp driving and dipped beam 45/40 watts   33 Front flasher lamp 5 watts   34 Front flasher lamp 20 watts
35 Side flasher lamps 5 watts   36 Engine compartment lamp 5 watts   37 Instrument lights 3 watts   38 Roof light 5 watts   39 Luggage compartment light 5 watts
40 Direction indicator warning light 5 watts   41 Tail light 5/20 watts   42 Reversing lamp 20 watts   43 Number plate lamp 5 watts   44 Direction indicator warning light 3 watts
45 Direction indicator warning light 3 watts   46 Ignition warning light 3 watts   47 Blower warning light 3 watts   48 Pilot warning light 3 watts   49 Fuel content
warning light 3 watts

Key to cable colour code   Verde=Green   Bianco=White   Rosso=Red   Nero=Black   Grigio=Grey   Rosa=Pink   Marrone=Brown   Giallo=Yellow
Giallo-nero=Yellow-black   Bianco-nero= White-black

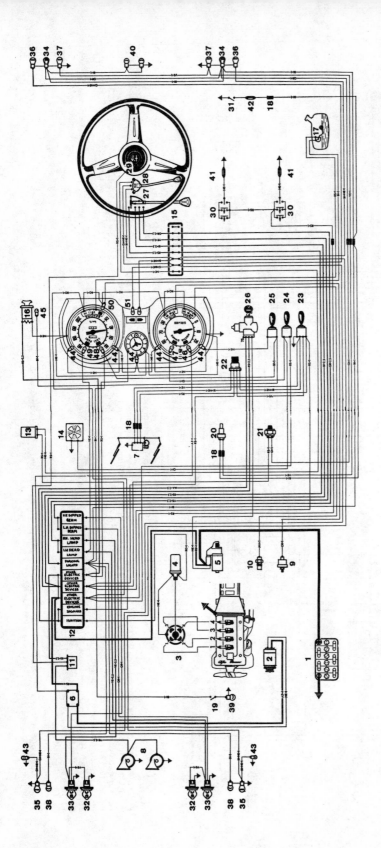

FIG 13:4   Wiring diagram for Giulia Super 1600

Key to Fig 13:4   1 Battery   2 Generator   3 Distributor   4 Coil   5 Starter   6 Regulator   7 Windscreen wiper   8 Horn   9 Oil pressure switch   10 Temperature switch
11 Electromagnetic relay   12 Fuse box   13 Flasher unit   14 Fan motor   15 Connector plate   16 Cigar lighter   17 Petrol gauge tank unit   18 Connectors

Switches   19 Bonnet light   20 Reverse light   21 Stop switch   22 Windscreen washer, foot controlled   23 Windscreen wiper motor   24 Fan motor
25 Facia light (rheostat)   26 Ignition/starter switch   27 Side light, headlight and flashers   28 Direction indicators   29 Horns   30 Interior light (on door post)   31 Boot light
Bulbs   32 Headlight beam small model 45/40 watts asymmetric   33 Headlight beam large model 45/40 watts asymmetric   34 Side and stoplight, rear, 5/20 watts
35 Direction indicator, front 20 watts   36 Direction indicator, rear 20 watts   37 Reverse light 20 watts   38 Side light, front, spherical bulb 5 watts   39 Bonnet light,
spherical bulb 5 watts   40 Number plate, spherical 5 watts   41 Interior light, cylindrical 5 watts   42 Boot light, cylindrical 5 watts   43 Flasher repeater, tubular 3 watts
44 Speedometer/petrol gauge light, tubular 3 watts   45 Cigar lighter light, tubular 3 watts   46 Generator control lamp, tubular 3 watts   47 Fan control lamp, tubular 3 watts
48 Dipped headlight control lamp, tubular 3 watts   49 High beam control lamp, tubular 3 watts   50 Petrol reserve control lamp, tubular 3 watts   51 Flasher control lamp,
tubular 3 watts

Key to cable colour code   **AZ** Pale blue   **GR** Grey   **RO** Pink   **BI** White   **MA** Brown   **RS** Red   **NE** Black   **VE** Green
The figure after the colour code letters indicates the section of the wire in mm²

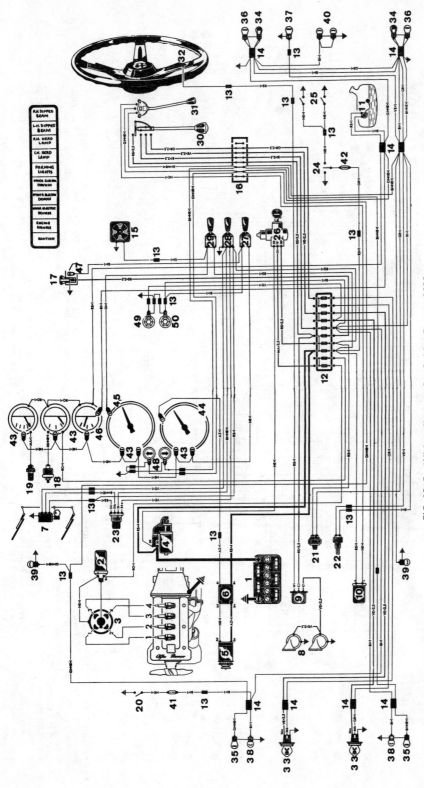

FIG 13:5 Wiring diagram for Spider Duetto 1600

Key to Fig 13:5 1 Battery 2 Coil 3 Distributor 4 Starter 5 Generator 6 Regulator 7 Windscreen wiper 8 Horn 9 Electromagnetic relay 10 Flasher unit 11 Petrol gauge tank unit 12 Fuse box 13 Connectors (1-pole) 14 Connector block 15 Fan motor 16 Connector plate 17 Cigar lighter 18 Oil pressure switch 19 Temperature (water) switch

Switches 20 Bonnet light 21 Stop switch 22 Reverse light 23 Windscreen washer foot switch 24 Fan motor 25 Interior light switch (on rear view mirror) 26 Ignition/starter switches 27 Instruments light 28 Windscreen wiper motor 29 Fan motor 30 Side, headlights and flashers 31 Direction indicators 32 Horns

Bulbs 33 Headlights 45/40 watts asymmetric 34 Direction indicators, front 20 watts 37 Reverse light 20 watts 38 Side light, front 5 watts spherical 39 Flasher repeater 5 watts spherical 40 Number plate 5 watts spherical 41 Bonnet light 5 watts cylindrical 42 Interior light 5 watts cylindrical 43 Instrument combinations 3 watts tubular 44 Generator control lamp 3 watts tubular 45 Fan control lamp 3 watts tubular 46 Petrol reserve light 3 watts tubular 47 Cigar lighter 3 watts tubular 48 Direction indicator control lamp 1,2 watts tubular 49 High beam control lamp 1,2 watts tubular 50 Side light control lamp 1,2 watts tubular

Key to cable colour code **AZ** Pale blue **GR** Grey **RO** Pink **BI** White **MA** Brown **RS** Red **GI** Yellow **NE** Black **VE** Green
The figure after the colour code letters indicates the wire section in mm^2

ARG1600

149

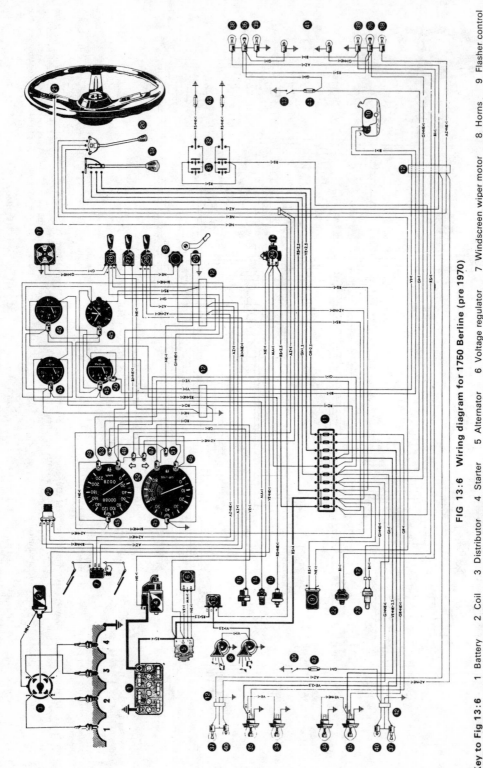

FIG 13:6 Wiring diagram for 1750 Berline (pre 1970)

Key to Fig 13:6 1 Battery 2 Coil 3 Distributor 4 Starter 5 Alternator 6 Voltage regulator 7 Windscreen wiper motor 8 Horns 9 Flasher control 10 Fuel gauge transmitter 11 Fuse box 12 Connectors 13 Horn relay 14 Water temperature transmitter 15 Oil pressure transmitter 16 Minimum oil pressure transmitter 17 Two-speed heater:ventilator motor 18 Cigar lighter 19 Side, head and head flash switch 20 Direction indicator switch 21 Horn switch 22 Stop light switch 23 Reverse light switch 24 Ignition and starter switch 25 Choke warning 26 Wiper motor switch 27 Panel lights switch 28 Heater: ventilator motor switch 29 Windscreen washer plunger switch 30 Engine compartment light switch 31 Door pillar light switch 32 Independent interior light switch 33 Boot compartment switch 34 Inner headlamps 35 Outer headlamps 36 Rear parking and stop lights 37 Front direction indicator lamps 38 Rear direction indicator lamps 39 Reverse lights 40 Front parking lights 41 Index plate lights 42 Engine compartment lamp 43 Interior lamps 44 Boot compartment lamps 45 Instrument panel lamps 46 Heater fan warning lamp 47 Alternator charge warning lamp 48 Parking light warning 49 Main head beam warning light 50 Low fuel warning light 51 Choke warning lamp 52 Flasher repeater lamps 53 Oil pressure warning lamp
Key to colour code **AZ** Blue **B1** White **G1** Yellow **GR** Grey **MA** Maroon **NE** Black **RO** Pink **RS** Red **VE** Green **V1** Violet
The number after the colour code letters indicates the thickness of the cable in sq mm

150

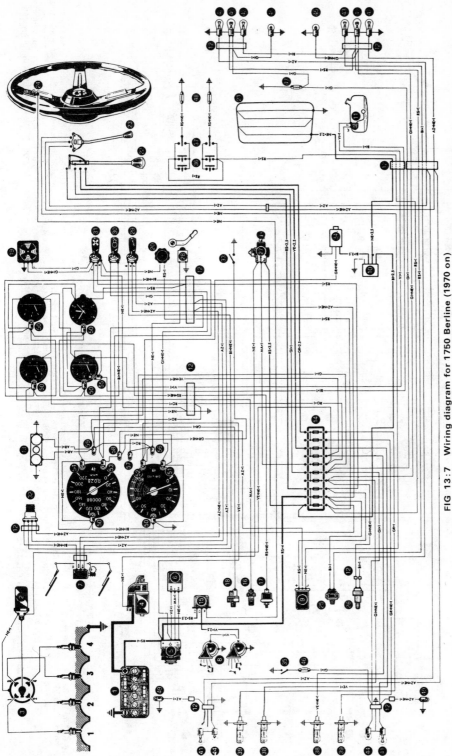

FIG 13:7 Wiring diagram for 1750 Berline (1970 on)

Key to Fig 13:7 1 Battery 2 Coil 3 Distributor 4 Starter 5 Alternator 6 Voltage regulator 7 Windscreen wiper motor 8 Horns 9 Flasher unit
10 Electro-magnetic relay for heated rear window (optional) 11 Fuel gauge transmitter 12 Connectors 13 Brake fluid (minimum) transmitter 14 Fuse box
15 Horn relay 16 Water temperature transmitter 17 Oil pressure transmitter 18 Oil pressure (minimum) transmitter 19 Two-speed heater ventilator motor
20 Cigar lighter 21 Heated rear window (option) 22 Side, head and head flash switch 23 Direction indicator switch 24 Horn switch 25 Stop light switch
26 Reverse light switch 27 Ignition and starter switch 28 Choke warning switch 29 Wiper motor switch 30 Instrument panel light switch 31 Heater-ventilator
motor switch 32 Windscreen washer plunger switch 33 Handbrake warning light switch 34 Rear window heater switch 35 Engine compartment light switch
36 Door pillar light switch 37 Interior light switch 38 Outer headlamp 39 Inner headlamp 40 Stop and tail light 41 Front direction indicators 42 Rear
direction indicators 43 Reverse lights 44 Front parking lights 45 Index plate lights 46 Engine compartment light 47 Boot compartment light 48 Interior lamps
49 Side repeater lamps 50 Instrument panel lights 51 Heater motor warning lamp 52 Alternator charge warning 53 Parking light warning 54 Headlamp warning
55 Low fuel warning light 56 Choke warning light 57 Handbrake warning light 58 Direction indicator warning repeater lamp 59 Minimum brake fluid
warning light
Colour code and cable thickness—see **FIG 13:6**

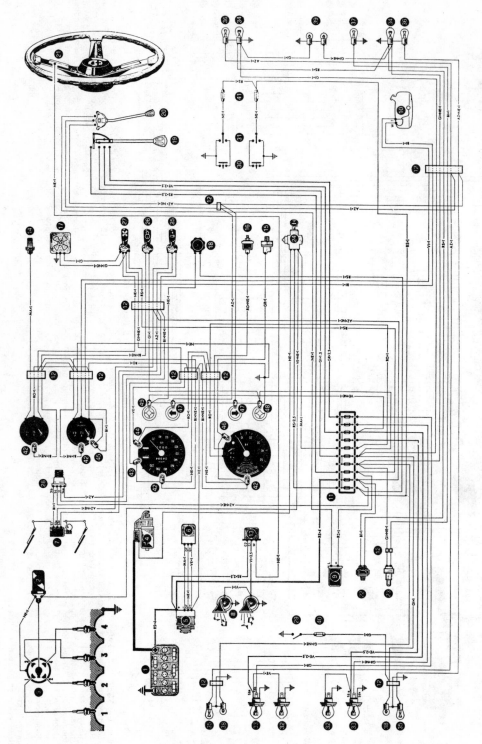

FIG 13:8 Wiring diagram of 1750 Coupe

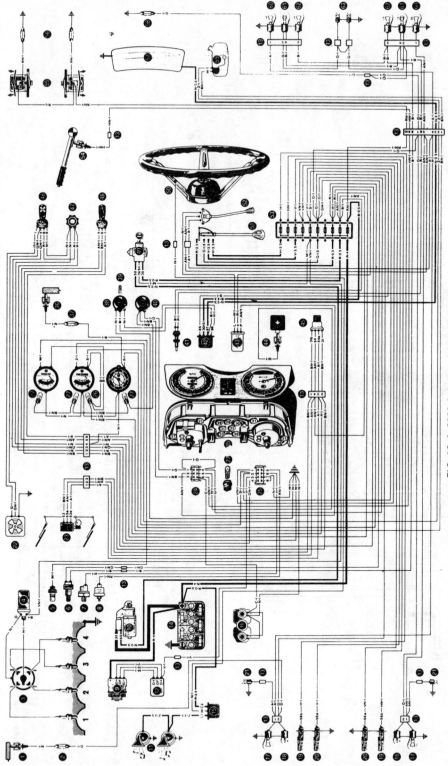

FIG 13:9 2000 Saloon wiring diagrams

Key to Fig 13:9
3 Distributor   4 Coil   5 Water temperature sender   7 Oil pressure warning sender   8 Oil pressure sender   9 Alternator   10 Starter   11 Horns
12 Voltage regulator   13 Connectors   14 Battery   15 Horn relay   16 Brake fluid warning sender   22 Two-speed heater fan   23 Wiper motor   24 Connector
(6-way)   25 Connector (8-way)   42 Heated window relay   43 Flasher control   47 Cigar lighter   53 Fuse box   57 Heated rear window   59 Fuel tank unit
Switches   1 Engine compartment light   6 Reverse lamp   36 Glove box   38 Rear window   40 Instrument panel lamps   41 Stop lamp   44 Choke warning lamp
45 Foot, windscreen wash   46 Heater fan   48 Wiper motor   49 Ignition and starter   50 Horn   51 Side, head and flasher   52 Direction indicators   54 Handbrake
warning   55 Interior lights
Lamps   2 Engine compartment   17 Front flashers   18 Side lamps   19 Dipped beam   20 Headlamp main beam   21 Side indicators   26 Reserve petrol warning
27 Instrument panel   28 Handbrake and fluid level warning   29 Flasher repeaters   30 Fan warning   31 Choke warning   32 Charge warning   33 Side flashers   61 Rear and
34 Headlamp warning   35 Low oil pressure warning   37 Glove box   39 Heated window warning   56 Interior lights   58 Boot   60 Rear flashers
stop lamps   62 Reversing lamp   63 Number plate
Key to colour code   A Blue   B White   C Orange   G Yellow   H Grey   M Maroon   N Black   R Red   S Rose   V Green   Z Violet
The number after the colour letter indicates the section of the wire in sq mm

ARG1600

153

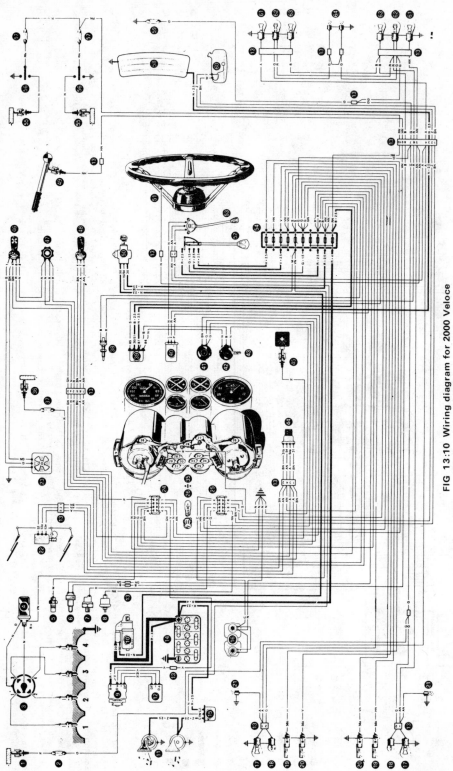

FIG 13:10 Wiring diagram for 2000 Veloce

Key to Fig 13:10

Equipment 3 Distributor 4 Coil 5 Water temperature sender 7 Oil pressure warning sender 8 Oil pressure sender 9 Alternator 10 Starter 11 Horns 12 Voltage regulator 13 Cable connectors 14 Battery 15 Horn relay 16 Brake fluid warning sender 22 Windscreen wiper 23 Two-speed heater fan 24 and 25 Connectors 39 Heated window relay 40 Flasher control 47 Cigar lighter 54 Fuse block 58 Heated rear window 60 Fuel tank unit

Switches 1 Engine compartment light 6 Reverse lamp 36 Glove box 38 Stop lamp 41 Instrument panel light 42 Rear window heater 44 Windscreen washer 45 Choke warning 46 Heater:ventilator motor 48 Wiper motor 49 Handbrake warning 50 Ignition and starter 51 Horns 52 Side, head and head flash 53 Direction indicator 55 Door pillar 56 Interior light

Lamps 2 Engine compartment 17 Direction indicator (front) 18 Front parking 19 Dipped beam 20 Main beam 21 Side repeater 26 Instrument panel 27 Reserve petrol warning 28 Flasher repeater 29 Battery charge warning 30 Choke engaged warning 31 Heater fan operating 32 Headlamp warning 33 Handbrake and fluid level warning 34 Low oil pressure warning 35 Parking light warning 37 Glove box 43 Rear window heater warning 57 Interior 59 Boot 61 Rear direction indicator 62 Rear and stop 63 Reversing 64 Index plate

Colour codes and cable thickness—see **FIG 13:9**

154

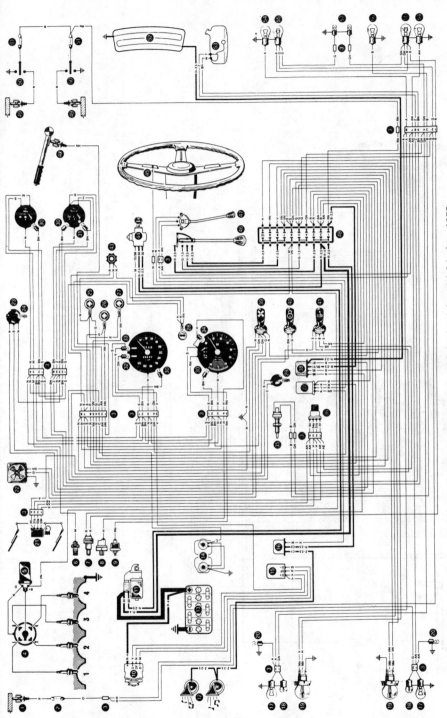

FIG 13:11   Wiring diagram for GT Junior 1.3 and 1.6 before 1975

Key to Fig 13:11   1 Engine compartment light switch   2 Engine compartment light bulb   3 Junction boxes and connectors   4 Distributor   5 Coil   6 Coolant thermometer sender   7 Reversing light switch   8 Pressure switch for oil pressure warning light   9 Oil pressure gauge sender   10 Alternator   11 Starter motor   12 Horn   13 Battery   14 Brake fluid level warning light switches   15 Voltage regulator   16 Horn relay   17 Front direction indicators bulb   18 Front parking light bulb   19 Headlamp high/low bulb   20 Side direction indicators bulb   21 Windscreen wiper   22 Blower motor   23 Heated rear window switch (with built-in telltale)   24 Heated rear window warning light bulb   25 Windscreen wiper   26 Parking brake warning light bulb   27 High beam warning light bulb   28 Direction indicators warning light bulb   29 Bulb for brake fluid level telltale   30 Instrument lights bulb   31 Reserve warning light bulb   32 Blower warning light bulb   33 Alternator warning light bulb   34 Oil pressure warning light bulb   35 Stop light switch   36 Windscreen washer, foot operated   37 Flasher unit   38 Heated rear window relay   39 Blower switch   40 Instrument lights switch   41 Windscreen wiper switch   42 Parking brake warning light switch   43 Cigarette lighter   44 Ignition and starting switch   45 Horn control switch   46 Parking lights, headlamps and flashing switch   47 Direction indicators switch   48 Fuse box   49 Button switch for courtesy lights on jamb   50 Toggle switch for courtesy lights in light unit   51 Courtesy light bulb   52 Heated rear window   53 Fuel level sender   54 Rear direction indicators bulb   55 Rear parking and stop lights bulb   56 Reversing light bulb   57 Number plate light bulb

Cable colour code   **A** Blue   **B** White   **C** Orange   **G** Yellow   **H** Grey   **M** Brown   **N** Black   **R** Red   **S** Pink   **V** Green   **Z** Violet   **AB** Blue/white   **AN** Blue/black   **BN** White/black   **GN** Yellow/black   **HN** Grey/black   **RN** Red/black   **VN** Green/black   **CN** Orange/black

The figure following the colour code indicates the wire cross-section in sq mm. Unmarked wires are 1 sq mm.

155

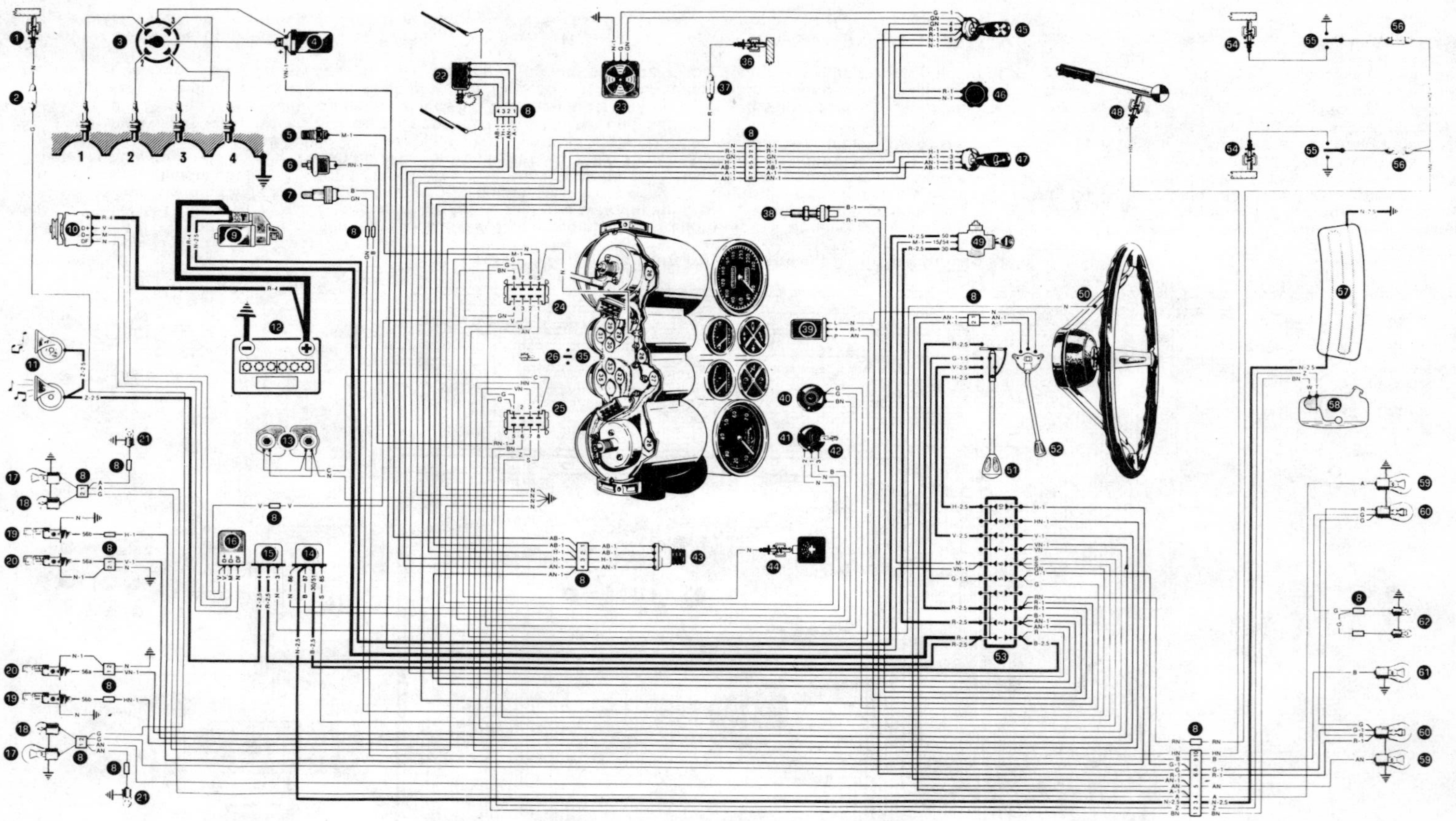

FIG 13:12 Wiring diagram for GT Junior 1300 and 1600, 1975 onwards

Key to Fig 13:12 1 Engine compartment light switch 2 Engine compartment light bulb 3 Distributor 4 Coil 5 Coolant thermometer sender 6 Oil pressure gauge sender 7 Reversing light switch 8 Junction boxes and connectors 9 Starting motor 10 Alternator 11 Horns 12 Battery 13 Switches for low brake fluid telltale 14 Heated rear window relay 15 Horn relay 16 Voltage regulator 17 Front direction indicators bulb 18 Headlamp low beam bulb, halogen 20 Headlamp high beam bulb, halogen 21 Side direction indicator bulb 22 Windscreen 23 Blower motor 24 Instrument panel connector 25 Instrument panel connector 26 Instrument light bulb 27 Fuel reserve warning light bulb 28 Direction indicator warning light bulb 29 Alternator warning light bulb 30 Choke warning light bulb 31 Blower warning light bulb 32 High beam warning light bulb 33 Handbrake and low brake fluid level telltale bulb 35 Parking light warning bulb 36 Glove box light switch 37 Glove box light bulb 38 Stop light switch 39 Flasher unit 40 Instrument light dimmer 41 Heated rear window warning light bulb 43 Windscreen washer switch, foot operated 44 Choke warning light switch 45 Blower motor switch 46 Cigarette lighter 47 Windscreen wiper motor switch 48 Handbrake warning light switch 49 Ignition and starting switch 50 Horn control switch 51 Parking lights, headlamps and flashing switch 52 Direction indicator switch 53 Fuse box 54 Courtesy light microswitch on door jambs 55 Courtesy light toggle switch in light unit 56 Courtesy light bulb 57 Heated rear window 58 Fuel level sender 59 Rear direction indicators bulb 60 Rear parking and stop lights bulb 61 Reversing lights bulb 62 Number plate light bulbs

Cable colour code **A** Blue **B** White **C** Orange **G** Yellow **H** Grey **M** Brown **N** Black **R** Red **S** Pink **V** Green **AB** Blue/white **AN** Blue/black **BN** White/black **GN** Yellow/black **HN** Grey/black **RN** Red/black **VN** Green/black **CN** Orange/black

The figure following the colour code indicates the wire cross-section in sq mm. Unmarked wires are 1 sq mm.

156

HINTS ON MAINTENANCE AND OVERHAUL

There are few things more rewarding than the restoration of a vehicle's original peak of efficiency and smooth performance.

The following notes are intended to help the owner to reach that state of perfection. Providing that he possesses the basic manual skills he should have no difficulty in performing most of the operations detailed in this manual. It must be stressed, however, that where recommended in the manual, highly-skilled operations ought to be entrusted to experts, who have the necessary equipment, to carry out the work satisfactorily.

Quality of workmanship:

The hazardous driving conditions on the roads to-day demand that vehicles should be as nearly perfect, mechanically, as possible. It is therefore most important that amateur work be carried out with care, bearing in mind the often inadequate working conditions, and also the inferior tools which may have to be used. It is easy to counsel perfection in all things, and we recognize that it may be setting an impossibly high standard. We do, however, suggest that every care should be taken to ensure that a vehicle is as safe to take on the road as it is humanly possible to make it.

Safe working conditions:

Even though a vehicle may be stationary, it is still potentially dangerous if certain sensible precautions are not taken when working on it while it is supported on jacks or blocks. It is indeed preferable not to use jacks alone, but to supplement them with carefully placed blocks, so that there will be plenty of support if the car rolls off the jacks during a strenuous manoeuvre. Axle stands are an excellent way of providing a rigid base which is not readily disturbed. Piles of bricks are a dangerous substitute. Be careful not to get under heavy loads on lifting tackle, the load could fall. It is preferable not to work alone when lifting an engine, or when working underneath a vehicle which is supported well off the ground. To be trapped, particularly under the vehicle, may have unpleasant results if help is not quickly forthcoming. Make some provision, however humble, to deal with fires. Always disconnect a battery if there is a likelihood of electrical shorts. These may start a fire if there is leaking fuel about. This applies particularly to leads which can carry a heavy current, like those in the starter circuit. While on the subject of electricity, we must also stress the danger of using equipment which is run off the mains and which has no earth or has faulty wiring or connections. So many workshops have damp floors, and electrical shocks are of such a nature that it is sometimes impossible to let go of a live lead or piece of equipment due to the muscular spasms which take place.

Work demanding special care:

This involves the servicing of braking, steering and suspension systems. On the road, failure of the braking system may be disastrous. Make quite sure that there can be no possibility of failure through the bursting of rusty brake pipes or rotten hoses, nor to a sudden loss of pressure due to defective seals or valves.

Problems:

The chief problems which may face an operator are:
1 External dirt.
2 Difficulty in undoing tight fixings.
3 Dismantling unfamiliar mechanisms.
4 Deciding in what respect parts are defective.
5 Confusion about the correct order for reassembly.
6 Adjusting running clearance.
7 Road testing.
8 Final tuning.

Practical suggestions to solve the problems:

1 Preliminary cleaning of large parts—engines, transmissions, steering, suspensions, etc.,—should be carried out before removal from the car. Where road dirt and mud alone are present, wash clean with a high-pressure water jet, brushing to remove stubborn adhesions, and allow to drain and dry. Where oil or grease is also present, wash down with a proprietary compound (Gunk, Teepol etc.,) applying with a stiff brush—an old paint brush is suitable—into all crevices. Cover the distributor and ignition coils with a polythene bag and then apply a strong water jet to clear the loosened deposits. Allow to drain and dry. The assemblies will then be sufficiently clean to remove and transfer to the bench for the next stage.

  On the bench, further cleaning can be carried out, first wiping the parts as free as possible from grease with old newspaper. Avoid using rag or cotton waste which can leave clogging fibres behind. Any remaining grease can be removed with a brush dipped in paraffin. If necessary, traces of paraffin can be removed by carbon tetrachloride. Avoid using paraffin or petrol in large quantities for cleaning in enclosed areas, such as garages, on account of the high fire risk.

  When all exteriors have been cleaned, and not before, dismantling can be commenced. This ensures that dirt will not enter into interiors and orifices revealed by dismantling. In the next phases, where components have to be cleaned, use carbon tetrachloride in preference to petrol and keep the containers covered except when in use. After the components have been cleaned, plug small holes with tapered hard wood plugs cut to size and blank off larger orifices with grease-proof paper and masking tape. Do not use soft wood plugs or matchsticks as they may break.

2 It is not advisable to hammer on the end of a screw thread, but if it must be done, first screw on a nut to protect the thread, and use a lead hammer. This applies particularly to the removal of tapered cotters. Nuts and bolts seem to 'grow' together, especially in exhaust systems. If penetrating oil does not work, try the judicious application of heat, but be careful of starting a fire. Asbestos sheet or cloth is useful to isolate heat.

  Tight bushes or pieces of tail-pipe rusted into a silencer can be removed by splitting them with an open-ended hacksaw. Tight screws can sometimes be started by a tap from a hammer on the end of a suitable screwdriver. Many tight fittings will yield to the judicious use of a hammer, but it must be a soft-faced hammer if damage is to be avoided, use a heavy block on the opposite side to absorb shock. Any parts of the

ARG1600

steering system which have been damaged should be renewed, as attempts to repair them may lead to cracking and subsequent failure, and steering ball joints should be disconnected using a recommended tool to prevent damage.

3 It often happens that an owner is baffled when trying to dismantle an unfamiliar piece of equipment. So many modern devices are pressed together or assembled by spinning-over flanges, that they must be sawn apart. The intention is that the whole assembly must be renewed. However, parts which appear to be in one piece to the naked eye, may reveal close-fitting joint lines when inspected with a magnifying glass, and, this may provide the necessary clue to dismantling. Left-handed screw threads are used where rotational forces would tend to unscrew a right-handed screw thread.

Be very careful when dismantling mechanisms which may come apart suddenly. Work in an enclosed space where the parts will be contained, and drape a piece of cloth over the device if springs are likely to fly in all directions. Mark everything which might be reassembled in the wrong position, scratched symbols may be used on unstressed parts, or a sequence of tiny dots from a centre punch can be useful. Stressed parts should never be scratched or centre-popped as this may lead to cracking under working conditions. Store parts which look alike in the correct order for reassembly. Never rely upon memory to assist in the assembly of complicated mechanisms, especially when they will be dismantled for a long time, but make notes, and drawings to supplement the diagrams in the manual, and put labels on detached wires. Rust stains may indicate unlubricated wear. This can sometimes be seen round the outside edge of a bearing cup in a universal joint. Look for bright rubbing marks on parts which normally should not make heavy contact. These might prove that something is bent or running out of truth. For example, there might be bright marks on one side of a piston, at the top near the ring grooves, and others at the bottom of the skirt on the other side. This could well be the clue to a bent connecting rod. Suspected cracks can be proved by heating the component in a light oil to approximately 100°C, removing, drying off, and dusting with french chalk, if a crack is present the oil retained in the crack will stain the french chalk.

4 In determining wear, and the degree, against the permissible limits set in the manual, accurate measurement can only be achieved by the use of a micrometer. In many cases, the wear is given to the fourth place of decimals; that is in ten-thousandths of an inch. This can be read by the vernier scale on the barrel of a good micrometer. Bore diameters are more difficult to determine. If, however, the matching shaft is accurately measured, the degree of play in the bore can be felt as a guide to its suitability. In other cases, the shank of a twist drill of known diameter is a handy check.

Many methods have been devised for determining the clearance between bearing surfaces. To-day the best and simplest is by the use of Plastigage, obtainable from most garages. A thin plastic thread is laid between the two surfaces and the bearing is tightened, flattening the thread. On removal, the width of the thread is compared with a scale supplied with the thread and the clearance is read off directly. Sometimes joint faces leak persistently, even after gasket renewal. The fault will then be traceable to distortion, dirt or burrs. Studs which are screwed into soft metal frequently raise burrs at the point of entry. A quick cure for this is to chamfer the edge of the hole in the part which fits over the stud.

5 **Always check a replacement part with the original one before it is fitted.**

If parts are not marked, and the order for reassembly is not known, a little detective work will help. Look for marks which are due to wear to see if they can be mated. Joint faces may not be identical due to manufacturing errors, and parts which overlap may be stained, giving a clue to the correct position. Most fixings leave identifying marks especially if they were painted over on assembly. It is then easier to decide whether a nut, for instance, has a plain, a spring, or a shakeproof washer under it. All running surfaces become 'bedded' together after long spells of work and tiny imperfections on one part will be found to have left corresponding marks on the other. This is particularly true of shafts and bearings and even a score on a cylinder wall will show on the piston.

6 Checking end float or rocker clearances by feeler gauge may not always give accurate results because of wear. For instance, the rocker tip which bears on a valve stem may be deeply pitted, in which case the feeler will simply be bridging a depression. Thrust washers may also wear depressions in opposing faces to make accurate measurement difficult. End float is then easier to check by using a dial gauge. It is common practice to adjust end play in bearing assemblies, like front hubs with taper rollers, by doing up the axle nut until the hub becomes stiff to turn and then backing it off a little. Do not use this method with ballbearing hubs as the assembly is often preloaded by tightening the axle nut to its fullest extent. If the splitpin hole will not line up, file the base of the nut a little.

Steering assemblies often wear in the straight-ahead position. If any part is adjusted, make sure that it remains free when moved from lock to lock. Do not be surprised if an assembly like a steering gearbox, which is known to be carefully adjusted outside the car, becomes stiff when it is bolted in place. This will be due to distortion of the case by the pull of the mounting bolts, particularly if the mounting points are not all touching together. This problem may be met in other equipment and is cured by careful attention to the alignment of mounting points.

When a spanner is stamped with a size and A/F it means that the dimension is the width between the jaws and has no connection with ANF, which is the designation for the American National Fine thread. Coarse threads like Whitworth are rarely used on cars to-day except for studs which screw into soft aluminium or cast iron. For this reason it might be found that the top end of a cylinder head stud has a fine thread and the lower end a coarse thread to screw into the cylinder block. If the car has mainly UNF threads then it is likely that any coarse threads will be UNC, which are not the same as Whitworth. Small sizes have the same number of threads in Whitworth and UNC, but in the $\frac{1}{2}$ inch size for example, there are twelve threads to the inch in the former and thirteen in the latter.

7 After a major overhaul, particularly if a great deal of work has been done on the braking, steering and suspension systems, it is advisable to approach the problem of testing with care. If the braking system has been overhauled, apply heavy pressure to the brake pedal and get a second operator to check every possible source of leakage. The brakes may work extremely well, but a leak could cause complete failure after a few miles.

Do not fit the hub caps until every wheel nut has been checked for tightness, and make sure the tyre pressures are correct. Check the levels of coolant, lubricants and hydraulic fluids. Being satisfied that all is well, take the car on the road and test the brakes at once. Check the steering and the action of the handbrake. Do all this at moderate speeds on quiet roads, and make sure there is no other vehicle behind you when you try a rapid stop.

Finally, remember that many parts settle down after a time, so check for tightness of all fixings after the car has been on the road for a hundred miles or so.

8 It is useless to tune an engine which has not reached its normal running temperature. In the same way, the tune of an engine which is stiff after a rebore will be different when the engine is again running free. Remember too, that rocker clearances on pushrod operated valve gear will change when the cylinder head nuts are tightened after an initial period of running with a new head gasket.

Trouble may not always be due to what seems the obvious cause. Ignition, carburation and mechanical condition are interdependent and spitting back through the carburetter, which might be attributed to a weak mixture, can be caused by a sticking inlet valve.

For one final hint on tuning, never adjust more than one thing at a time or it will be impossible to tell which adjustment produced the desired result.

NOTES

GLOSSARY OF TERMS

Allen key Cranked wrench of hexagonal section for use with socket head screws.

Alternator Electrical generator producing alternating current. Rectified to direct current for battery charging.

Ambient temperature Surrounding atmospheric temperature.

Annulus Used in engineering to indicate the outer ring gear of an epicyclic gear train.

Armature The shaft carrying the windings, which rotates in the magnetic field of a generator or starter motor. That part of a solenoid or relay which is activated by the magnetic field.

Axial In line with, or pertaining to, an axis.

Backlash Play in meshing gears.

Balance lever A bar where force applied at the centre is equally divided between connections at the ends.

Banjo axle Axle casing with large diameter housing for the crownwheel and differential.

Bendix pinion A self-engaging and self-disengaging drive on a starter motor shaft.

Bevel pinion A conical shaped gearwheel, designed to mesh with a similar gear with an axis usually at 90 deg. to its own.

bhp Brake horse power, measured on a dynamometer.

bmep Brake mean effective pressure. Average pressure on a piston during the working stroke.

Brake cylinder Cylinder with hydraulically operated piston(s) acting on brake shoes or pad(s).

Brake regulator Control valve fitted in hydraulic braking system which limits brake pressure to rear brakes during heavy braking to prevent rear wheel locking.

Camber Angle at which a wheel is tilted from the vertical.

Capacitor Modern term for an electrical condenser. Part of distributor assembly, connected across contact breaker points, acts as an interference suppressor.

Castellated Top face of a nut, slotted across the flats, to take a locking splitpin.

Castor Angle at which the kingpin or swivel pin is tilted when viewed from the side.

cc Cubic centimetres. Engine capacity is arrived at by multiplying the area of the bore in sq cm by the stroke in cm by the number of cylinders.

Clevis U-shaped forked connector used with a clevis pin, usually at handbrake connections.

Collet A type of collar, usually split and located in a groove in a shaft, and held in place by a retainer. The arrangement used to retain the spring(s) on a valve stem in most cases.

Commutator Rotating segmented current distributor between armature windings and brushes in generator or motor.

Compression ratio The ratio, or quantitative relation, of the total volume (piston at bottom of stroke) to the unswept volume (piston at top of stroke) in an engine cylinder.

Condenser See capacitor.

Core plug Plug for blanking off a manufacturing hole in a casting.

Crownwheel Large bevel gear in rear axle, driven by a bevel pinion attached to the propeller shaft. Sometimes called a 'ring gear'.

'C'-spanner Like a 'C' with a handle. For use on screwed collars without flats, but with slots or holes.

Damper Modern term for shock-absorber, used in vehicle suspension systems to damp out spring oscillations.

Depression The lowering of atmospheric pressure as in the inlet manifold and carburetter.

Dowel Close tolerance pin, peg, tube, or bolt, which accurately locates mating parts.

Drag link Rod connecting steering box drop arm (pitman arm) to nearest front wheel steering arm in certain types of steering systems.

Dry liner Thinwall tube pressed into cylinder bore

Dry sump Lubrication system where all oil is scavenged from the sump, and returned to a separate tank.

Dynamo See Generator.

Electrode Terminal, part of an electrical component, such as the points or 'Electrodes' of a sparking plug.

Electrolyte In lead-acid car batteries a solution of sulphuric acid and distilled water.

End float The axial movement between associated parts, end play.

EP Extreme pressure. In lubricants, special grades for heavily loaded bearing surfaces, such as gear teeth in a gearbox, or crownwheel and pinion in a rear axle.

Fade	Of brakes. Reduced efficiency due to overheating.
Field coils	Windings on the polepieces of motors and generators.
Fillets	Narrow finishing strips usually applied to interior bodywork.
First motion shaft	Input shaft from clutch to gearbox.
Fullflow filter	Filters in which all the oil is pumped to the engine. If the element becomes clogged, a bypass valve operates to pass unfiltered oil to the engine.
FWD	Front wheel drive.
Gear pump	Two meshing gears in a close fitting casing. Oil is carried from the inlet round the outside of both gears in the spaces between the gear teeth and casing to the outlet, the meshing gear teeth prevent oil passing back to the inlet, and the oil is forced through the outlet port.
Generator	Modern term for 'Dynamo'. When rotated produces electrical current.
Grommet	A ring of protective or sealing material. Can be used to protect pipes or leads passing through bulkheads.
Grubscrew	Fully threaded headless screw with screwdriver slot. Used for locking, or alignment purposes.
Gudgeon pin	Shaft which connects a piston to its connecting rod. Sometimes called 'wrist pin', or 'piston pin'.
Halfshaft	One of a pair transmitting drive from the differential.
Helical	In spiral form. The teeth of helical gears are cut at a spiral angle to the side faces of the gearwheel.
Hot spot	Hot area that assists vapourisation of fuel on its way to cylinders. Often provided by close contact between inlet and exhaust manifolds.
HT	High Tension. Applied to electrical current produced by the ignition coil for the sparking plugs.
Hydrometer	A device for checking specific gravity of liquids. Used to check specific gravity of electrolyte.
Hypoid bevel gears	A form of bevel gear used in the rear axle drive gears. The bevel pinion meshes below the centre line of the crownwheel, giving a lower propeller shaft line.
Idler	A device for passing on movement. A free running gear between driving and driven gears. A lever transmitting track rod movement to a side rod in steering gear.
Impeller	A centrifugal pumping element. Used in water pumps to stimulate flow.

Journals	Those parts of a shaft that are in contact with the bearings.
Kingpin	The main vertical pin which carries the front wheel spindle, and permits steering movement. May be called 'steering pin' or 'swivel pin'.
Layshaft	The shaft which carries the laygear in the gearbox. The laygear is driven by the first motion shaft and drives the third motion shaft according to the gear selected. Sometimes called the 'countershaft' or 'second motion shaft.'
lb ft	A measure of twist or torque. A pull of 10 lb at a radius of 1 ft is a torque of 10 lb ft.
lb/sq in	Pounds per square inch.
Little-end	The small, or piston end of a connecting rod. Sometimes called the 'small-end'.
LT	Low Tension. The current output from the battery.
Mandrel	Accurately manufactured bar or rod used for test or centring purposes.
Manifold	A pipe, duct, or chamber, with several branches.
Needle rollers	Bearing rollers with a length many times their diameter.
Oil bath	Reservoir which lubricates parts by immersion. In air filters, a separate oil supply for wetting a wire mesh element to hold the dust.
Oil wetted	In air filters, a wire mesh element lightly oiled to trap and hold airborne dust.
Overlap	Period during which inlet and exhaust valves are open together.
Panhard rod	Bar connected between fixed point on chassis and another on axle to control sideways movement.
Pawl	Pivoted catch which engages in the teeth of a ratchet to permit movement in one direction only.
Peg spanner	Tool with pegs, or pins, to engage in holes or slots in the part to be turned.
Pendant pedals	Pedals with levers that are pivoted at the top end.
Phillips screwdriver	A cross-point screwdriver for use with the cross-slotted heads of Phillips screws.
Pinion	A small gear, usually in relation to another gear.
Piston-type damper	Shock absorber in which damping is controlled by a piston working in a closed oil-filled cylinder.
Preloading	Preset static pressure on ball or roller bearings not due to working loads.
Radial	Radiating from a centre, like the spokes of a wheel.

Radius rod	Pivoted arm confining movement of a part to an arc of fixed radius.
Ratchet	Toothed wheel or rack which can move in one direction only, movement in the other being prevented by a pawl.
Ring gear	A gear tooth ring attached to outer periphery of flywheel. Starter pinion engages with it during starting.
Runout	Amount by which rotating part is out of true.
Semi-floating axle	Outer end of rear axle halfshaft is carried on bearing inside axle casing. Wheel hub is secured to end of shaft.
Servo	A hydraulic or pneumatic system for assisting, or, augmenting a physical effort. See 'Vacuum Servo'.
Setscrew	One which is threaded for the full length of the shank.
Shackle	A coupling link, used in the form of two parallel pins connected by side plates to secure the end of the master suspension spring and absorb the effects of deflection.
Shell bearing	Thinwalled steel shell lined with anti-friction metal. Usually semi-circular and used in pairs for main and big-end bearings.
Shock absorber	See 'Damper'.
Silentbloc	Rubber bush bonded to inner and outer metal sleeves.
Socket-head screw	Screw with hexagonal socket for an Allen key.
Solenoid	A coil of wire creating a magnetic field when electric current passes through it. Used with a soft iron core to operate contacts or a mechanical device.
Spur gear	A gear with teeth cut axially across the periphery.
Stub axle	Short axle fixed at one end only.
Tachometer	An instrument for accurate measurement of rotating speed. Usually indicates in revolutions per minute.

TDC	Top Dead Centre. The highest point reached by a piston in a cylinder, with the crank and connecting rod in line.
Thermostat	Automatic device for regulating temperature. Used in vehicle coolant systems to open a valve which restricts circulation at low temperature.
Third motion shaft	Output shaft of gearbox.
Threequarter floating axle	Outer end of rear axle halfshaft flanged and bolted to wheel hub, which runs on bearing mounted on outside of axle casing. Vehicle weight is not carried by the axle shaft.
Thrust bearing or washer	Used to reduce friction in rotating parts subject to axial loads.
Torque	Turning or twisting effort. See 'lb ft'.
Track rod	The bar(s) across the vehicle which connect the steering arms and maintain the front wheels in their correct alignment.
UJ	Universal joint. A coupling between shafts which permits angular movement.
UNF	Unified National Fine screw thread.
Vacuum servo	Device used in brake system, usihg difference between atmospheric pressure and inlet manifold depression to operate a piston which acts to augment brake pressure as required. See 'Servo'.
Venturi	A restriction or 'choke' in a tube, as in a carburetter, used to increase velocity to obtain a reduction in pressure.
Vernier	A sliding scale for obtaining fractional readings of the graduations of an adjacent scale.
Welch plug	A domed thin metal disc which is partially flattened to lock in a recess. Used to plug core holes in castings.
Wet liner	Removable cylinder barrel, sealed against coolant leakage, where the coolant is in direct contact with the outer surface.
Wet sump	A reservoir attached to the crankcase to hold the lubricating oil.

NOTES

INDEX

NOTES